W9-ACU-495

DATE DUE

SEP 2 4 2007	
MAR 2 4 2008	
April/9/08	
MAR 3 0 2011	
MAY 0 5 2011	
NOV 0 7 2012	
DEC 1 2 2013	

DEMCO, INC. 38-2931

BUDDHISM
IN
AMERICA

BUDDHISM IN AMERICA

The Social Organization of an Ethnic Religious Institution

by

Tetsuden Kashima

Contributions in Sociology, Number 26

ST. JOSEPH'S UNIVERSITY

BLQ 8712.9 .U6 K37   STX

Buddhism in America :

3 9353 00046 6829

BQ
8712.9
.U6
K37

170702

GREENWOOD PRESS
Westport, Connecticut • London, England

Library of Congress Cataloging in Publication Data

Kashima, Tetsuden.
    Buddhism in America.

    (Contributions in sociology ; no. 26)
    Bibliography: p.
    Includes index.
    1. Buddhist Churches of America. 2. Sociology,
Buddhist—United States. 3. Japanese in the United
States. I. Title.
BQ8712.9.U6K37   294.3'0973   76-57837
ISBN 0-8371-9534-9

Copyright © 1977 by Tetsuden Kashima

All rights reserved. No portion of this book
may be reproduced, by any process or technique,
without the express written consent of the
publisher.

Library of Congress Catalog Card Number: 76-57837
ISBN: 0-8371-9534-9
ISSN: 0084-9278

First published in 1977

Greenwood Press, Inc.
51 Riverside Avenue, Westport, Connecticut 06880

Printed in the United States of America

To my father, the late Reverend Tetsuro Kashima,
and my mother, Yoshiko

Contents

Tables and Figures

Preface

This book is about an ethnic religious institution and an ethnic group's attempts over the years to maintain its integrity within a usually hostile social environment. Most Americans are aware of the Japanese Americans as a racial and ethnic minority. Very few, however, can claim a thorough understanding of either the Japanese American people or the institution that has played a key role in their sociocultural survival and adaptation. This institution is the Buddhist Churches of America (BCA), a unique collection of religious and ethnic organizations almost unknown outside the Japanese American community.

An alien group in America, especially one with a radically different language and religion, is peculiarly vulnerable to attempts at exploitation and discrimination. The Japanese Americans are no exception. In the face of acts of subjugation such as the Oriental Exclusion Act, the Alien Land Laws, and the evacuation during World War II, the groups involved often made collective efforts to maintain a sense of personhood and group cohesion. The groups' various organizations usually provided some measure of social support, either as protective associations or as havens from the turmoil and uncertainty that the ethnic groups encountered in their daily lives.

For the Japanese in America, the BCA, representing the Jodo Shinshu branch of Buddhism, has been an extremely important institution. It has allowed this ethnic minority to retain its religious beliefs and practice, and to find and preserve a large degree of community solidarity.

The BCA represents an alien religion in America—one that has continued for seventy-six years. An understanding of the reasons for its continued existence will elucidate the general relationship between racial and ethnic groups in this country. How has the BCA aided the Japanese in their survival and adaptation in America? How have the Japanese American Buddhist churches maintained themselves throughout their turbulent history? Where there have been social changes, what has been the precise nature of these changes, and what explanations can be offered concerning their particular forms? Who are the members? What suborganizations are involved? Who are the priests? What is the future of this particular institution in America? This study attempts to answer these and similar questions.

The following chapters are empirical case studies of social change within a religious institution. They are based on my personal experiences and impressions as a participant in the church for thirty years and as a participant-observer for the last six of these years. Other data in this book derive from formal and informal interviews, responses to a questionnaire, and library and church documents.

My interest and participation in the Buddhist churches has been long and continuous. My father was a priest within the institution, and I spent all of my childhood years living in or near a Buddhist church. In my adult years, I have attended services and ceremonies, and have participated in the secular activities sponsored by the church: picnics, bazaars, movies, sports activities, and so on. I have been acquainted with many ministers and have taken advantage of this acquaintance in seeking and obtaining information.

During the last six years, I have attended and participated in the various BCA national, district, and temple level meetings and conferences, and I have been asked to give lectures or to sit as a panel member at many Buddhist conferences. These assemblies have ranged from the annual ministers' conferences, Sunday School teachers' conferences, and district Buddhist seminars to various youth-oriented conferences.

Besides using the participant-observation technique, with informal interviews, I have conducted formal interviews. By formal interviews, I mean those centering on questions posed in advance; in most cases, the responses were recorded on tape. Here I concentrated on the priests of the Buddhist church as well as the presiding bishop. My selection of interviewees was not random; rather, I deliberately sought out representatives of the different groupings found within the priesthood: Issei, Nisei, and Sansei priests, a non-Japanese American priest, and a woman priest. Precisely because most priests were inaccessible for formal interviews, a questionnaire (reproduced at the end of this book) was devised and sent to the then seventy-six active and twenty-five inactive ministers. In addition, although little has been written about the BCA, whatever has been published, either by the institution or by outside researchers and writers, I have accumulated and scrutinized.

Formal interviews were not conducted with members of the church because, with over 43,000 members, a random sample (without adequate survey analysis support) would have been difficult, if not impossible. For the member's perspective, I have relied upon the many informal interviews I have conducted throughout the various states where the Buddhist churches are situated as well as the various conferences I have attended.

Entering an ethnic institution for study and research purposes is often difficult. An initial problem is to gain entrance. Almost any non-Japanese, non-Buddhist researcher should expect to meet some resistance as he/she attempts to obtain information. The BCA members and priests have been traditionally reticent about answering questions from outside inquirers. A problem in basic communication is also quickly encountered. Although English has come to be the predominant language, conversational Japanese is an absolute necessity when speaking to the Issei (immigrant Japanese). A non-Japanese-speaking researcher would have access to most Nisei (second generation, Japanese American) members and priests but to very few of the Issei. For convenience, interviews conducted in Japanese have been translated or paraphrased into English.

Acknowledgments

This book could not have been written without the kind assistance of many individuals. It was during my freshman year at Berkeley, some time ago, that I first took a course from Professor Stanford M. Lyman, who has played a major part in formalizing my interest in the field of sociology. Moreover, his outstanding works in race relations have been a prime example of what studies in this field should be. I am deeply grateful to Professor Lyman; his incisive, penetrating critiques, unstinting encouragement, and kind and generous support have been important factors in the completion of this work. I cannot adequately acknowledge his help.

During my years as a graduate student in sociology, I was privileged to study with Professors Carl Backman, David Harvey, and Paul Secord at the University of Nevada, Reno. At the University of California, San Diego, Professors Jack Douglas and Joseph Gusfield were very instrumental in furthering my knowledge of sociology, and these two scholars have given me continual encouragement and advice. I would also like to acknowledge the support of Professors Anthony Ngubo, Michael Parrish, and Nolen Penn. Professor Tamotsu Shibutani, University of California, Santa Barbara, read the initial product and gave me some very useful suggestions for its improvement.

While doing the research for the book, I benefited from the assistance of many BCA members and priests. Numerous priests have subjected themselves to intensive interviews and have completed the questionnaire. I am grateful to Bishop Kenryu Tsuji, and to Reverends Shingetsu Akahoshi, John Doami, Hogen Fujimoto, Bunya Fujimura,

Kakumin Fujinaga, Masami Fujitani, Sekan Fukuma, Hakushi Futaba,
Julius Goldwater, Akira Hata, Shojo Hondo, Shirei Iwai, Tesshin
Kakimoto, Zeisei Kawasaki, Masao Kodani, Haruyoshi Kusada, Yurii
Kyogoku, George Matsubayashi, William Masuda, Kyogyo Miura, Ronald
Miyamura, Keisho Motoyama, Toshio Murakami, Gyosei Nagafuji,
Ensei Nekoda, Koshin Ogui, Seiko Okahashi, Shojo Oi, Sadamaro Ouchi,
Shawshew Sakow, Shintatsu Sanada, Laverne Sasaki, Shinryo Sawada,
Hozen Seki, George Shibata, Hideo Shimakawa, Unryu Sugiyama,
Kakuyei Tada, Arthur Takemoto, Zuikei Taniguchi, Koju Terada,
Chonen Terakawa, Eiyu Terao, Junjo Tsumura, Shodo Tsunoda, Enryo
Unno, Kosho Yukawa, Tetsuya Yukawa, and Haruo Yamaoka.

In addition, many members of the Buddhist church have assisted me
in this project—too many to list completely. I would like, however, to
acknowledge the assistance of Mr. and Mrs. Zenbei Iwashita and family,
Mr. and Mrs. Harry Kajihara, Mr. and Mrs. Tetsuyo Kashima, and Mr. and
Mrs. George Kido and family.

To Dr. and Mrs. Ryo Munekata, I would like to give special thanks.
Dr. Munekata generously offered his materials on the Buddhist church
and was helpful in going through the manuscript of this work.

When there was a need to translate difficult Japanese materials,
Katsuhiko Abe was always willing and able to help. I gratefully acknowledge his enthusiastic assistance. I am also indebted to Patricia
Morgan, Janet Shishino, Carol Tanaka, and Elaine Forester for their
excellent typing. John Forester has been of immeasurable help in giving
excellent editorial advice. I am also grateful for the assistance and encouragement of the personnel at Greenwood Press.

For any errors or misinterpretations, I alone am responsible.

List of Abbreviations

ABA	Adult Buddhist Association
BBA	Buddhist Brotherhood of America
BBE	Bureau of Buddhist Education
BCA	Buddhist Churches of America
BCFF	Buddhist-Christian Clergy Fellowship of Southern California
IBS	Institute of Buddhist Studies
ICSC	Interreligious Council of Southern California
JACP	Japanese American Curriculum Project
JARF	Japanese American Religious Federation
NABM	North American Buddhist Mission
RAB	Relevant American Buddhist
WABL	Western Adult Buddhist League
WRA	War Relocation Authority
YABL	Young Adult Buddhist League
YBA	Young Buddhist Association
YMBA	Young Men's Buddhist Association
YMWBA	Young Men and Women's Buddhist Association
YWBA	Young Women's Buddhist Association

BUDDHISM
IN
AMERICA

CHAPTER 1 | *The Religions of Japan at the Time of the First Japanese Migrations to America and the Beginning of the NABM and BCA in America*

The religious ties of the Japanese immigrants to America were to their native religions of Buddhism and Shintoism.[1] In the course of its long history, Buddhism in Asia has divided into many denominations. Stressing different scriptures and practices to attain Enlightenment (Nirvana), the two major divisions of Buddhism are Theravada (or Hinayana) and Mahayana Buddhism. Theravada Buddhism is found in Southern Asia, Ceylon, Burma, Thailand, Laos, Cambodia, and neighboring regions. Mahayana Buddhism is found in Northern Asia, especially China, Korea, and Japan. However, Buddhism in Japan is not a single unified religion: fifty-six primary, formal divisions have been catalogued, with more than 170 subdivisions. Anesaki describes the many divisions:

> Their practices range from the quiet meditation of Zen to the frantic drum beating of Nichiren and from sophisticated Tendai discussions of reality to the Shingon performances of elaborate rituals. Their tenets are no less diverse than their practices, while the adherents comprise philosophical minds of high standing as well as the most superstitious of the populace. Buddhism in Japan is a vast system, such a conglomerate of many trends that no observer, without an ample knowledge of its historical background, could escape bewilderment trying to find out what it all meant.[2]

Among the Japanese immigrants to the United States, five subdivisions of Buddhism are represented in America: Tendai, Shingon, Nichiren, Zen, and Amida (or Pure Land Buddhism). Tendai Buddhism, founded in Japan by Dengyo Daishi (767–822), is considered the fountainhead of most Buddhist subdivisions in Japan.

> *Tendai* philosophy was eclectic. It embraced almost all of the contradictory sectarian teachings of Chinese Buddhism and it left the choice of a method of salvation largely to the individual. Its comprehensive teachings included esoteric mysteries, abstract contemplation, and faith in the saving grace of the Buddha-Amida— in short, all the basic *Mahayana* doctrines. . . . Essentially, however, *Tendai* emphasized the Lotus Sutra [holy words of the Buddha], which it considered the greatest of all Buddhist scriptures, and taught that the "supreme truth" can be realized only through meditation.[3]

Shingon Buddhism, founded by Kobo Daishi (774–835), is based on the *Dainichi* Sutra (the Great Sun Sutra). "In the *Shingon* Buddhism, it is believed that chanting of *Mantras* (True words) in the form of Chinese transliterations of the original Sanskrit phrases has great efficacy for the welfare and happiness of mankind in this world."[4]

Nichiren Buddhism, founded by Nichiren (1222–1283), is based on the *Hokke* Sutra (the Lotus of the Wonderful Law). "Nichiren strongly advocated that it must be on this earth where one must try to attain Buddahood through the whole-hearted reliance on the . . . *Hokke* sutra, by chanting [the Japanese phrase 'Namu-Myohorenge Kyo' (Reliance goes to the Lotus Sutra of the Wonderful Law)]. . . which brings happiness to both nation and people."[5]

Zen Buddhism, established in Japan by Eisai (1141–1215), Dogen (1200–1253), and Ingen (1592–1673), has as its core the belief that personal salvation comes from self-enlightenment. This perfection of one's inner self is attained through meditation or concentration and discipline.

Amida Buddhism, or Pure Land Buddhism, has its roots in Tendai Buddhism. It was founded by Genshin (942–1017), who advocated faith (*shinjin*) as the path to salvation. Jodo, or "Pure Land," is the place where Buddhist followers expect to be "reborn" through the

Amida Buddha's powers of salvation. Based essentially on the *Daimuryoju* Sutra, Amida Buddha, a personification of limitless wisdom and compassion, "made a . . . vow to attain the state of enlightenment not for his sake, but for those who are unable to become Buddhas through their own efforts and practices. . . . Through sincere faith in the Amida Buddha, the followers . . . are enabled to be born in the Pure Land [where there are neither cravings nor defilements to obstruct the attainment of enlightenment]."[6] In Amida Buddhism, an important practice is the recitation of the *Nembutsu*, "*Namu Amida Butsu*" (Homage to the Amida Buddha).

In America, two of the four denominations of Japanese Amida Buddhism are represented: Jodo and Jodo Shinshu. The Jodo denomination, founded by Honen (1133–1212), teaches that individuals can attain the Pure Land after death through faith while continually reciting the *Nembutsu* without distraction, throughout one's life. The Jodo Shinshu or Shinshu denomination was founded by Shinran (1173–1262) and is practiced by the majority of Japanese Buddhists. Shinran, a disciple of Honen, believed that "the *Nembutsu* was not a practice, but the expression of gratitude to the all-embracing compassion of Amida Buddha. It is not necessary, therefore, to recite the *Nembutsu* to be saved by Amida Buddha. Nevertheless, according to him, the *Nembutsu* will be a spontaneous expression when one realizes the compassionate original vow of Amida Buddha and has a sincere faith in it."[7]

The Buddhist denomination predominant among the Japanese immigrants to America and their children is Jodo Shinshu. Although in Japan there are ten sects of Shinshu Buddhism,[8] only two of these are found in America: Nishi Hongwanji (literally, West School of the Original Vow of Amida Buddha) and Higashi Hongwanji (East School). Of these two sects, Nishi Hongwanji, incorporated as the BCA, has represented an estimated 75[9] to 90 percent[10] of the Japanese Buddhists in America.

From early studies, it appears that the Japanese immigrants emigrated primarily from four prefectures: Hiroshima, Kumamoto, Yamaguchi, and Fukuoka. These prefectures have always been identified with the Jodo Shinshu sect. This is especially true of Hiroshima, "which is known as the place of 'Aki-monto,' the fervent Shinshu believers of Aki Province, and where there exists more than eight hundred Shinshu parish temples with about an equal number of small temples. It is generally granted that if a Japanese is a native of the Hiroshima Prefecture

it is safe to assume that he belongs to Shinshu."[11] The number of passports issued from Japan during the period 1889 to 1903 were as follows:[12]

Prefectures	Migrants
Hiroshima	21,861
Kumamoto	12,649
Yamaguchi	11,219
Fukuoka	7,698
Thirty-nine other prefectures	31,135
Total migrants	84,562

Since the first four prefectures represent 63 percent of the immigrants during this fourteen-year period, it is not surprising that their
predominant religious sect should have gained an ascendancy in America. During the early years of Japanese immigration, from 1889 to
1924, with the Oriental Exclusion Act, few Japanese communities had
sufficient numerical and monetary resources to support more than one
religious organization. With the arrival of the Nishi Hongwanji missionary priests in 1899, this Buddhist sect began to attend to the religious
needs of the immigrants. The Nishi Hongwanji had crossed the Pacific
Ocean even earlier, having sent priests to administer to the Japanese in
Hawaii in 1889. Two factors—Japanese immigrants coming from Jodo
Shinshu strongholds in Japan and the early arrival of their priests—gave
this sect an early lead over other sects in establishing a Buddhist organization in America.

Neither the religious beliefs of Jodo Shinshu Buddhism nor the effects of the early Japanese immigrants' beliefs in and practice of a particular form of Buddhism, important though they are, are our main object of attention in this study. Rather, our focus is on the institution
housing this sect of Buddhism in America so that we might explain the
various changes and adaptations that have been a continual feature of
its history in this country. The Buddhist beliefs of the Japanese immigrants and of their children have been institutionalized as an ethnic religious organization—formerly (1899–1944) the *Hokubei Bukkyo Dan*
(North American Buddhist Mission or NABM) and presently (since
1944) known as the Buddhist Churches of America.

The BCA is an incorporated religious organization of Buddhist churches or temples[13] in the United States, maintaining Jodo Shinshu beliefs. The BCA is presently composed of fifty-nine main churches (independent and dues-paying), with thirty-nine branches (attached to the independent churches), two "gatherings," and a headquarters at San Francisco. (See Appendix 1 for a list of BCA churches and temples).[14] The membership is composed primarily of Japanese Americans, although there are some Caucasians, Chinese Americans, Filipino Americans, and black Americans.[15] The organization supports approximately eighty active ministers, and the chief religious and administrative leader is the bishop.

The institution has its roots, philosophically and organizationally, in Japan. While the religious beliefs have remained for the most part untouched, the forms of presentation have changed over the years. The primary reason for these changes is clear: the change of membership from the first immigrants (the Issei) to their children (the Nisei) and grandchildren (the Sansei). With the Nisei came a problem of language and of translation difficulties from Japanese to English. Many Japanese terms or concepts are difficult to translate properly; consequently, the BCA has utilized a combination of English and Japanese in its services.

There have also been changes in the organizational structure. From its beginnings in 1899 with one church, the American Buddhist institution proliferated into many churches. Then, in 1942, with the internment of almost all the Japanese and Nikkei (Americans of Japanese ancestry) population, the Buddhist organization was also removed to the Assembly Centers and Relocation Camps. The result was a complete dislocation of established everyday habits and lifestyles. After 1945, the Jodo Shinshu institution returned to the West Coast and also opened new churches and temples in the eastern states. The traumatic events and movements during the early 1940s resulted in the birth of a new organization, the BCA, from the earlier *Hokubei Bukkyo Dan*; however, the pattern for the new organization originated from the old.

Another continual theme in the history of this institution is its importance as a force for ethnic social solidarity. Until World War II, the Buddhist church was the sole social center for many Japanese communities. By offering a central locale for the Japanese congregation, through its picnics, religious services, Japanese language school, Japanese cinema, and so on, the church provided a friendly environment for an ethnic group that often encountered hostility from the society at large. The need for a territorial center to escape discrimination and prejudice began to fade in the 1950s, and other Japanese American organizations have come into existence to serve the non-Buddhists. Nevertheless, in the minds of its members and other Nikkei, the Buddhist church continues to be their institution, to be operated and controlled by and for the Japanese and their offspring.

Each of the three themes enumerated above—the roots of the institution in Japan, the structural changes that have occurred during its existence in the United States, and the importance of the institution for ethnic social solidarity—will be detailed in the following chapters. We will show that important elements within the institution, especially those related to the religion of Buddhism, have remained constant and unchanging. Other social changes within the BCA are best understood as adaptations to practical problems that arose within the Japanese and Japanese American Buddhist institution.

The Development of the NABM and the BCA

The development of the organization known first as the NABM and then as the BCA can be divided into five phases. The first phase, covering the period 1899 to 1920, starts with the origin of the San Francisco Buddhist temple, and thus of the NABM, and culminates with the end of the "picture-bride" era. The second phase, beginning in 1920 and extending to the beginning of World War II, goes from the passage of the Oriental Exclusion Act and the Alien Land Law to the cessation of Japanese immigration to the United States. The third phase, from 1941 to 1945, encompasses the complete evacuation of the Buddhists and Japanese Americans into concentration camps and the resultant movement of the BCA away from their physical structures along the Pacific Coast. The fourth phase, from 1945 to 1966, covers the period following the Japanese Americans' release from the camps and the inception of the Institute for Buddhist Studies. The fifth phase includes the period from 1966 to the present, during which the third-generation Japanese Buddhists have come of age, some of whom have embraced the ministry and others of whom have become involved with church and temple affairs.

The following chapters detail these five phases and also discuss the changing role of the priesthood, the present status of the BCA, its organizational structure, and its future.

Notes

1. Although many Issei had Shinto shrines in their homes, there is no large-scale organized religious organization in the United States comparable to the BCA.

2. Masaharu Anesaki, *Religious Life of the Japanese People* (Tokyo: Kokusai Bunka Shinkokai, 1970), p. 45.

3. William C. Bunce, *Religions in Japan* (Rutland, Vt.: Charles E. Tuttle Co., 1955), p. 62.

4. Shoyu Hanayama, "Buddhism in Japan," in *A Guide to Buddhism*, edited by Terukatsu Okano (Yokohama, Japan: International Buddhist Exchange Center Press, 1970), p. 84.

5. Ibid., p. 101.

6. Ibid., pp. 87–88.

7. Ibid., p. 93.

8. "Altogether there are now approximately 16,500,000 Jodo Shin believers divided among ten sects. Two of the sects, the Hongwanji and Ohtani sects, between them claim roughly 16,000,000 followers and are the only sects of major importance." See Bunce, op. cit., p. 86.

9. A. Freed and K. Luomala, "Buddhism in the United States." Community Analysis Report No. 9. Washington, D.C.: War Relocation Authority, May 15, 1944, p. 3.

10. Tamotsu Shibutani, "The Buddhist Youth Movement in Chicago," Typescript, University of Chicago, October 1944, p. 1.

11. Paul T. Tajima, "Japanese Buddhism in Hawaii: Its Background, Origins and Adaptation to Local Conditions," Master's Thesis, University of Hawaii, Honolulu, 1935, p. 16.

12. Computed from Yamato Ichihashi, *The Japanese in the United States* (Stanford, Calif.: Stanford University Press, 1932), p. 80. Ichihashi quotes M. Togo, *Nihon Shokumin Ron* (Tokyo: 1906), pp. 269–271. Yosaburo Yoshida quotes similar statistics from T. Togo but gives as his dates 1899–1903, with a total of 84,576. Yoshida also states that of the 84,576 migrants, more than 80 percent came to the United States. See "Sources and Causes of Japanese Emigration," *Annals of the American Academy of Political Science* (September 1909: 380–381; reprint ed., San Francisco: R and E Research Associates, 1970).

13. The terms *church* and *temple* are used synonymously within the BCA. A discussion of this lingustic problem is found in Chapter 7.

14. For a detailed examination of church and temples, see Chapter 7.

15. An examination of non-Japanese members is found in Chapters 5 and 7. See Appendix 1 for a list of BCA churches and temples.

CHAPTER 2 | *Buddhism Among the Japanese Americans to the Time of the Oriental Exclusion Act*

The Issei immigrants to America arrived with their Japanese cultural and social institutions, bringing with them their language, their life-style,[1] their pattern of interaction,[2] their economic institutions,[3] and their religious organization. Few of these immigrants understood either the American social lifestyle or the English language.

The first crisis these immigrants experienced in America was the disruption of their everyday life. The Issei had little preparation for the "taken-for-granted" social world that had evolved along the Pacific Coast states when they migrated to America. Aside from sporadic reports and writings of earlier sojourners, which suggested that they would encounter a totally different culture and society than that from which they came, until they arrived they had no realization of just how different life would be for them.

An understanding of this initial crisis explains why the Japanese Americans created a lifestyle different from that they had known in their traditional Japanese society. Unlike many of America's other settlers, they did not come to the New World as a body of persecuted people fleeing their homeland with the wish to maintain their religious beliefs; they came, in many instances, to gain a modicum of economic success so that they could return to Japan to live in a style that would have been unattainable had they remained in their home country. Thus, the complete preservation of their traditional organizations and culture was not a primary consideration. Indeed, flexibility and adaptation are probably the key concepts accounting for their behavior in America as they set out to attain their economic goals.

11

After the initial entrance of the Issei in the 1870s, Buddhist priests came to minister to their spiritual and religious needs. So long as the Issei remained in the United States, the Buddhist associations also remained and were sustained by the immigrants. The first missionary, Reverend Shuye Sonoda, reached a few non-Japanese through religious services, lectures, and meetings, but it was the Japanese population that provided the economic and social support necessary to the *bukkyokais* (literally, Buddhist Association church or temple).

At the time of the first large Japanese influx into America (the late 1890s), religion, especially the Buddhist faith, was probably not an important issue in the minds of the immigrants. As one Issei pointed out, when he arrived in San Diego as a young man of sixteen in 1919, there were few Japanese families, mostly young single males in their twenties and early thirties.[4] Farmwork took up much of their time, and whatever leisure time they had was spent drinking *sake*, gambling, and taking occasional Saturday rides into the city of San Diego to enjoy a meal or to meet other friends. There was little need for religion. A missionary would occasionally come down from Los Angeles to conduct services for the devout Buddhists who assembled from the various farms in the area.

The first religious organizations for the Japanese in America were not Buddhist, but Protestant, missions. The first Protestant mission church was started in San Francisco in 1877, both to aid the Japanese who had been converted to Christianity while in Japan and to proselytize among the newly arriving immigrants: "The first to extend a hand of welcome to them [Japanese] were the Christian churches on the coast. The mission buildings of the churches became hostels for the newcomers. They also functioned as schools of English and of American customs, and later as clearing houses for employment."[5]

For the very early immigrants, the hostels and missions were places where friendship and acceptance were no doubt unstintingly offered. From the mission's perspective, however, social services were of much less importance than converting the Japanese: "Another important characteristic of the Japanese church was the evangelistic zeal of its leaders. That the mission premises served as centers of orientation to American life as well as social centers was secondary in importance."[6] The Issei were never converted to Christianity in large numbers, and as the various *bukkyokais* were formed within the Issei communities, Christian evangelism became less and less effective.

The Japanese population in the United States was not large from 1870 to 1880. From 1890 until 1930, however, there was a continual increase, as can be seen from Bureau of the Census data.[7] (The following figures exclude Hawaii and Alaska.)

Year	Total	Year	Total
1870	55	1930	138,834
1880	148	1940	126,947
1890	2,039	1950	168,773
1900	24,326	1960	260,195
1910	72,157	1970	373,983
1920	111,101		

A conservative estimate of religious orientation among Japanese immigrants indicates that two-thirds came from prefectures dominated by the Jodo Shinshu faith.[8] The eventual arrival of Jodo Shinshu missionary priests to care for the religious needs of the immigrant can be traced to the efforts of a twenty-one-year-old immigrant, Nisaburo Hirano.[9] When he arrived in San Francisco in 1891, he apparently availed himself of the Christian missionary services. Although acknowledging the kind help he had received from the missionaries, he declined conversion and baptism into Christianity since he considered himself a Buddhist. Hirano returned to Japan in 1896 and, together with Hideshima Yoshida of San Francisco, requested an audience with Reverends Kakuryo Nishijima and Shoi Yamada to discuss the need for Jodo Shinshu missionaries in America. The two priests, in turn, obtained an audience with Lord Abbot Myonyo Shonin, who sent Reverends Eryu Honda and Ejun Miyamoto on a goodwill and reconnaissance trip to the United States. The pair arrived in San Francisco on July 6, 1898, and after meeting with the resident Buddhists aided in forming the *Bukkyo Seinen Kai*, or Young Men's Buddhist Association (YMBA), of San Francisco. The YMBA, initially composed of thirty members, met on July 14, 1898, at the home of Dr. Katsugoro Haida at 303 Market Street; they later rented the Pythian Castle auditorium[10] at 909 Market Street. An inaugural ceremony was held on July 30, 1898, with the adoption of a constitution and election of a board of directors; thus began the first Jodo Shinshu organization in the continental United States. On September 17, 1898, the YMBA moved to 7 Mason Street, meeting on a weekly basis for religious discussions and study of the Buddhist sutras. The two priests stayed in San Francisco for about two weeks and then left for other areas of Japanese Buddhist concentration, including Sacramento; Seattle, Washington; and Vancouver, Canada.

During their visit, the two priests realized that the introduction of Buddhism to the North American continent would not be easy. While the immigrant Japanese Buddhists desired to practice their religion, the entire surrounding religious community might oppose the establishment of this "exotic" religion. Honda recalls a conversation with the Japanese consul Miki Saito in Seattle on this point:

> When I discussed about the proposed Buddhist Missionary work in the United States, Consul Saito with an expression of annoyance on his face and while thumbing through a number of documents, asked whether the United States government would allow the entrance of a "foreign religion." He also expressed his feelings about the numerous problems which might arise from the entrance of a "foreign religion," when the Japanese and Americans are presently coexisting peacefully. Since I felt that such expressions came from an individual who did not know the Buddadharma [Sanskrit term for Buddhism], I took the opportunity to explain some salient points about the religion. Because of such attitudes on the part of the leadership in the Japanese community, I felt that missionary work will be difficult. Yet, somehow, agreement was reached that missionary work may be started. And, since I was able to see the establishment of the San Francisco YMBA, I returned to Japan with a strong conviction that missionary work must be started in the United States.[11]

Although Consul Miki Saito might have been aware of the American constitutional guarantees concerning freedom of worship, his statement to Honda indicates a belief that Buddhism could in some way be a threat to relations between Japan and America. Nevertheless, Miyamoto and Honda returned to Japan and presented a detailed report and recommendation that missionary activity be started in the United States.

Meanwhile the San Francisco YMBA met on September 1, 1898, to discuss relations with the Nishi Hongwanji headquarters in Japan. Bearing the signatures of eighty-three persons, a petition was sent to Japan requesting the establishment of a Buddhist center headed by a Buddhist missionary sent from the homeland. Written in formal Japanese, the petition reads in part: "In the eight directions are non-Buddhist forces surrounding the Japanese Buddhists, and we cannot be at ease. It is as if we are sitting on the point of a pin; no matter how we move, we will be pricked. Our burning desire to hear the Teachings [of the Buddha] is about to explode from every pore in our body."[12]

With the report by Miyamoto and Honda, and the petition made by the San Francisco YMBA tempered by Consul Saito's statement, the Nishi Hongwanji officials initially decided to send two missionaries, Shuye Sonoda and Kakuryo Nishijima. A large missionary effort had been initially considered with a monetary budget of 12,000 yen for 1899. For unknown reasons this plan was rejected.[13] Two possible reasons for curtailing the initial missionary activity were the headquarters' concern that such activities in the United States might meet with limited success among the Japanese, and the fear that they might encounter resistance from the United States government. For the latter possibility, we need only look at the observation of Consul Saito; for the former, we may assume that if the missionary activity failed, it would be a reflection upon the Nishi Hongwanji leadership.

Nevertheless, the San Francisco YMBA continued its activities. On April 8, 1899, the first *Hanamatsuri* ceremony (to honor Sakyamuni Buddha's birth) was held, and on May 21, *Gotan-E* (birthday of Shinran Shonin) was observed.[14] On May 25, the Japanese imperial naval fleet, on a world tour, entered San Francisco Harbor; on board was a Jodo Shinshu *guntai fukyoshi* (literally, naval chaplain), Jundo Fujita.[15] During the five-day stay by the fleet, Fujita gave nightly sermons to the YMBA.

The first official Jodo Shinshu missionaries assigned to the United States, Shuye Sonoda and Kakuryo Nishijima, arrived on September 1, 1899,[16] and by September 14, they had rented a building in San Francisco. Their arrival thus constitutes the officially recognized beginning of the NABM. On September 24, a sign was posted announcing the "Hongwanji Branch Office" with the necessary attendant ceremonies and services.[17] Before coming to America, Sonoda was the director of the Academy of Literature at the Hongwanji and Nishijima had been his student.[18]

Sonoda and Nishijima were soon conducting services and study classes, Sonoda for the Japanese, and Nishijima for the American public. The offering of some services and lectures in English has led one researcher, William Rust, to conclude that "the evidence of the amount of Americanization which has taken place among the Japanese population is indicated by the establishment of services in English. On November 24 [?], 1899, the first Buddhist service was conducted in English. After this day, in addition to the Japanese services, a regular service was held each Sunday in English."[19] Rust gives no reference for this conclusion. It would be more accurate to view the English service not as a desire to "Americanize" Buddhism, but rather as an opportunity to introduce the religion to Caucasians who desired to learn about Buddhism. Unlike most of the later Issei priests, Reverend Sonoda was able to give talks in English. In addition, some works on Buddhism written in English[20] were already extant, a fact that indicates the prior interest of some Occidentals in the Buddhist religion. The sermons were given in Japanese; not until the birth of the Nisei generation was there any large attempt to give services and sermons in English.

Sonoda and Nishijima also went to other areas with Buddhist populations; they dedicated a *Bukkyo Seinen Kai* in Sacramento on December 17, 1899. Back in San Francisco, they conducted the first *Ho onko* ceremony (celebration of gratitude to Shinran Shonin), published a magazine, the *Bukkyo Seinenkai Kaiho* (YMBA Newsletter), created the Buddhist Women's Association (*Fujinkai*) in 1900, and conducted their first *Hanamatsuri* service on April 18, 1900.[21] By 1901, four other *kaikyoshi* (missionaries) had arrived in the United States, two of whom were assigned to San Francisco, and one each to Sacramento and Fresno. The missionaries attempted to fulfill the religious needs of the Buddhist adherents by giving sermons and conducting services and ceremonies; they also created new Buddhist centers in their locales. From 1898 to 1971, new churches or temples were created or founded at the rate of at least one per year until 1946. In some years, three churches were founded per year (1905, 1909, 1931), while others saw four per year (1929, 1945). After World War II, twelve new churches were established, bringing the total to sixty-four. There are in addition thirty-nine smaller Buddhist group entities, some with actual church buildings affiliated with a central church. For instance, the Los Angeles Betsuin Temple staffs and maintains four other structures not counted in the present fifty-nine "official" dues-paying churches or temples under the BCA umbrella structure.

The early pattern for the creation of churches and temples was as follows: with any sizable number of Japanese in any sector a *Bukkyo Seinen Kai* was formed, in the main by young male Issei. As the group became larger with the influx of Japanese, splinter groups were established, each with the capacity to support a resident *kaikyoshi.* Thus, there were established clusters of related organizations around the new temples in the San Francisco Bay area, Los Angeles, Fresno, lower central California, and Seattle. This pattern in which the churches and priests follow, rather than precede, their membership continues to this day. In Seabrook, New Jersey, for example, the Japanese population was almost nonexistent until after the post-World War II migration when a large number came to work in the nearby frozen-food processing plant. By 1965, the Japanese population in that area had stabilized and had accumulated the funds necessary to construct and maintain a church building.

Meanwhile, in the early 1900s, the NABM headquarters became formally situated in San Francisco. The headquarters in Japan first gave the chief Buddhist official the designation *kantoku* (director) and later, in 1918, *socho* (bishop), and assigned him to the San Francisco temple. In 1905, Reverend Koyu Uchida became the fourth *kantoku.* Among his decisions he changed the previous designation of "Hongwanji Branch Office" to the "Buddhist Church of San Francisco," and he allowed other organizations in other locales to call themselves Buddhist churches.[22]

The rationale for this title change to Buddhist church is not clear. One probable explanation may have been the desire to lessen the "exotic" nature of a foreign religion. By utilizing the words "Buddhist church," a designation familiar to the American population, the emphasis would be placed on the religious activities of the Japanese organization. Closely related to this explanation is that the years 1900 to 1905 in San Francisco saw the early rise of anti-Japanese agitation among the American population:

> The Western Central Labor Union in Seattle started the anti-Japanese movement (April 18, 1900). In California the first gun was fired, in San Francisco, when, on May 7, 1900, Dr. A. E. Ross at a meeting of the State and San Francisco Building Trades Council criticized unrestricted immigration and labor's exposure to the competition of cheaply paid foreigners . . . although in the

beginning it was emphasized that there was no prejudice against Orientals and that the motive was only an economic one, racial feelings were appealed to almost immediately. The "treacherous, sneaking, insidious, betraying and perfidious nature and characteristics of the Mongolian race" were emphasized. . . . Japan's successes in the Russo-Japanese War and the warnings by Kaiser William II of the "Yellow Peril" increased apprehension in California. . . . The San Francisco *Chronicle* in February 1905 carried a vigorous campaign against the "little yellow man," and the state legislature passed a resolution demanding of Congress that action be taken immediately to restrict further immigration of Japanese labourers.[23]

It was in 1905 that racial antagonisms against the Japanese resulted in physical attacks against them: "The local press (several organs of which were owned or controlled by political factions) continued to keep the issue before the public and in 1905 the Asiatic Exclusion League was organized in San Francisco. Gangs of 'hoodlums' (probably not officially connected with the League but not publicly repudiated by it either) made repeated and unprovoked attacks on Japanese laundries, restaurants, and other places of business, sometimes completely wrecking the buildings."[24] As was to be the case again in the 1920s and the early 1940s, all things Japanese came under suspicion. It could well be assumed, then, that the Japanese, especially in San Francisco, wanted to be careful not to cause further unwarranted antagonisms between themselves and the American populace.

Let us return to Reverend Uchida's decision concerning the use of the title Buddhist church. Apparently, the use of the word "church" was not consistent, for the words "Buddhist Mission" were utilized to designate the San Francisco headquarters relocated after the 1906 earthquake.[25] The Issei still refer to their place of reverence as the *bukkyo kai* (Buddhist association), and after 1914 the overall Buddhist organization encompassing all the Buddhist churches was the *Hokubei Bukkyo Dan* (literally, North American Buddhist Mission). It is the Nisei and Sansei who most often refer to their religious establishment as the Buddhist church. Thus, the term *church* came after the original *bukkyokai*, the *bukkyokai* term constituting the habit and *church* possibly arising from a crisis of anti-Japanese agitation.

The Start of the Bukkyokais — *Buddhist Association Need*

Soon after the Japanese arrived in America, they realized their need for the *bukkyokai*. Anti-Japanese agitation, from 1900 to 1907, was one early sign that they would not receive easy acceptance in America. Fortunately, the Buddhist institutions were able to create a familiar religious refuge that accepted the immigrants and helped offset their feelings of isolation and alienation in the new land. This early hostility led to the creation of more and more *bukkyokais* as increasing numbers of Japanese entered the United States until the Oriental Exclusion Act of 1924.

The hardships faced by the immigrants were many and varied.[26] A tract from the Tri-State Buddhist Church (centered in Denver, Colorado) pointed out that "at that time [1915], there were many immigrants in Denver who came from localities in Japan where the Jodo Shinshu Teachings were predominant. Although these persons may not have had a zealous faith burning in their hearts, they must have been very lonesome. Consequently, when they heard the Teachings of Buddhism, their hearts must have been as refreshed as the dry desert is by the gentle rains."[27]

In various locales in California, too, a *bukkyokai* was established primarily to give spiritual leadership or comfort to the surrounding population. The responses to the questionnaire administered to present BCA ministers revealed the following reasons:[28]

Buddhist Church of San Francisco (organized in 1898): "To provide spiritual comfort to the Japanese." (Reverend Keshin Ogura)

Oakland Buddhist Church (1903): "Around 1901, Reverend Tetsuei Mizuki resided in San Francisco. He was asked to take charge of memorial services for the deceased wife of Itaro Harada of Oakland. This service held in Oakland has led those Buddhists to establish a *Bukkyo kyudo kai* (Buddhist study group). Since then once a month a *Howakai* [Buddhist gathering to hear Buddhist sermons] meeting was held. This was the start of the Oakland Buddhist Church." (Reverend Zuikei Taniguchi)

Placer Buddhist Church (1902): "Many Japanese [were in the

area] and they wanted their religion which they had in Japan. The Christian church did a lot of propagation among the Japanese immigrants but most held back and did not go into the Christian Church." (Reverend Akira Hata)

Berkeley Buddhist Church (1911): "In 1908, a decade after the beginning of the Buddhist movement in America, Buddhist families in Berkeley began to gather together and to hold occasional services. On the occasion of the Shinran Shonin's Memorial Service, the Young Men's Buddhist Association composed of 73 members, was organized in 1911." (Reverend Toshio Murakami)

Palo Alto Buddhist Church (1914): "A group of young Isseis needed spiritual strength and opportunities to listen to the Dharma [the teachings of the Buddha]." (Reverend Keisho Motoyama)

With regard to the *bukkyokais* organized before 1924, the only explicit mention in the questionnaires of the church or temple as other than a place of religious worship was by Reverend Toru Kakimoto for the San Mateo Buddhist Church (1910): he stated that its function was to "serve as a religious social center for the Japanese community Buddhists."

Yet, interviews with these and other ministers showed that the division between the purely religious and the social for the early immigrants was difficult, if not impossible, to explicate. The reason is that many of the Japanese holidays or social events are religious in nature. For example, the New Year's holiday has both Shinto and Buddhist roots.

Aside from the *bukkyokais*, the only other large organization for the early Japanese was the Japanese Association.[29]

Each Buddhist organization was started in a time of crisis. Diverse events at each locale contributed to the consolidation of the Japanese populace, which raised the monies necessary for building the physical structure and for sustaining and maintaining a minister. In San Diego, for instance, prior to 1916, a Buddhist minister would sporadically travel from the Los Angeles temple to conduct services. But on January 27, 1916, the nearby Otay Dam overflowed, resulting in the death of some Japanese farmworkers. The residents of San Diego met and decided that a Buddhist Association was thus necessary, and by the tenth

anniversary of the disaster they had founded a church and had acquired
the necessary support to have a permanent resident minister.[30]

Just before 1909, in the area surrounding Guadalupe, California, approximately 500 Japanese workers labored on sugarbeet farms. The
farmers and workers began to press for their own religious organization,
as the sporadic visitations by both Christian and Buddhist missionaries
from Los Angeles were becoming inadequate for the growing Japanese
populace of the area. After some community meetings recognizing the
need for an organization and ascertaining the ability to support a resident religious personage, the community leaders sent both the Christian
mission and the Buddhist temple in Los Angeles an almost identical
letter indicating their desire for a full-time resident minister. The Guadalupe community leaders had decided that whichever religious organization responded positively to the letter would be given the assent and
the support of the community. One day before the Christian church
sent its positive reply, the Buddhist Association in Los Angeles sent its
consent. Thus it is that the Buddhist church in Guadalupe has been the
sole Japanese religious association in that city since January 1909.[31]
Undoubtedly, then, each church had its roots in a crisis. To generalize
further about the actual origins of each of the fifty-nine churches and
temples comprising the BCA would be difficult, since, as is evident
from the San Diego and Guadalupe cases, the precipitating events were
divergent. Nevertheless, each area must have had a group of Japanese
motivated by a strong sense of community. These two factors—crisis
and sense of community—were the crucial forces enabling the *bukkyokais* to start, flourish, and financially maintain a resident minister
and necessary religious and social programs.

Shashinkekkon: The "Picture-Bride" Era

A second important event within the crisis of organization was the
1907 Gentleman's Agreement. This agreement was an "understanding"
between the two countries, Japan and America, that they would restrict
Japanese immigration, in effect, to nonlaborers. This agreement apparently arose out of an attempt, made in 1906 by anti-Japanese forces
in San Francisco, to segregate the small number of Japanese school-
children in the schools in the Chinese part of town. This attempt was
duly noted in a Tokyo newspaper and led to sending an official protest

to President Theodore Roosevelt. As a result of the ensuing negotiation, the segregation order was rescinded, and new Japanese laborers were discouraged from migrating. Under the Gentleman's Agreement, passports could be issued only to workers who had already been in America and the wives and children of workers residing in America. The *Shashinkekkon* (Picture-Bride) system allowed Japanese wives to migrate to America, thus setting the conditions for the start of many Japanese families in America. In pre-World War II Japan, marriage was a contract between families rather than between individuals. That is, marriages were usually arranged by the families of the individuals, sometimes without the individuals knowing each other. This practice enabled marriage *baishakunins* (go-betweens) to arrange suitable matches between males in America and females in Japan. Many of these marriages were conducted in Japan, with a proxy standing in for the groom; the bride could then cross the Pacific as the legal spouse of the immigrant.[32] As a result of the Gentleman's Agreement, large-scale importation of Japanese labor was effectively curtailed in 1908. Japanese immigration declined to less than 10,000 per year, except in 1918 and 1919, "and in every year without exception, women out-numbered male immigrants, often by a more than two to one margin."[33] The effect upon the NABM was to cut off the increasing numbers of new Japanese immigrants desiring and needing the services of the temple. By 1910, however, there were already 72,157 Japanese and Japanese Americans within the continental United States.

The *Shashinkekkon* era extended from 1908 to 1921; in 1921, the issuance of passports for brides was voluntarily stopped by the Japanese government.[34] The actual number of "picture-bride" passports is difficult to determine, since many Japanese laborers returned to Japan to marry, while others who were already married simply sent for their wives. As Ichihashi states, "In consequence, estimates vary widely; those made by the advocates of exclusion insist upon figures altogether unwarranted on the basis of immigration statistics."[35] The two figures he cites are 5,273, from the Immigration Station at San Francisco for the period 1912–1919; and 2,175 for those admitted in Seattle, as listed by the commissioner general of immigration, for the period 1912–1920, excluding the year 1914.[36] Nevertheless, "in 1900 there were 410 married women in a Japanese population of 24,326; in 1910 there were 5,581 in one of 72,157; and in 1920 there were 22,193 in one of 111,010."[37] Although a sizable number of the immigrants could start a more stable family life in the United States, 42.5 percent of the Japanese adult males were still single by 1921.[38]

The outcome of the Gentleman's Agreement was detrimental to the NABM, for the flow of immigrants, most of whom were Buddhists, was in effect stopped. However, the "picture-bride" era did make possible the start of the progeny necessary for the continuation of the Buddhist institution. The influx of women into the harsh male-oriented environment had important effects on the Buddhist institution. The Japanese Buddhist Women's Association (*Fujinkai*) has always been one organization within each temple or church that has strongly supported the NABM and the BCA.[39]

During the early 1900s, the temple was the ideal, and in many cases the only, meeting place for social activities at a single locale. Especially in the agricultural communities, it alone provided a chance for the women to gather and talk, for the children to play with other Japanese children, and for the men to reminisce and to socialize. The Japanese Association was less family- and more male-centered, and consequently the main topic of conversation there revolved around economic and political questions. In contrast, the *bukkyokais* offered interesting Japanese sermons for the adults and sports and other recreational activities for the family as a whole.

Within other organized Japanese communities, the prefectural associations (*Kenjinkais*) were important, but as they restricted membership to persons from certain areas in Japan, they were not able to unify the entire Japanese populace as could the Buddhist organizations. Japanese communities have traditionally tolerated the coexistence of all such organizations, which in some cases aid different portions of the Japanese population. But even until recent times, the Buddhist church in some communities has been the only important center for religious and social gatherings. Befu, in contrasting two communities, speaks about the importance of the Buddhist organization in one community:

> Nearly all important social and recreational activities of the Japanese community are sponsored and organized by the Buddhist Church. These include annual bazaars, dance parties, ball games, and film showings, as well as more religious oriented activities such as funerals, weddings and memorial and Sunday services.

> . . . It is evident that the social functions of the church are just as important, if not more so, in holding the community together as is the religious faith of the members. At present, the Buddhist Church alone among all formal associations, has any significance for the community as a whole; and it has achieved a monolithic dominance over the entire community.[40]

This unique dominance of the Buddhist temple over social activity cannot be found in all the major urban areas of Japanese concentration. Such urban areas have competing organizations that offer other and similar social programs. Yet, historically, unlike the Buddhist temples of Japan, the Buddhist institution in America from its start was able to offer its adherents not only a religious service but also more secular activities.

The Headquarters at San Francisco

From 1899 to 1920, the headquarters in San Francisco grappled with the difficult problem of organization. By the time Reverend Sonoda left the United States in December 1900, the position of director had become increasingly important, for a large number of missionaries were coming to take charge of the growing Buddhist membership. After Reverend Sonoda, two other directors served until the arrival of Reverend Koyu Uchida in San Francisco on August 14, 1905. By the end of 1909, under Uchida's supervision, the number of churches and temples had increased to twenty and covered an area on the Pacific Coast from Seattle to Los Angeles. It was during his tenure that the present San Francisco Buddhist Church and the headquarters building (no longer remaining) were initiated and completed in January 1914 at a total cost of $33,000.[41]

By 1914, there were twenty-five churches and branches. In that year, the first general meeting of ministers and lay representatives was held to formally organize the Buddhists in America as the NABM. It was further agreed at the meeting to host and to sponsor the World Buddhist Conference (*Bankoku Bukkyo Taikai*) during the 1915 celebration of the opening of the Panama Canal Exposition in San Francisco. To this conference came Buddhist representatives from the Far East, the Indochina area, Mexico, and Hawaii. The 1914 conferees also decided to develop future missionary programs for the youths, such as Sunday Schools, as well as to draft a constitution that would officially recognize the NABM as the Jodo Shinshu organization.

This meeting marked the first official recognition of a need for an organizational structure. However, the NABM did not become an official organization until the constitution and articles of incorporation were submitted and accepted by the California state agency in 1924.[42] The bishop remained the leader of the organization, but had little direct authority over the individual member temples since they were incorporated as independent religious organizations. The bishop has always controlled the placement of the resident missionaries, and at that time he did make at least yearly visits to the temples.

Notes

1. Ruth Benedict, *Chrysanthemum and the Sword* (Boston: Houghton Mifflin Co., 1946).

2. See Stanford M. Lyman, "Generation and Character: The Case of the Japanese Americans," in *The Asian in the West* (Reno, Nev.: Desert Research Institute, 1970), pp. 81–89.

3. Ivan H. Light, *Ethnic Enterprise in America: Business Among Chinese, Japanese and Blacks* (Berkeley: University of California Press, 1972).

4. Personal interview with Zenbei Iwashita, Coronado, Calif., on December 27, 1973.

5. Reverend Seizo Abe, quoted in Toru Matsumoto, *Beyond Prejudice: A Story of the Church and Japanese Americans* (New York: Friendship Press, 1946), p. 2; also Alpha H. Takagi, "Mini-Sermon: 95th Anniversary of Christian Churches," San Francisco *Hokubei Mainichi*, October 30, 1972, p. 2.

6. Matsumoto, op. cit., p. 2.

7. U.S. Bureau of the Census, *Statistics of the Population* (Washington, D.C.: U.S. Government Printing Office).

8. Kosei Ogura, "A Sociological Study of the Buddhist Churches in North America," Master's thesis, University of Southern California, Los Angeles, 1932, p. 84.

9. Ryo Munekata (ed.), *Buddhist Churches of America: Vol. I, 75 Year History* (Chicago: Nobart, Inc., 1974), pp. 44–45.

10. There is some doubt as to the exact name of the rented hall. The Japanese transliteration is Peshon Castle found in Kozen Tsunemitsu,

Nippon Bukkyo To-Bei Shi [History of Japanese Buddhism in America] (Tokyo: Bukkyo Shuppan Kyodo, 1964), while the word Pythian Castle is used in the National Young Buddhist Association, *Young Buddhist Handbook*, mimeographed (San Francisco: Western Young Buddhist League Handbook Committee, 1958), p. 5.

11. Quoted by Munekata, op. cit., p. 46.

12. Ibid.

13. Ibid.

14. Ibid., p. 47.

15. Ibid. The ship was the *Hiei*.

16. Reverend Takashi Tsuji, *An Outline of Buddhism* (Toronto: Eastern Canada Publications, 1966), p. 23. The initial missionary office was at 807 Polk Street.

17. Munekata, op. cit., p. 47.

18. An American newspaper referred to them as Doctor Shuye Sonoda and Reverend Kakuryo Nishijima. In fact, their Japanese title was *kaikyoshi*, a title granted only to Jodo Shinshu ministers entering into missionary service. "Missionaries of the Buddhist Faith," San Francisco *Chronicle*, September 12, 1899, p. 1.

19. William C. Rust, "The Shin Sect of Buddhism in America: Its Antecedents, Beliefs, and Present Conditions," Ph.D. dissertation, University of Southern California, Los Angeles, 1951, pp. 142–143.

20. There have been translations of Buddhist works into English as early as 1853. "In 1853, the *Journal of the American Oriental Society* published a translation of the *Life of Buddha* from Burmese." Philipp K. Eidmann, *Young People's Introduction to Buddhism: A Sangha Award Study Book for Shin Buddhist Scouts* (San Francisco: BCA, n.d.), p. 62. Other translated works on Buddhism were available in the late 1800s: for example, T.W. Rhys Davids (trans.), *Buddhist Sutras* (Oxford: Clarendon Press, 1881), and Henry Alabaster, *The Wheel of Law* (London: Trubner, 1871).

21. Munekata, op. cit., p. 48. The observance date is April 8; however, many temples schedule the special ceremonies on convenient days close to the prescribed date.

22. Ibid., p. 49.

23. B. Schrieke, *Alien Americans: A Study of Race Relations* (New York: Viking Press, 1936; reprint ed., San Francisco: R and E Research Associates, 1971), pp. 26–27.

24. Jean Pajus, *The Real Japanese California* (Berkeley: James J. Gillick Co., 1937; reprint ed., San Francisco: R and E Research Associates, 1971), p. 7.

25. See picture inset of the headquarters building at 1617 Gough Street, San Francisco, occupied after the earthquake. Munekata, op. cit., p. 49.

26. See any of the basic texts on the Japanese Americans. For example, William Hosokawa, *The Nisei: The Quiet Americans* (New York: William Morrow and Co., 1969), or Roger Daniels, *The Politics of Prejudice* (Gloucester, Mass.: Peter Smith, 1966).

27. Anonymous, "Brief History of the Tri-State Buddhist Church," pamphlet, n.p., n.d.

28. See Appendix 2 for the questionnaire.

29. The Japanese Association was organized in 1900 to "protect the 'rights' of the Japanese. . . . Upon renewal of this agitation in 1905 (strong anti-Japanese movement) the association was reorganized and extended its activity to the entire state of California. . . . Its objects . . . are: 1) to elevate the character of the Japanese immigrants, 2) to promote association between Japanese and Americans, 3) to promote commerce, agriculture, and other industries, and 4) to further Japanese interests." Robert E. Park and Herbert A. Miller, *Old World Traits Transplanted* (New York: Harper and Bros., 1921), pp. 169–170.

30. Personal interview with Z. Iwashita, December 24, 1973; and Reverend Giko Yamamoto, "Church History: Buddhist Church of San Diego," typescript, April 1966.

31. Personal interview with Reverend Hiroshi Futaba, Guadalupe Buddhist Church, October 16, 1972.

32. Daniels, op. cit., p. 44.

33. Hosokawa, op. cit., p. 96.

34. Edward K. Strong, *The Second Generation Japanese Problem* (Stanford, Calif.: Stanford University Press, 1934), p. 50. See also, Ichihashi, op. cit., p. 296. Ichihashi dates the government proclamation as February 29, 1921, with the last date of issuance on September 1, 1921.

35. Ichihashi, op. cit., p. 292.

36. Ibid.

37. Ibid., p. 291.

38. Hosokawa, op. cit., p. 97.

39. The *Fujinkai* organization will be discussed later. Many such organizations did start soon after the formation of the *bukkyokai*. In the Oakland Buddhist Church, for example, the *Fujinkai* was started one year after the *bukkyokai*. Buddhist Church of Oakland, "70th Anniversary Booklet: 1901–1971," pamphlet, Oakland, Calif., pp. 8–9.

40. Harumi Befu, "Contrastive Acculturation of California

Japanese: Comparative Approach to the Study of Immigrants," *Human Organization* 24 (Fall 1965): 214.

41. Munekata, op. cit., p. 50.

42. Ibid., p. 51.

CHAPTER 3 | *Religious Changes in Response to Generational Changes: The 1920s and 1930s*

In the early 1900s, the Japanese immigrants experienced the outcome of American prejudice and discrimination. The 1906 San Francisco school segregation issue, which precipitated the Gentleman's Agreement in 1907, was one important outward sign of the racial prejudice manifested against the Japanese. During this period, not only the Japanese immigrants but also those within the Buddhist institution had to defend themselves against the hostile reactions of those outside the racial and religious group. The crisis of early organization was passed; during the 1920s another round of extreme anti-Japanese feelings arose within the Pacific Coast states which resulted in another crisis for the *Hokubei Bukkyo Dan.*

Anti-Japanese Period

Since numerous other source materials have fully documented hostility toward the Japanese culminating in the passage of the Alien Land Laws and the Oriental Exclusion Law of 1924, we need not give a detailed presentation of the problem here.[1] By 1923, two Anti-Alien Land Laws had been passed in California (1913 and 1920) which were designed not only to terminate whatever control of California farmlands the Japanese had managed, but also to discourage or to stop further Japanese immigration. The 1907 agreement between Japan and America did not completely eradicate the immigration of the Japanese. The furor raised concerning the approximately 118,000 Japanese immigrants between 1909 and 1925 cannot be understood merely in terms of actual numbers. When the 1861–1908 Japanese immigration figure of approximately 157,000 is added to the 1909–1925 figure of 118,000, the total, 275,000, is a mere pittance in comparison to the more than thirty million immigrants from Europe who arrived on these shores between 1856 and 1924.[2]

> When compared with the total populations of California and the United States, the figures show that at the time of their highest incidence in the population, Japanese immigrants and native-born comprised two and one-tenth percent (.021) of the population of California and one tenth of one percent (.001) of the population of the continental United States.[3]

But as students of race relations know, numerical statistics say little about the social impact of the situation on the involved groups. That manifold use was made of the issue of Japanese immigration by California politicians and labor organizers to garner support and votes is undeniable. The restrictive and exclusionary aspects of anti-Japanese legislation had as its core interracial conflict:

> It was fear of what might happen, together with fresh memories of mob action against the Chinese and consideration of the unresolved race problems in the South that governed the thinking of the better element and led to the almost unanimous conclusion that a large number of Japanese could not live in harmony with the whites in California.[4]

Racial prejudice against the Japanese immigrants was exacerbated by increasing political fear of Japan. Through the Japanese-Russian War (1904–1905), Japan had attained status as a world military power, whose ultimate intentions with regard to the rest of the world remained a mystery. The Japanese intrusion into Korea in 1910,[5] their 1914 capture of Tsingtau, as well as their 1918 entrance into Siberia, were given worldwide publicity. These military successes ultimately aroused the suspicions of the American press and populace regarding not only the nation of Japan but also her emigrants in the United States.

John S. Chambers in 1921 summarized the American fears of the Japanese in California concerning their potential for controlling the

farmlands, the projected takeover of the population of California, and
the anti-American nature of their religion:

> According to the official report of the State Board of Control of
> California, the Japanese now own or control in this state 458,056
> acres. My personal opinion is that the acreage owned and con-
> trolled by them far exceeds this figure. Just as they evade census
> returns so do they cover up their land holdings. . . .

> In ten years the Japanese births in California have increased from
> one in forty-four to one in thirteen, with only one Japanese woman
> to four Japanese men in population, while there is one white woman
> to one white man here. At this rate, in ten years there will be
> 150,000 Japanese born here and by 1949 they will outnumber the
> white people. . . .

> Not only are these people claimed as citizens of Japan, not only is
> their first allegiance to Japan and not to America, but they have
> not only in the Islands but here in the state of California, their own
> language schools and their Buddhist temples. . . . In their churches
> they are taught the religion of Japan, that the Mikado, called by
> them "Tenno," is the "bodily representation on earth of the King
> of Heaven"; that he is above evil, can do no wrong and must be
> worshipped as a God. . . . But as these people in the main, stay
> apart socially, industrially, politically, so do they religiously.[6]

In the California of the early twentieth century, people with "different" social, political, or religious views were at a great disadvantage. The
Japanese with differences in all three areas were particularly discrimin-
ated against. Some politicians even distrusted those Japanese who were
Christians or who had converted to Christianity: "Our missionaries here
and across the Pacific make occasional converts, *some of whom are sincere*, at the time, and some of whom, *perhaps*, remain so unto death"
[emphasis added].[7] The racial antagonisms were so strong that all
spheres of Japanese life were attacked as alien or "strange." The immigrant's tie with his homeland was continually used as a justification for
discriminatory laws and practices.

The Buddhist religion was continually misunderstood or deliberately mistaken for or lumped together with the state Shinto religion. For example, in July 1920, Senator James D. Phelan (California) testified before a subcommittee of the House Committee on Immigration. He stated in the San Francisco hearings that "there are seventy-six Buddhist temples in California and I am told that they are regularly attended by 'Emperor worshippers' who believe that their Emperor is the over-lord of all."[8]

Another strong proponent of Japanese exclusionary laws was Valentine S. McClatchy, publisher of the Sacramento *Bee*:

> The Japanese hold that their Mikado is the one living God to whom they owe their very existence, and therefore all obedience. . . . This worship of the Mikado (Mikadoism, or Shintoism) is a part of the education of each child in Japan, and school children are by government decree forced to worship at the Shinto shrines. Buddhism, which is tolerated in Japan, has Shintoism grafted onto it.[9]

Both Phelan and McClatchy considered the Japanese to be undesirables, and their arguments reflected a distaste for all aspects of the Japanese immigrant presence in America. Their attack on the religious life of the Japanese immigrants was but one facet of their position. Their remarks on the religion of the Japanese immigrants were not left unanswered.[10] The most authoritative rebuttal was made by Bishop Koyu Uchida in his statement to the House Committee:

> We wish to strongly emphasize that our Churches have nothing to do whatsoever with Shintoism, politics or any imperialistic policy formulated by the Japanese government. Our mission is to elevate the spiritual life, not to dictate politics or policies of any government. We should also like to point out that Buddhism is Democratic, an ideal long held by the citizens of the United States of America. All the clergy in charge of churches are ordained by Hongwanji as priests, and authorized to preach our religion, and are duly appointed as missionaries in this country by the Missionary Superintendent who is president of the Headquarters. The missionaries are required to have sufficient knowledge and information of America and American customs before being sent

here, and are requested to perfect themselves as soon as possible after their arrival.[11]

Bishop Uchida, as did other Shinshu Buddhists, believed in the inherent adaptability and democratic nature of the religion. They encouraged their adherents to lead exemplary Buddhist lives regardless of the country in which they lived or the social situation they encountered: "For some time special emphasis has been laid on the necessity of the Americanization of our people, and all the clergy located at different churches strive to educate the members in the American way of life."[12]

The Japanese language schools started by the Buddhist temples and the Christian missionaries also came under attack by those desiring to exclude the Japanese immigrants: "The two most persistent baiters of California Japanese, Senator Phelan and Mr. McClatchy, denounced the language schools as dangerous and un-American growths. McClatchy, in the face of Japanese denials stoutly maintained that the institutions were hotbeds of Buddhism and Mikado worship, founded for the express purpose of thwarting the Americanization of the younger generation of Japanese."[13]

The fundamental object of the Japanese schools was to teach the children the language of their parents, but for the anti-Japanese groups the schools constituted tools for indoctrination and propagandizing of the Japanese culture and moral system. There is little doubt that Japanese values were taught. The fact is, however, that there were several other ethnic language institutions in America at that time, none of which experienced such extreme political attacks on the "foreign" and therefore "subversive" nature of their schools. These foreign language schools were not perceived as undermining the American society. Thus, the Japanese were compelled to defend their homeland culture. Another factor overlooked by those attacking the Japanese language schools was that some of the schools also offered instruction in English and American culture.[14]

The success of the Japanese language schools was very limited. Beyond a few Japanese ideographs and a rudimentary vocabulary, the Nisei students never acquired any great facility in their parents' language. In many cases, the instruction was accepted with less than wholehearted cooperation. Children saw Japanese school, or Nihongakko, as an intrusion into their playtime. As one Nisei writer reports,

"Above everything, I didn't want to go to Japanese school."[15] In most cases, then, the instruction was an aid only in casual home conversations. Despite the limited success of the schools, however, even today in the large urban and sometimes rural Japanese population centers, many Sansei and fourth-generation children ritually go to Japanese schools after "regular" schools or on Saturdays. Personal communication with students, teachers, and parents indicate that the parents want their children to retain some aspects of their grandparents' tradition. Ironically, this desire is in the face of their own reluctance to learn Japanese when they were children. More importantly, they want their offspring to have an opportunity to meet and play with other Japanese Americans. The children, however, view the schools as irrelevant to their everyday lives and as an intrusion upon their social life. Whether they interact with other Japanese children makes no difference to them. The teachers are thus faced with a group of disinterested students who are resistant to any serious study of the Japanese language.[16]

During the 1920s, however, these schools were viewed as a threat to California's social order. Many Buddhist temples with increasing numbers of Nisei instituted the language schools for three reasons: first, the schools augmented the revenue of the minister and his wife, who often served as the principal instructors; second, the parents desired their children to retain their language to facilitate communication; and third, the schools helped to preserve the tie between young children and the Buddhist institution. With sparse English literature on Jodo Shinshu and with the Buddhist priests unable to communicate effectively in English, the language schools enabled the young to learn enough Japanese to understand the sermons and teachings of the priests until adequate English translations were made available. The schools thus helped to bring the young to the church for a secular purpose and simultaneously kept them in contact with the religious institution.

Some language schools attempted to include rudiments of the Japanese culture along with the language.[17] By 1932, the NABM had, as part of its program for the Nisei, thirty-one weekday and Saturday language schools.[18] In one Buddhist temple, a minister made explicit the relationship of the instruction found within the schools to the Nisei and to the Buddhist teachings:

It aims to teach the Japanese language to the children of the members of the Gardena Buddhist Church, *together with moral ideals based on Buddhist doctrine.* Among the Japanese who live in America, the Japanese language is more than essential, for its knowledge on the part of the second generation is probably the only means of saving the Japanese family's disintegration, and from many other sorry misfortunes, as the immigrants are not proficient in English, and their children, being educated in American public schools, speak English more than Japanese. . . . Naturally, the language instructions include education in such traditional Japanese virtues as honesty, chastity, ambition, equipose, patience, etc., which are recognized in the world.[19] [emphasis added]

Buddhist meditation was also part of the training at the Gardena Japanese school. The students started and ended their Saturday school within the temple, and Buddhist mottoes or sayings were interwoven with the language instruction. It is difficult to document whether all Buddhist church-sponsored language schools did in fact include religious instruction, but the assertion made by the anti-Japanese politicians in California politics that all the schools taught extreme Japanese nationalistic ideas and Japanese emperor worship is without foundation.[20]

Conflicts with the Japanese Community: 1920–1930

The discriminatory laws and prejudicial statements against the Japanese during the 1910s thus placed the immigrants within a hostile environment. Not only in California but in the states of Washington (1921 and 1925), Oregon and Idaho (1923), and Nebraska and Texas (1923), Alien Land Laws which had special effects on the Japanese[21] were passed. Takao Ozawa, an Issei, a resident of the United States for twenty years applied for citizenship in 1914. His request was denied ultimately by the Supreme Court in 1922. The privilege of naturalization, argued the court, was reserved for "free white persons" or aliens from Africa or of African descent. Ozawa did not fit into any of these categories; he was a Japanese. Thus, the Japanese immigrants were precluded from gaining naturalization. These cases, along with the Immigration Act of 1924, affected the entire Japanese community in the United States. The 1924 act, often called the Oriental Exclusion Act, set fixed quotas for immigrants from various countries and also excluded aliens ineligible for citizenship. The Chinese had already been excluded in 1882. Since the Japanese could not be naturalized, they saw the immigration act as an attempt to stop them from immigrating further.

The hostility of the wider society sometimes made it difficult, if not impossible, for the Japanese Buddhists to erect temples on the Pacific Coast in 1923 and 1924. Speaking on the interethnic religious conflict, Elliott Mears writes:

> In Hollywood, the Japanese attempted to buy a piece of property to use for a Japanese Presbyterian church; in Long Beach, three Presbyterian churches tried to buy property for a Japanese mission; and in Pasadena, the Japanese wished to establish a Buddhist temple in the same block with two Christian churches. In all three cases, ministers and church members of certain other faiths sided with anti-Japanese groups in preventing the erection of new churches; and in two cases their efforts were successful.[22]

The extreme anti-Japanese atmosphere pervading the Pacific Coast in the 1920s accounts in no small way for the immigrants' banding together.

The Buddhist churches became increasingly important during the 1920s for the immigrants and their children. Since the parents could not, except in isolated instances, enter the American mainstream society, they created their own social, political, and economic organizations. Therefore, many community organizations revolved around the Buddhist churches. Twenty-one new Buddhist churches were established from 1920 to 1941. Through their attendant women's group (*Fujinkai*), church picnics, language schools, and rotating credit systems (*tanomoshi*), the NABM combined secular activities with religious.

Various activities were instituted for the Nisei which, when compared to the various activities in Japan, can be best described as social adaptations. The *Bukkyo Seinen Kai*, Sunday Schools, church socials, and athletic events were important activities instituted for the youth. In later years, with the inclusion of Boy Scout functions and American dancing in the temples, the Buddhist organization adapted even further to American ways. As Takahashi writes, the kind of activities offered by a church is all important:

For the first generation the selecting of a sect is no problem at all, for it was predetermined in his village life, but for the second generation the selecting of churches is relatively free and there are no coercive factors of predetermination. Because he has no traditions, memories and morals connected with the church, his choice mainly depends on his personal response to the church. If his father's church has no attraction in its activities he may choose another church which is more attractive to him.[23]

With the increasing Nisei population in the 1920s, it soon became apparent that some changes had to be made in the NABM. The Nisei's increasing use of English and Americanization, together with the differing needs of the Issei and Nisei, created a crisis within the NABM just when the anti-Oriental climate was at its harshest.

The passage of the 1924 Oriental Exclusion Law, aimed at excluding the Japanese from America,[24] was the culmination of the anti-Japanese sentiment that had been festering since the late 1890s. The curtailment of Japanese immigrant labor was very ominous for the Japanese in America, for the population could not replenish itself or increase except by birth, illegal immigration, or a small influx of nonquota immigrants.

However, for the NABM the 1924 act was a windfall. The Issei interpreted the passage of the law as an extreme injustice to their nation and people, demonstrating the extent to which anti-Oriental sentiment could be manifested within the political arena. As Ogura shows, the law was beneficial to the membership of the Gardena Buddhist Church:

After the passage of the Immigration Law of 1924 discriminating against the Japanese, the number of Buddhists increased rapidly, and so did that of the Buddhist churches. Before that event, some of them had been hesitant in declaring themselves Buddhists, considering such an act impudent in a Christian country. But the immigration law made them more defiant and bold in asserting what they believed to be their rights; it made them realize the necessity of cooperation for the sake of their own security and welfare, and naturally they sought the centers of their communal activity in their Buddhist churches.[25]

Ogura's statement on the increasing number of Buddhist churches and temples after the 1924 law is well-founded. The last two temples constructed prior to 1924 were in 1918 (Florin) and 1922 (Santa Barbara). No other temple was built until that of March 1924 in Salinas. The El Centro temple was established in 1925, San Diego in 1926, two more in 1927, four in 1929, and between 1929 and the start of World War II, eleven temples were constructed. Thus, twenty of the present total of fifty-nine temples or churches presently in the BCA were built during this period.

New churches were not established solely because of the Exclusion Act. For one thing, the Issei were now growing older and were turning more to religious matters. For another, the social and religious services offered by the temples became increasingly important to the Nisei's attempt to maintain their ethnic culture.[26] The NABM and its ministers were able to meet the social and religious needs of its adherents by instituting dual programs, one for the Issei and another for the Nisei. During this period, most of the Nisei spoke enough Japanese to allow communication with the Japanese-speaking ministers. Through its ministers, the NABM expanded the organization into newer territory and created an atmosphere for ethnic and religious security.

With the passage of the 1924 law, the vitriolic anti-Japanese agitation subsided somewhat. The Japanese already in America could not be deported since they were law-abiding, exemplary persons. While there were many instances of discriminatory acts against individuals, no other large-scale laws affecting the entire group were passed until the attack on Pearl Harbor in 1941.[27]

Intraracial Conflicts: 1920–1930

During the 1920s, religious conflicts within the Japanese community aggravated the already tense situation existing in the larger society. The large urban areas of Japanese settlement were able to support both Christian ministers and Buddhist missionaries, but in rural areas, the communities were usually either strongly Buddhist or strongly Christian. One extreme consequence of the difference in religious feelings took place in Steveston, British Columbia, Canada, around the year 1933. Reverend Zesei Kawasaki recalls that "there was a split in the community as one group strongly opposed the continuation of the monthly *howakai* [literally, sermon meeting]. In those days I had to attend these services with a bodyguard."[28] The majority of the Japanese were Christians who were strongly anti-Buddhist; physical threats against Reverend Kawasaki necessitated the bodyguard.[29] Threats against physical safety because of religious beliefs, however, were rare among the Japanese.

The predominant religion of the Japanese who had settled in the rural areas of the Pacific Coast was Buddhism. To this day, in some locales the Buddhist temple or church is the only ethnic religious institution within the Japanese community. In Japanese communities located in Reedley, Guadalupe, Salinas, and Parlier, California; Honeyville, Utah; and Cleveland, Ohio, there are only Buddhist institutions and no Japanese Christian churches.[30]

Even in the Japanese communities where one religious faith was predominant, religious tensions often arose. In one sector of Hawaii, for example: "The children of Christian parents . . . were not treated in a friendly manner by the children of the Buddhist parents. They were looked upon as 'sissies'; they had to endure being teased and called 'Christo' and were excluded from participation in many childhood activities."[31]

For the Buddhists, the period after 1924 was one of exclusion and adjustment. As the Issei grew older, some returned to their homeland while others passed away. The most striking phenomenon during this time was the increase in the Nisei population and the establishment of the Japanese American family in the United States. The average age of the Issei male in 1930 was forty-two, and of the Issei female, thirty-five.[32] There were 138,836 Japanese in the United States in 1930, and of that number, 48.5 percent, or 68,375, were Nisei. By 1940, there were 12,947 Japanese, 47,305 of whom were Issei and 79,642, or 62 percent, their offspring.

The Start of the Nisei Generation

Prior to the 1920s, the Buddhist church membership was predominantly Issei. After the *Shashinkekkon* period, a new generation of Nisei children necessitated the creation of Buddhist programs aimed at educating the young about the religion of their parents. The establishment of Japanese language schools, as previously noted, was one method used to counteract the prevalent use of English by the Nisei.

The inception of Sunday Schools, sports activities, and Nisei youth organizations was a further attempt by the *Bukkyokais* to solve this problem.

The problem of the Nisei became critical as more Nisei were born and as English became the prevalent language among them. Prime difficulties were the insufficient English-language texts and the Issei priests' inability to communicate with the young. The birth of the Nisei ultimately altered the church institution as the Issei knew it: the churches now instituted programs, suborganizations, and activities oriented to the Nisei. These changes were incorporated into the activities of the church, in addition to those for the Issei, and formed the basis for the later changes that would come with the start of the Sansei generation.

It was during the 1920 to 1941 period that the NABM recognized the growing needs of the Nisei. One important change instituted for the Nisei was the rejuvenation of the *Bukkyo Seinen Kai.* With so many individual Young Men's Buddhist Associations (YMBAs) in existence at various churches or temples, the Nisei recognized the need for a coordinated group. Thus, in January 1926, eight YMBA organizations met in San Francisco to form a federated league.[33] By 1934, the league had held nine national conferences represented by the Nisei within the NABM temples. This national organization allowed the Nisei males to have contact with the NABM, thus giving the youth a voice in the decisions made by the Issei. At various temples, the Nisei women were gathering and forming their own Young Women's Buddhist Associations (YWBAs). In July 1927 fifty-two delegates met in San Pedro, California, to initiate a women's national Buddhist league. By 1933, six national YWBA conferences had been held. Separate organizations arose for males and females because the Issei frowned on the social intermingling of the sexes. "In 1926, a league of YMBA's was formed, with fourteen member organizations. Only two of these were designated YMWBA [Young Men and Women's Buddhist Association]. Apparently the Japanese culture of that period did not encourage or sanction boy-girl integrated social gatherings."[34]

It was not until 1937, when the Nisei began to dominate the Issei organization, that the Young Buddhist Association (YBA) was formed, sponsoring both men's and women's activities.[35]

The activities of the YMBA and YWBA were socially and religiously oriented: "YMBA functions covered social and cultural activities, athletics and academic-religious resources. The idea of devotional obligation to the organization appeared to be significant in extent, for accounts of the first YMBA's abound with descriptions of loyalty in the membership and of many regularly scheduled activities."[36] The YMBA had basketball teams and held Buddhist study classes, dances, and other social events with the YWBA.

Communication continued to be a problem during the rise of the Nisei. The ministers could speak only Japanese, and the Nisei, raised and educated in an American social environment, were more comfortable speaking and writing in English. As the Nisei became older, the importance of Buddhist materials in English became crucial. A training program in 1926 to teach Nisei Sunday School instructors was instituted as the *Koshukai*, or Teachers' Training Program, by the San Francisco headquarters. Some Nisei of high school or college age were recruited as potential teachers for the younger Nisei; yet, their teachers were still the Japanese-speaking ministers.

A major difficulty concerned the translations of Buddhist words and concepts from Japanese, Chinese, or Indian origins. To facilitate communications, two methods were employed. First, English words bearing close literal translatability to their Buddhist counterparts were accepted. The use of "bishop" for *socho*, "hymns" for *gathas*, "minister" or "Reverend" for *kaikyoshi* or *jushoku*, "church" for *bukkyokai* or *otera*, and "faith" for *shinjin* are a few but salient examples. The second method, when no easy English equivalent was available, was to provide transliterations of the words or concepts. Words such as *Sangha* (Brotherhood of Buddhists), *dana* (offerings or charity), *Bodhisattva* (a Buddha-to-be), and *Dharma* (Teachings of the Buddha) are still used today. Some Buddhists considered the English translations to be less than adequate because of their etymological origins. The main problems centered on the derivation of the translations from words having a Judeo-Christian base:

> In 1933, the leaders at the annual [YMBA] conference stressed the use of English terminology different from that used in Christian churches. A look at books on Shinshu published in English during that period shows that there was a definite need for such a separate identity. For anyone with a Christian background reading such books would tend to interpret Buddhist teachings in a Christian context.[37]

The problem of proper translation is still discussed today.[38] For example, a word found in Jodo Shinshu Japanese, *shinjin* (literally, believing-mind), has no adequate English equivalent, although the word itself is easily translated as "faith."[39] "Faith," in Christian terminology, connotes the trust in God and His promises as presented through Jesus or the Holy Bible. *Shinjin*, in contrast, is "the awakening to the nature of the blind self [desire] and simultaneous awakening to the compassionate vow of Amida Buddha,"[40] or the "moment we are free from all selfishness."[41] For the Buddhist, there can be no belief or trust in a God since there is none in this religion. A better term for *shinjin* is perhaps "understanding," yet it does not highlight the sacred or religious meaning inherent in the concept. However, since *shinjin* has implicit in it a belief or trust in the Teachings of the Buddha (*Dharma*), the word "faith" is partially applicable.

The translation of *shinjin* as "faith" was accepted by the NABM and later by the BCA because "faith" connoted the sacred nature of the Japanese word. The English-speaking Buddhist followers were expected to realize the "real" meaning of "faith" as it applied to their religion; that is, they knew the common meaning of the word "faith," but they were then expected to relearn the Buddhist definition of the term. Unfortunately, many Nisei and Sansei Buddhists may not be aware of the other meaning of the word, and the word "faith" is used as if the Christian connotations of trust and belief were paramount. For instance, the three most repeated sentences in Jodo Shinshu Buddhist, besides the name of the Buddha, are the three homages.[42] The original words are in the Pali language, and the translations used by the Nikkei are: "I put my faith in Buddha, I put my faith in Dharma, and I put my faith in Sangha."

This long example on the Buddhist concept of "faith" suggests the immigrants' inherent difficulty in teaching their religion to their children. Before adequate translations can be inaugurated, the translator should be conversant in both languages; however, the missionary *kaikyoshi* were conversant only in Japanese. The *kaikyoshi* were unable to cross-check the adequacy of the translations since they had not mastered the English language.[43]

Many Issei returned to their Jodo Shinshu institution, especially with their increasing years and anti-Japanese agitation against them during the 1920s and 1930s. Although the NABM attempted to attract the Nisei, many of them were only potential church goers whose families were Buddhist. Many Nisei did not in fact become active church members. To conclude that the non-church goers were converted to Christianity is unwarranted; rather, the Nisei were likely to abstain from ritual attendance and from joining organized Buddhist youth activities.

The temples were oriented toward the Issei; the local temple's policy and organizations were dominated by them, and the priests spoke in Japanese. The only effective organizations for the young were the YMBA and the YWBA. Although many Nisei remained active church supporters, the NABM was not successful in retaining and attracting an overwhelming number of Nisei supporters. However, the events of World War II dramatically changed the Japanese communities in the western states as well as the NABM and the status of the Nisei within it.

By the 1940s, the remaining Issei were acknowledging their permanent relationship with the United States. Although their dream may have been to return to Japan, and their cultural ties remained with their home country, the passing years and the birth of their children strengthened their actual ties to America. The Issei's new feeling about America in 1939 is exemplified at a White River Valley, Washington, party for two Nisei draftees:

> I shall never forget the message of the village elder, who was not a Christian. It was to the effect that the Issei was wedded to the United States and therefore, though Japan had remained his "original" home for these many years, his "true" home was none other than the United States. The traditional Japanese teaching emphasizes that once married, the bride must accept her husband's parents as her own, his home as hers; and her primary and ultimate loyalty must be to his parents and his home. . . . When he saw his son standing proudly in a U.S. Army uniform, he knew that he had been wedded to the United States for all these years, even though there had been many in-laws, as it were, who mistreated him. Characteristically Japanese, he would say, "If I were alone, I might choose to return to Japan, but now I have these children, for whose sake I will stick it out to the bitter end."[44]

This is not to say that the Issei ever felt at home or at ease in America. This was an adopted country, but they knew that the adoption was only one-way; America had often indicated to them their impermanent status. But the familial ties with the American Nisei, the economic ties to their occupations and farmlands, the social ties to the community, the psychological ties, binding the group together through suffering and endurance of anti-Japanese prejudice, were all factors keeping them in America. Ironically, in the homeland, Japan was undergoing a period of extreme nationalism. The country that the immigrants left was no longer the same, and was in the process of preparing itself for war with the United States.

Notes

1. See, for example, Ichihashi, op. cit., and Daniels, op. cit.
2. Daniels, op. cit., p. 1.
3. Ibid., pp. 1–2.
4. Strong, op. cit., p. 46.
5. See Sidney L. Gulick, *American-Japanese Relations 1916–1920: A Retrospect*, Report to the Federal Council of Churches of Christ in America, n.d., pp. 7–11.
6. John S. Chambers, "The Japanese Invasion," *Annals of the American Academy of Political and Social Sciences* 93 (January 1921): 26–27. Chambers occupied the office of the California state controller in 1919. At that time, "saving California from the Japs" was an important political movement with both Democrats and Republicans attempting to capitalize on the issue. See Daniels, op. cit., p. 84.
7. Daniels, op. cit., p. 2.
8. Kiichi Kanzaki, *California and the Japanese* (San Francisco: Japanese Association of America, 1921), p. 24.
9. Valentine S. McClatchy, "Japanese in the Melting Pot," in *Present Day Immigration with Special Reference to the Japanese, Annals of the American Academy of Political and Social Sciences* 93 (January 1921): 30.
10. See for example, Kanzaki, op. cit., pp. 24–25; and E. Manchester Boddy, *Japanese in America* (Los Angeles: E. M. Boddy, 1921), pp. 114–117.
11. Quoted in K. K. Kawakami, *The Real Japanese Question* (New York: Macmillan Co., 1921), p. 154.
12. Ibid.
13. Pajus, op. cit., p. 181.
14. See Kanzaki, op. cit., pp. 34–35; and Kanzaki, "Is the Japanese Menace in America a Reality?" *Annals of the American Academy of*

Political and Social Sciences (January 1921): 95–96; H. A. Millis, *The Japanese Problem in the United States* (New York: Macmillan Co., 1920), p. 268.

15. Monica Sone, *Nisei Daughter* (Boston: Little Brown and Co., 1953), p. 19. For the "success" of the Japanese schools, see Ichihashi, op. cit., pp. 331–333.

16. There are Japanese language schools in Los Angeles, Gardena, Oxnard, San Francisco, etc. I am indebted to K. Abe, past instructor of the Oxnard Buddhist Church Japanese School, Oxnard, Calif., for this suggestion.

17. See Sone, op. cit., pp. 20–27, for an autobiographical account: "As time went on I began to suspect that there was more to *Nihon Gakko* [Japanese School] than learning the Japanese language. There was a driving spirit of strict discipline behind it all which reached out and weighed heavily upon each pupil's consciousness."

18. Ogura, op. cit., p. 21.

19. Ibid., pp. 71–72.

20. John Modell (ed.), *Kikuchi Diary* (Urbana: University of Illinois Press, 1973), p. 82n.

21. Ichihashi, op. cit., p. 280.

22. Eliot Grinell Mears, *Resident Orientals on the American Pacific Coast: Their Legal and Economic Status* (New York: Institute of Pacific Relations, 1927), p. 381.

23. Kyojiro Takahashi, "A Social Study of the Japanese Shinto, and Buddhism in Los Angeles," Master's Thesis, University of Southern California, Los Angeles, January 1937, p. 92.

24. See Ichihashi, op. cit., pp. 298–318.

25. Ogura, op. cit., pp. 85–86.

26. Ibid., p. 86.

27. See Modell, op. cit., pp. 1–40.

28. Recollections of Reverend Zesei Kawasaki, a *kaikyoshi* in the NABM and BCA since 1929. "A Discussion on Early Missionary Work with Three Senior BCA Ministers," *Buddhist Churches of America Newsletter* 10, no. 3 (March 1973): 4.

29. Additional material from personal correspondence with Dr. Ryo Munekata, August 17, 1973.

30. Responses from the Minister's Questionnaire; see Appendix 2.

31. William Carlson Smith, *Americans in Process: A Study of Our Citizens of Oriental Ancestry* (Ann Arbor, Mich.: Edward Brothers Inc., 1937; reprint ed., New York: Arno Press, 1970), p. 144.

32. Hosokawa, op. cit., p. 151. The following figures are also from Hosokawa.

33. National Young Buddhist Association, op. cit.

34. Paul Andrews, "A Brief Look at Young Buddhist Association History," Typescript, n.d., p. 1.

35. Ibid., p. 2.

36. Ibid., p. 1.

37. Ibid., p. 20.

38. Reverend Masami Fujitani, "English Nomenclature for *So-cho*," mimeographed, February 24, 1971, for the BCA Ministerial Study Committee. The linguistic problem will be further explored in Chapter 5.

39. Nishu Utsuki, *The Shin Sect: A School of Mahayana Buddhism* (Kyoto, Japan: Publication Bureau of Buddhist Books, Hompa Hongwanji, 1937), pp. 1–2 and 7–22. See also *The Jodo Shinshu Book* (Los Angeles: Nembutsu Press, 1973), p. 58.

40. Taitetsu Unno, "Shin Buddhism Questions and Answers," in BCA, *Shin Buddhist Handbook* (San Francisco: 1972), p. 95.

41. Eidmann, op. cit., p. 2.

42. Shoyu Hanayama, *Buddhist Handbook for Shin-shu Followers* (Tokyo: Hokuseido Press, 1969), p. 53. The words in Pali are: *Buddham Saranam Gacchami* (I put my faith in Buddha), *Khamma Saranam Gacchami* (I put my faith in Dharma), *Sangham Saranam Gacchami* (I put my faith in Sangha).

43. Only since the 1950s, and most recently in the 1960s, have there been available Shinshu texts written in English and sanctioned by the Hompa Hongwanji and the BCA. See, for example, Hompa Hongwanji Mission of Hawaii, *The Shinshu Seiten* (Honolulu: Hompa Hongwanji, 1955); Shodo Tsunoda, Shoko Masunaga, and Kenryo Kumata, *Buddhism and Jodo Shinshu* (San Francisco: BCA, 1955); Hanayama, op. cit.; Eidmann, op. cit.; and BCA, *Shin Buddhist Handbook.* The problem is far from resolved at the present time (see Chapter 4).

44. Daisuke Kitagawa, *Issei and Nisei: The Internment Years* (New York: Seabury Press, 1967), p. 32.

CHAPTER 4 | *The Catastrophic Events of World War II: 1941-1945*

On December 7, 1941, the Japanese military forces attacked the American naval fleet at Pearl Harbor. The effect on the Japanese communities nestled on the Pacific Coast was instantaneous. Almost immediately there followed a roundup of Issei community leaders, businessmen, teachers of Japanese martial arts, leaders of the Japanese Association, and Shinto and Buddhist priests. Thus began a period of fear, insecurity, and anxiety about the future for the Japanese Americans.

The evacuation and its effects on the Japanese Americans have been studied in great detail, and we need not enter into a lengthy discussion here.[1] The overall outcome for the Buddhist churches was threefold: first, a crisis arose for the ministers as to their conduct during the war; second, the Nisei gained a position of limited prominence and importance within the religious institution; and third, the resettlement pattern of the Buddhists after the war created changes in the temple organizations.

The Crisis of the NABM

The outbreak of the war allowed the American anti-Japanese sentiment of the early 1900s to resurface. Members of the Buddhist faith, along with the followers of Shintoism, were suspected of harboring Japanese nationalistic and anti-American feelings.

[In 1942] a spokesman for the California Joint Immigration

47

Committee . . . [stated] the religion of emperor worship similarly led people away from Americanism. This last point was apparently a reference to Shintoism. An Oregon State Senator extends the danger classification to Buddhists, stating that "the Buddhist religion is looked on as a national Japanese custom," and "even among the children there isn't much social mixing between the Buddhists and the Christian children."[2]

The response by the NABM to the pro-Japanese allegation was a clear and unequivocal denial of such charges:

The Buddhist Mission of North America released a statement to the effect that "the suddenness and the unwarranted and inhumane attack upon these United States of America leave us, the Buddhists in America, with but one decision: the condemnation of that attack." One duty remained for American Buddhists: "The loyalty to the United States which we have pledged at all times must now be placed into instant action for the defense of the United States of America."[3]

The need for releasing some kind of statement was clear: from the start of the war, the FBI had questioned Buddhists and had taken some into custody for early internment. With their priests and community leaders under investigation or in jail, the Buddhist members themselves could only assume that they too were under suspicion. Many Japanese destroyed items that might be regarded as incriminating: some burned Sutra books, while others concealed their family Buddhist altars.[4]

The officers at NABM headquarters were cognizant of the fears and anxieties of the Buddhist community, but the NABM priests were incarcerated and so could not immediately aid their followers. It is safe to assume that the NABM officers were experiencing their own share of fear and anxiety. The priests, undoubtedly moral and law-abiding,[5] had been suddenly arrested by the FBI without notice or justification. The Japanese community was thus faced with the question of how best to deal with this seemingly irrational oppression.

During this period of confusion and uncertainty, the personnel at NABM headquarters took positive steps to emphasize the organization members' loyalty to the United States. The Reverend Kenryo Kumata, a Nisei minister, and the Reverend Zenkai Okayama acted for the then ill and bedridden Bishop Ryotai Matsukage. They made frequent calls to the San Francisco FBI and the Naval Intelligence Bureau to explain the activities of the Buddhist organization.

The Reverend Kumata, as information officer of the NABM, sent questionnaires to the member temples and churches to gather data on their activities and loyalty. One of the reply letters came from the Oakland Buddhist Church on January 8, 1942. The Reverend Tetsuro Kashima wrote:

> The following is a report of the activities now in progress by the members of the Oakland Buddhist Church, which includes both citizens and non-citizens of the United States in doing defense work and Red Cross work.
>
> 1. The Buddhist Church of Oakland has urged its members to show their loyalty and patriotism by helping to buy defense bonds and enrolling and giving all their time to doing Red Cross and defense work. It has already donated $150.00 to the Oakland Red Cross. It is willing to lend the use of its building for any defense work.
>
> 2. The Young Men's Buddhist Association of Oakland has bought $200.00 worth of defense bonds. The young men are canvassing the neighborhood to collect old clothes, newspapers, books, magazines, etc., to be used for the defense program of America.
>
> 3. The Young Women's Buddhist Association has signed up to do Red Cross work and will meet every week.
>
> 4. The Older Women's Club of the Oakland Buddhist Church are giving their time in doing Red Cross work.
>
> 5. The members of the Oakland Buddhist Church have given their boys who have been drafted send-off parties and gifts in appreciation for the duties they are to perform as American soldiers. In order that they keep up their morale, and to let

them know that they are not forgotten, the Older Women's Club are sending gifts twice a year to these boys stationed at the various camps.[6]

This letter, and others received from the various temples and churches, were utilized by the NABM to demonstrate the patriotic activities and basic loyalty of the collective religious body. That Reverend Kashima wrote and signed this letter in English, though as an Issei he was more fluent in Japanese, suggests that he knew the final recipient would probably not be Bishop Matsukage but the authorities investigating the NABM.

On February 7, 1942, another letter was sent to the NABM from the Oakland Buddhist Church. The format was question-and-answer, and the relevant portion reads:

2. Q: How many families did you visit to encourage the spirit of loyalty to this country?

A: Approximately ninety families.

3. Q: How often did you give patriotic lectures to encourage members of your church to be or become loyal and high moral citizens and residents of this country?

A: I have always included the above in my sermons, but since the emergency, only about sixteen times as the opportunity of gatherings was few.

8. Q: How many members of your church are now serving in [the] Armed Forces of this country?

A: Thirteen members.

9. Q: State other measures and activities undertaken by your church to meet this emergency.

A: 1) The Church has signed over its two Sunday school busses to the States call.

2) The church building and facilities to be offered to citizens defense and the Red Cross.

3) The YMBA building now being used by the Red Cross workers.

4) Part of the offerings will be devoted to the buying of defense stamps and bonds.

The district in which our Church building stands has been declared by the Federal Government to be within the forbidden area after February 24. This ruling naturally means the curtailment of activities.

Respectfully submitted,

(signed) Reverend T. Kashima[7]

The NABM and the individual churches and temples continued to proclaim their basic loyalty to the United States. For the first time, the Nisei, able to speak English, were encouraged to participate more fully in church-related activities, and for the first time, too, sermons in English were sanctioned by the NABM.[8]

Despite all such efforts, on February 19, 1942, President Roosevelt signed Executive Order 9066, authorizing

The Secretary of War, and the Military Commanders whom he may from time to time designate . . . to prescribe military areas . . . from which any or all persons may be excluded, and with respect to which, the right of any person to enter, remain in or leave shall be subject to whatever restriction the Secretary of War or the appropriate Military Commander may impose in his discretion.[9]

On March 2, Lieutenant General John L. DeWitt, the commanding general of the Western Defense Command, prescribed that the western third of Washington, all of Oregon, the western half of California, and the southern quarter of Arizona would be Military Area No. 1, from which all alien Germans and Italians, and all persons of Japanese ancestry, would be removed. The NABM wrote a mimeographed letter on March 4, 1942, addressed to the Buddhist churches in the United States:

Your attention is called to the Proclamation of Lt. General J. L. DeWitt outlinin[g] the Military Zone. In keeping with this proclamation it behooves the Buddhists to:

1. Respect the Government of the United States and its laws and regulations; to hold fast to your religious faith in Buddhism, and to be calm and collected at all times.

2. Cooperate with the Defense of the United States of America and as loyal citizens and residents understand the vital necessity of and conform with the regulations pertaining to evacuation.

3. Make all preparations within each Buddhist Church to be able to cope with problems arising from evacuation.

4. Prepare for the evacuation of the Buddhist Churches itself, if the need arises.

May we remind you to complete the survey of your community as has been suggested to you in our communication No. 11, and be ready to evacuate in a quiet and orderly manner.

> With the Blessing of the Buddha
> (signed) Rev. K. M. Kumata
> Buddhist Churches of America[10]

This letter contains three items of importance. First, in the letterhead and signatory block, Reverend Kumata designated the institution as the Buddhist Churches of America instead of the NABM, for possibly the first time. This change of official designation from the *Hokubei Bukkyo Dan* was made without official approval from the constituent churches.[11] Second, the headquarters continued to emphasize the basic loyalty of the NABM to the United States and its war cause. Third, the NABM was warning its ministers of a possible evacuation, although the exact time and place of internment were still unknown. Thus, some preparations could be made; some churches were later used to store their members' personal belongings, while other buildings were loaned to various governmental or war-related organizations.[12] The War Relocation Authority (WRA) was created by the president on March 18, and evacuation to the assembly centers was effected by Civilian Defense Order No. 1 on March 24, 1942. After Exclusion Order 99, on June 6, 1942, 100,313 persons had been removed from Military Area No. 1. Between March 2 and October 31, 1942, a total of 117,116 persons came under the evacuation program, and 110,723 actually entered assembly or the ten relocation centers.[13]

Japanese was still a suspect language, and English was initially mandated by the Wartime Civil Control Authority (WCCA) as the official language. The Nisei ministers in the NABM, apparently numbering only four,[14] were thus given the greatest opportunity to be spokesmen for the group. Services at the assembly centers were conducted in English—first in the grandstands and later in the recreational centers. Services in Japanese were not allowed until WCCA authorities had been convinced that many Issei could not understand English.

Churches and temples in the evacuated areas were entrusted to the care of responsible persons; some were used by governmental authorities but others were left boarded up and unprotected. For instance, in Los Angeles, the main temple (*betsuin*) was watched during the war by the Reverend Julius Goldwater, an ordained Jodo Shinshu priest. Reverend Goldwater was also able to supply Buddhists, especially at the Santa Anita Race Track Assembly Center, with *ojuzu* (Buddhist beads), Buddhist altars, and other necessary religious materials. According to the Reverend Arthur Takemoto, this period was "the true beginnings of the English gatherings." Services in English, innovative teaching methods such as the use of flannel boards for story-telling, and puppetry were now inaugurated for the Buddhist ceremonies. Previously, religious services and activities, except for the national YBA conferences, were predominantly Issei-controlled and Issei-oriented.

Most of the Japanese interned in the camps were Buddhists. The statistics[15] are as follows:

	No.	Pct.	American Born	Pct.	Foreign Born	Pct.
Buddhist	61,719	55.5	35,327	48.7	26,392	68.5
Protestant	32,131	28.9	23,712	32.6	8,419	21.9
Catholic	2,199	2.0	1,735	2.4	464	1.2
Tenri-Kyo and similar sects (popular Shinto)	422	0.4	164	0.2	278	0.7
Seicho Noiye	37	(less than 0.05)	4	(less than 0.05)	33	0.1
Not Given	14,642	13.2	11,708	16.1	2,934	7.6
Total	111,170	100.0	76,650	100.0	38,520	100.0

These figures, obtained through interviews with the evacuees, indicate large differences between the Issei and Nisei Buddhists. Many Nisei Buddhists apparently were afraid to attend the religious institution of their parents: thousands listed "no preference" in their religion, and many even became Christians. Leighton reports that "there was a marked increase in church attendance. Buddhists and Shintoists went to the Christian churches because they felt that there would be more protection for them."[16]

By World War II, there were four major subdivisions, with Amida Buddhism plus two denominations—Jodo and Jodo Shinshu—represented in America. Before the war, these different subdivisions had had relatively little contact with each other; but when they were thrown together in some camps, a United Buddhist church was formed. Of the main Buddhist divisions represented in the relocation centers Jodo Shinshu had two (Nishi and Higashi Hongwanji), followed by Shingon, Zen, Nichiren, Tendai, and Jodo.[17] The mixture of denominations and sects created conflicts among the Buddhists and at certain relocation centers resulted in compromises. For example, in one of the three camps at Poston, Arizona, the priests of the Shingon, Nichiren, and NABM sponsored joint services. At that camp, instead of reciting "*Namu Amida Butsu*," as in the NABM and Jodo Shinshu liturgies, the priests substituted "*Namu Shaka-muni Butsu.*" Overall, in the United Buddhist church,

> Priests of the different groups took turns in conducting the services but at each service the particular ritual needs of each sect were given consideration. The tendency was not toward the elimination of all sectarian differences of doctrine and rites. Still the fear that such a leveling might occur as a result of the newly organized United Buddhist Church led to anxieties and conflicts.[18]

At Poston, and at most other camps, the predominance of the Jodo Shinshu followers became apparent soon after the initial confusion abated, especially because most Buddhist priests were by this time allowed to join their followers. Many Jodo Shinshu priests withdrew from the United Buddhist church to resume their own denominational services. The conflicts centered not only upon doctrinal but also financial and even political differences. For example, monetary disputes arose over whether offertory receipts were to be distributed according to the relative size of sects or divided equally among all. In the former case, the Jodo Shinshu priests would always receive the greater share, but in the latter, they could object because most of the Buddhists were originally Jodo Shinshu adherents.[19] Money was not the only source of discord. A purely political difference arose in Jerome, Arkansas, concerning the loyalty questionnaire:

> Until registration for the army occurred, the course of the [United Buddhist] Church was fairly smooth, but at that time twelve of the trustees of the Church requested three other board members to resign. The twelve members feared that the hostility of the three to registration would make Buddhism appear to be a pro-Japanese religion. The three dissenters resigned, and with three priests and a following of about three-hundred people established the Daijo Bukkyo Church.[20]

Another important inter-Buddhist religious event in the early 1940s was the establishment of a nonsectarian Buddhist organization. The Buddhist Brotherhood of America (BBA), an organization led by Reverend Julius Goldwater and assisted by Arthur Takemoto, later ordained a Jodo Shinshu priest, and Reverend Gyomei Kubose, a Nisei minister of the Higashi Hongwanji temple, was formed to create an American Buddhism, unhampered by denominational differences:

> Slowly but surely, a number of American students were absorbing Buddhist thought, and striving to practice the Buddhist philosophy in their daily living. So, it is not surprising that during this time of stress and upheaval, that these students . . . should become united in the purpose of preserving and fostering Buddhism in America, and it was in this manner, that the Buddhist Brotherhood in America came into being as an organization . . . it is up to us to carry the torch of Buddhism forward and on high. In this endeavor there can be no thought of discrimination in sect, race or color; the teachings must be paramount, combining the best of both Hinayana and Mahayana School, and in so doing, reaching that equilibrium so necessary for completeness and growth.[21]

The BBA was intended as a nonsectarian Buddhist organization that would spread Buddhism to all Americans. Although Reverend Goldwater had aided the NABM, and had known and been influenced by various Jodo Shinshu priests, he had received only the rites of ordination (*tokudo*). Since he had never become a *kyoshi*, with the right to do missionary work,[22] he was not a registered priest of the NABM.

The history of the BBA begins in Hawaii, with Bishop Yemyo Imamura investing the ordination rites upon Ernest H. and Dorothy Hunt at the Honolulu Hompa Nongwanji (Nishi Hongwanji headquarters in Hawaii) on August 11, 1924. Hunt, an Englishman,

> affirmed that Buddhism and genuine Americanism had much in common. He wrote that a true American, like a good Buddhist, was one who believes in absolute religious freedom and equal opportunity for all irrespective of race, color or creed. A true American, like a good Buddhist was one who "tries by his words and actions to hasten the day of universal brotherhood and peace."[23]

Occidental interest in Buddhism was already awakening by the late 1920s and early 1930s: "A large new monastery had been built in Hamburg, and two Buddhist societies had been founded in England—the Buddhist Lodge in London and the British branch of the Maha Bodhi Society in Liverpool. The Dharma was beginning to 'catch on' in the United States also, especially in New York and on the West Coast."[24] In Hawaii, Hunt and Bishop Imamura established the Hawaiian Branch of the International Buddhist Institute, dedicated to teaching a nonsectarian and united Buddhism.

The significance of Hunt's movement and the later BBA lay in their attempt to free the Buddhists of Hawaii and the continental United States from their sectarian traditions and history. From the Jodo Shinshu perspective, sectarian differences in Japanese Buddhism are very important. All the denominations in Japan had their own founders, histories, and emphases. If Hunt had been successful in making Hawaiian Jodo Shinshu Buddhism truly nonsectarian, a great change in Buddhism could have been effected. But Hunt's views were not fully accepted by the Hompa Hongwanji Mission of Hawaii officials. In December 1934, Bishop Imamura passed away; and in March 1935, the third bishop,

Gikyo Kuchiba, opposed to Imamura's policies and desirous of restricting Jodo Shinshu Buddhism to the Japanese, fired Ernest Hunt.[25]

Yet, the Reverend Hunt's message was not lost on the Hawaiian Nisei, and it even influenced some Nisei in America. In 1930, a Pan-Pacific YMBA conference, attended by the NABM-YMBA, was held in Honolulu. The topics revolved around the spreading of Buddhism to the youth and the easing of sectarian differences within Buddhism. Hunt spoke for more English texts and materials, and advocated "Christian" methods of proselytizing, such as organizing young men's groups, Sunday Schools, women's associations, and social work projects.[26]

One person profoundly influenced by Reverent Hunt was Julius Goldwater. Adopting Hunt's policies and ambitions, Goldwater helped to inaugurate the BBA. During the 1940s, with the rise of more Nisei spokesmen in the Jodo Shinshu institution, the BBA and its leaders advocated and aided in the reactivation of the national Young Buddhist Association.

The National Young Buddhist Movement in the Camps

In the 1940s, the YBA, as the youth organizations of the member Jodo Shinshu temples, started to push for a nonsectarian or "all-sectarian" Buddhist organization to bring together all the Buddhists in America. Their reasons were twofold: "Many YBA leaders held high hopes that this would provide for a greater development of Buddhism in the United States. There was also the factor that many thought that an all-sectarian policy would tend to diminish the identification of Buddhism strictly with Japan."[27] There were few YBA chapters in the other Buddhist denominations, primarily because of their small membership. As pointed out earlier, the YBA had been formed to meet the social and religious needs of English-speaking children of Japanese immigrants. In its collective membership, it was probably the largest Nisei organization.[28] The national YBA, inactive since the late 1930s, was essentially reestablished at a Salt Lake City conference of YBA leaders called from the various relocation camps in May 1943.

At this conference, Nisei YBA representatives met with various Nisei and Issei Jodo Shinshu priests to coordinate Buddhist youth activities in the camps and to encourage and survey the activities of all Buddhist organizations.[29] Various problems confronted these organizations, not the least of which was a decline in membership: "in fact, . . . even Buddhists [admitted] that there [was] a growing tendency for young American-born Japanese to turn away from Buddhism. A unique example, seven Nisei soldiers in the United States Army returned to Salt Lake City to be baptised in the Church of Jesus Christ of Latter Day Saints (Mormon Church)."[30]

The loss of Nisei adherents to Buddhism was viewed as only one symptom of a basic generation dilemma: the NABM was Issei- and Japanese-oriented, and there had been no effective Nisei Buddhist countermeasures.[31] By the 1930s, the NABM had realized the need to include more Nisei activities and ministers in the institution, but with the Nisei yet so young and with the difficulty of training English-speaking Nisei in a Japanese-oriented religion, it was not until relocation that the Nisei attained some decision-making rights.

One major issue that disrupted the camp but aided the Nisei in the NABM concerned the "loyalty" questionnaires presented to the evacuees in February and March 1943.[32] The WRA decided to use the questionnaire to distinguish potentially "loyal" from "disloyal" evacuees, to gather volunteers for military service, and to permit the resettlement of some evacuees into such nonsensitive areas as the Midwest or the East Coast. Two questions on the form, numbers twenty-seven and twenty-eight, became issues of controversy: the first dealt with the respondent's willingness to serve in the armed forces of the United States, and the second, in essence, asked for a renunciation of any allegiance to Japan. To ask the Issei, aliens ineligible for citizenship in the United States, to volunteer for military duties and to forswear allegiance to their nation of birth and citizenship was to place them in a very difficult position. Most Nisei responded positively, but many Issei did not, until the controversy brought a modification in the questions.

As a consequence, a further population shift took place in the camps. Those persons answering "no" to both questions twenty-seven and twenty-eight were, in the main, segregated in the Tule Lake, California, camp, while most of those responding "yes" at Tule Lake were shipped to the other nine camps. The majority of the negative respondents were vocal Issei and Kibei (Nisei who had spent part or most of their early years in Japan) leaders. The loss of these vocal Issei from the camps aided in the rise of the Nisei leadership in the Buddhist institutions by effectively silencing anti-American and anti-Nisei sentiments.

Another consequence of the affirmative responses by the majority of the Nisei was the start of their release from the camps in 1943 to Chicago, Denver, Cleveland, St. Louis, New York, Philadelphia, and Seabrook, New Jersey. By 1944, hundreds of evacuees were able to relocate into the eastern states, creating pockets of Japanese American populations. To these centers the NABM would soon follow.

Buddhist Churches of America: February to June 1944

An important series of meetings was initiated in 1944 that would have far-reaching consequences for the NABM. On February 28, 1944, at the Topaz, Utah, camp where Bishop Matsukage was interned, a meeting of Jodo Shinshu ministers and lay representatives was held concerning the NABM institution.[33] A study of the institution and its by-laws was continued on April 19 and 21. The April 21 meeting was called the *Kaikyoshi Shinto Daihyosha Kaigi* (Ministers and Lay Representatives Conference). By April 28, at another ministers and lay representative meeting, a new institution, the Buddhist Churches of America (*Beikoku Bukkyo Dan*), was already in the final stages of discussion, with final approval coming at the meeting on April 29.[34] The Reverend Shintatsu Sanada was asked by Bishop Matsukage to serve as the headquarters secretary under the new institution, and the official appointment was made on May 2, 1944. On May 29, the BCA institution board met, and an election was later held for the officers on June 5. On June 13, notice of the election was written, translated into English, and mailed to the other camp churches in the name of the bishop. By June 17, a board of trustees of the BCA was selected, consisting of two representatives from Topaz and five from the other camps. Final approval for the BCA had not yet been sent to all the churches, although the 1944 Topaz meetings clearly indicate that the groundwork for the organization had been laid by the Issei and the ministers and bishop of the NABM.

The Nisei officially entered the NABM reorganization in July 1944 at a YBA meeting held in Salt Lake City.

Buddhist Churches of America—July 1944

A conference important for the future of the NABM, following the May 1943 session, was held in Salt Lake City in July 1944. YBA representatives of the NABM, and the Higashi Hongwanji and the ministers, who were predominantly Nisei, gathered together to ratify the new general institutional organization under the title Buddhist Churches of America. The delegates agreed that the new organization should repudiate all ties with Japan, that relations with the Jodo Shinshu religious headquarters in Kyoto, Japan, should be minimized, and that the two Jodo Shinshu religious sects (Nishi and Higashi) should be united. An advisory council of fifteen Nisei, three of these to be priests, would be elected to administer the new Buddhist organization.[35] The new constitution stipulated that all offices in the organization would be occupied by Nisei, though they would be aided by an Issei advisory group. It also called for the election of the bishop (*socho*) by the members of the affiliated churches, whereas in the past, the bishop had been appointed from Japan. The other officials of the central organization were to be elected by postal ballot.[36]

The new constitution was submitted to the various Buddhist organizations, both within and outside the camps.[37] It was duly ratified, though not without opposition from some Issei ministers and former church leaders. These few Issei ministers felt that the changes would drastically alter the Jodo Shinshu faith as well as give complete control to the Nisei. Ratification was effected because the delegates to the conference were able to convince the various YBA organizations that there was a necessity for change. Other Issei ministers already saw the need to adapt their religion in the United States to maintain the immigrants' children in the religious organization. Moreover, the new organization voted to reappoint Bishop Matsukage as the chief leader of the Buddhist Churches of America, and this eased some tensions.[38]

The BCA retained the ideas of Buddhism as its core. The aim was to make Buddhism more acceptable, more understandable, more inclusive of all Buddhist thoughts, as well as less sectarian, less restrictive in membership, and more adaptable to the changing needs of the Nisei and Sansei. The Buddhists in America desired to lift, for the Nisei and their children, the veil of foreignness cast over their religion by the language and customs of the Issei. The predominant language was to be English, not Japanese, and the changes would aid in conveying the religion to the Nisei and Sansei.

Ratification of the new constitution was not followed by an immediate, wholesale reconstruction of the NABM. One reason was that the ministers of the BCA were still the original Issei of the NABM. Regardless of the titular change, the Japanese priests still held sway in the temples and churches. A second reason was that although the Nisei were able to make their views known to the BCA, the adherents were still largely Issei. Third, with the retention of Bishop Matsukage, an Issei, the BCA did not effect a radical change in the organizational power structure. Fourth, since the Higashi Hongwanji had far fewer adherents and only a few ministers, the NABM was able to maintain its own sectarian doctrines. Fifth, there were still few Buddhist materials written in English for dissemination to prospective Nisei ministers or to the Nisei community. Finally, full implementation of the new constitution was delayed because the difficulties of resettlement outside the camps became an immediate and pressing issue in late 1944 and 1945.

The BCA remains a sectarian religious institution, tied to the Hompa (Nishi) Hongwanji in Kyoto, Japan. But more Buddhist materials are now available in English, and an institution for the training of English-speaking ministers has become a reality.

Resettlement Outside the Camps

After being cloistered on a reservation for a period ranging from one to four years, most often three, the interned Japanese would face another set of difficulties in resettlement. Although the Japanese began to be released from the camps in late 1943, the West Coast was not open to Japanese resettlement until January 1945. The WRA also announced that all the camps would be closed by January 2, 1946. For the evacuees, the camps had come to be a place where a reorganized social structure had replaced pre-1942 patterns. To resettle again, outside the camps, was to experience the personal insecurity inherent in leaving relative safety for the unknown and unknowable. For the Issei internment had erased much of their economic security, and for the Nisei it had obliterated the personal security they felt was their right by citizenship. The camp experience forced the quiescence of the Issei within the Japanese American community and raised the Nisei to positions of influence.

Fear and insecurity, coupled with the youth[39] and inexperience of the Nisei leaders, compounded the problem of resettling the camp population. Many persons were reluctant to leave the camps for fear of losing new-found friends and of meeting discrimination and organized opposition by anti-Japanese elements wherever they might resettle. Family ties would be strained as members left for different areas, and financial and occupational insecurity seemed inevitable.[40] But resettlement was equally inevitable. Many Nisei had already left the camps to serve in the armed forces, or had relocated to the eastern United States, and with the continual success of the Allied forces in the battlefield, the Issei realized that the WRA must eventually terminate its operations.

The BCA as an organization also initiated plans for the impending resettlement. The bishop and the ministers urged and planned for the return. They even sent ministers ahead of the returning evacuees to convert existing temple structures into hostels for the West Coast returnees.[41] Certain Jodo Shinshu organizations had been allowed to operate during the war because their relocation was outside the jurisdiction of West Coast military authorities. These were the six churches at Denver and Fort Lupton, Colorado; Mesa, Arizona; Salt Lake City and Ogden, Utah; and New York City.[42] Prior to and during the war, their congregations had been small compared to those of churches on the West Coast, but their membership increased as the resettlement program proceeded.

Other areas saw the inauguration and operation of new Jodo Shinshu activities. In March 1944, a YBA member was dispatched from the YBA headquarters, then located in Ogden, Utah, to investigate the possibilities of starting a Buddhist temple in Chicago.[43] Although most evacuees desired eventually to return to the West Coast, job opportunities were greater in the Midwest, where there was a labor shortage. The number of Nisei in Chicago continued to increase until, by the summer of 1946, four Buddhist churches were established.[44] The Nishi Hongwanji under Reverend Gyodo Kono, and the Higashi Hongwanji under Reverend Gyomei Kubose, were the two largest sects in membership. These two priests, encouraged by the spirit of cooperation at the July 1944 Salt Lake City conference, attempted to establish an interdenominational Jodo Shinshu temple in Chicago; however, problems of personality, language, and finances resulted in the establishment of two separate organizations.[45] Reverend Kubose's group inaugurated the

Chicago Buddhist Church, while Reverend Kono's instituted the Midwest Buddhist Temple.

The Midwest Buddhist Temple grew to over 500 members just after the war. It continues to flourish today with 225 member families and a broad program of religious and social activities for both young and old members.[46] Precise membership statistics are not available for the Chicago Buddhist Church, but it too is still functioning, though on a somewhat smaller scale than the Midwest Buddhist Temple.

The period just after 1944 was not easy for the leaders and members in Chicago. They were under constant scrutiny by the FBI regarding their activities, their membership, and their ministrations to the growing number of Japanese evacuees flowing into the city. Both the Midwest Buddhist Temple and the Chicago Buddhist Church aided Japanese resettlement into the state of Illinois, and both grew accordingly. The two institutions had much in common, although there were some differences: obviously, both were Buddhist, and their common objective was to spread the Teachings of the Buddha. But Reverend Kubose, a Nisei who had been affiliated with the BBA, advocated a nonsectarian position on Buddhism and thus looked to Caucasians and Japanese alike for converts and financial assistance. Reverend Kono, as part of the NABM, was an Issei, and was tied by necessity, if not choice, to the Hompa (Nishi) Hongwanji.[47] The changes that he advocated as an NABM member were regarded by the BCA as necessary to keep the growing Nisei population inside the Buddhist religion. English became the predominant language for both churches, but with the Nisei membership remaining generally within the BCA, since it was their parents' organization, the Midwest Buddhist Temple did not have to institute the nontraditional bases of support and membership advocated by Reverend Kubose for the Chicago Buddhist Church.

As more evacuees left the camps, YBA groups were also formed in St. Louis, Cleveland, and Philadelphia. The return to the West Coast in 1945 signaled another period of readjustment for the Japanese Americans and for the newly organized Buddhist Churches of America.

With the close of 1945, the BCA and its members were slowly entering the present era. The difficult time of resettlement was still ahead.

The next chapter takes a short break from the social history of the organization and deals with an important element within the BCA—

the priesthood. The changes in the priesthood parallel many of the changes in the organization itself, and thus elucidate the BCA's role in the ethnic adjustment of the Japanese Americans, which is the subject of Chapter 6.

NOTES

1. See, for example, Dorothy Swaine Thomas, *The Salvage* (Berkeley: University of California Press, 1952); Dorothy Swaine Thomas and Richard S. Nishimoto, *The Spoilage: Japanese-American Evacuation and Resettlement During World War II* (Berkeley: University of California Press, 1946); Morton Grodzins, *Americans Betrayed: Politics and the Japanese Evacuation* (Chicago: University of Chicago Press, 1949); Anne Reeploeg Fisher, *Exile of a Race* (Seattle, Wash.: F. and T. Publishers, 1965); Edward H. Spicer, Asnel T. Hansen, Katherine Luomala, and Mervin K. Opler, *Impounded People: Japanese Americans in the Relocation Centers* (Tucson: University of Arizona Press, 1969); Leonard Bloom and Ruth Reimer, *Removal and Return* (Berkeley: University of California Press, 1949); Audrie Girdner and Ann Loftis, *The Great Betrayal: The Evacuation of the Japanese Americans During World War II* (London: Collier Macmillan Ltd., 1969); Allan R. Bosworth, *America's Concentration Camps* (New York: Bantam Books, 1967, 1968); Roger Daniels, *Concentration Camps USA: Japanese Americans and World War II* (New York: Holt, Rinehart and Winston, Inc., 1971); Jacobus tenBroek, Edward H. Barnhart, and Floyd Matson, *Prejudice, War and the Constitution* (Berkeley: University of California Press, 1954); Carey McWilliams, *Prejudice/Japanese Americans: Symbol of Racial Intolerance* (Boston: Little, Brown and Co., 1945); Modell, op. cit.; Michi Weglyn, *Years of Infamy: The Untold Story of America's Concentration Camps* (New York: William Morrow and Co., 1976).

2. From the Select Committee Investigation National Defense Migration, known as the Tolan Committee, 1942. Quoted by Grodzins, op. cit., p. 408. Coupled with distrust of Buddhism *per se* was a widespread suspicion that the religious organization was a Japanese propaganda agency. The California State Board of Equalization and the State Personnel Board fired all civil service employees of Japanese ancestry. The board had mimeographed stock dismissal forms with blanks appearing where the employee's name would be filled in. One item used to justify the termination of employment dealt with the employee's religious background:

That _____ while an employee of the State of California did attend a Japanese school conducted by the officials of the Buddhist church . . . and that the teachings of said school were in conflict with the political and social doctrines of the United States, which did adversely influence the loyalty and fidelity of (the) defendant to the United States of America. Ibid., p. 126.

3. Grodzins, op. cit., p. 186.
4. See Munekata, op. cit., p. 61.
5. I have been unable to find exceptions to the exemplary conduct of the NABM ministers during this period.
6. From the library of the late Reverend Tetsuro Kashima.
7. Ibid. Since such personal documents of the period are rare, the complete text, minus the portion related above, will be given:

(to) Buddhist Mission of NA   (from) Buddhist Church of
      1881 Pine Street   Oakland
      San Francisco, California   181 Sixth Street
                                        Oakland, California

Sirs:

Replying to your inquiries I wish to answer as follows:

1. Q: How many times have you distributed circulars to the various members of your Church?
   A: Eight times.
4. Q: State the total amount of Defense Bonds purchased by your Church and affiliated organizations.
   A: $200.00
5. Q: What is the stand taken by your church in connection with the Red Cross?
   A: 1) The Oakland Buddhist Church donated the sum of $100.00
      2) The Young Women's and Older Women's organizations have signed up with the Red Cross and are now engaged in sewing and knitting various articles.
      3) The Young Men's Association is collecting old magazines and newspapers and donating some to the Red Cross.
      4) Each Sunday school pupil donates one cent toward Red Cross every Sunday.

6. Q: Besides yourself, has any member of your church, i.e., any officer ever encouraged or addressed the church gatherings to be loyal citizens and law abiding residents? If so, give names.

A: The following officers of the church have done so on various occasions: [list of seventeen names included].

7. Q: With reference to question six, give names of church members.

A: [list of six names included].

8. See Shibutani, op. cit., p. 11.

9. Thomas and Nishimoto, op. cit., p. 9.

10. From the library of the late Reverend Tetsuro Kashima.

11. Within the next two years, the name change to the BCA would become a reality; however, this appears to be the first use of the BCA name.

12. The San Diego Buddhist Church, for example, was used by the USO for black servicemen.

13. John L. DeWitt, *Final Report: Japanese Evacuation from the West Coast, 1942* (Washington, D.C.: U.S. Government Printing Office, 1943), p. 356. The ten relocation centers were Central Utah (Topaz); Colorado River (Poston); Gila River, Ariz.; Granada, Colo.; Heart Mountain, Wyo.; Manzanar, Calif.; Jerome, Ark.; Rohwer, Ark.; Tule Lake, Calif.; and Minadoka, Ida.

14. Reverends K. Kumata, S. Tsunoda, K. Imamura, and N. Ishiura. Ishiura is now the *socho* of the Buddhist Churches of Canada.

15. War Relocation Authority, *The Evacuated People—A Quantitative Description* (Washington, D.C.: U.S. Department of the Interior, 1942), Table 24, p. 79. "Religious Preference by Nativity, Under 14 and 14 Years Old and Older: Evacuees to WRA in 1942."

16. Quoted in Alexander Leighton, *The Governing of Men: General Principles and Recommendations Based on Experience at a Japanese Relocation Camp* (Princeton, N.J.: Princeton University Press, 1945), p. 35.

17. For a description of the Buddhist denomination, see Bunce, op. cit., pp. 58–92.

18. Freed and Luomala, op. cit., p. 5.

19. The offertory was important not so much for the money itself but for the uses for the monies. Most camp churches purchased their own materials, reproduced *gathas*, sutra books, and altar materials. With limited church income the offertory became a significant church problem.

20. Freed and Luomala, op. cit., p. 6.

21. Buddhist Brotherhood of America, *Buddhist Gathas and Ceremonies* (Los Angeles: The Buddhist House, 1943), pp. 65–66.

22. For a more detailed explanation of these two terms, see Chapter 5.

23. Louise H. Hunter, *Buddhism in Hawaii: Its Impact on a Yankee Community* (Honolulu: University of Hawaii Press, 1971), p. 159.

24. Ibid., p. 164.

25. Ibid., p. 171. After his dismissal, Hunt was associated with the Soto Zen Temple of Hawaii, still teaching Buddhism to the young, officiating at weddings and funerals, and aiding in the Sunday Schools. During the war, he conducted services in private homes and in the temples of Oahu and Hawaii. In 1953, he was ordained a Soto Zen priest. He passed away at the age of ninety on February 7, 1967.

26. Ibid., p. 167.

27. Andrews, op. cit., p. 4.

28. Shibutani, op. cit., p. 15.

29. Munekata, op. cit., p. 64.

30. "Relocated Buddhists," *Newsweek* 23, no. 1 (January 3, 1944): 62.

31. "Many Nisei, despite the language schools, do not know enough Japanese to follow the services led by priests so unfamiliar with English as to be unable to translate from Japanese for the benefit of the younger members of the congregation. Then too as the young people marry, they tend to withdraw from the church societies, thus breaking the social and recreational tie which had been stronger than the religious bond in holding them to the Buddhist church." Freed and Luomala, op. cit., p. 11.

32. For a detailed explanation and assessment of the loyalty questionnaire issue, see Thomas and Nishimoto, op. cit., especially pp. 54–84.

33. This material was obtained from the personal correspondence of the Reverend Sanada, now at the Parlier Buddhist Church, in a letter dated December 13, 1973. Reverend Sanada has kept a diary of the events at Topaz, and was an active member in the creation of the BCA. The diary is in Japanese; relevant portions were translated through the assistance of Dr. R. Munekata and K. Abe.

34. The diary entry reads: "April 29 [1944, Friday]. Ministers and Lay Representatives Meeting (First Day). Opening service at the Topaz Buddhist Church. After 1-10-B.C. [building number to which they went for meeting] approximately forty people in attendance. Rev. [Joshin] Motoyoshi Chairman and Mr. Harada, Vice-chairman. Discussion on the establishment of the corporation took morning to afternoon.

April 29 . . . after morning service transferred to meeting room. During the morning, the BCA corporation was passed. In the afternoon discussions, etc., on other matters. In the evening minister's meeting."

35. Robert Spencer, "Japanese Buddhism in the United States, 1940–1946: A Study in Acculturation," Ph.D. dissertation, University of California, Berkeley, September 1946, p. 182.

36. Ibid., pp. 183–184.

37. Ibid., p. 186. One new organization had been started in Chicago, two in Utah, and three in Colorado.

38. Ibid., p. 179.

39. The Nisei were quite young, around sixteen and twenty-four years of age.

40. War Relocation Authority, "Evacuees Resistance to Relocation," Community Analysis Report No. 5, June 1943.

41. See the individual church histories in Munekata, op. cit.

42. Freed and Luomala, op. cit., p. 4.

43. Shibutani, op. cit., p. 23.

44. U.S. Department of the Interior, War Agency Liquidation Unit, *People in Motion: The Postwar Adjustment of the Evacuated Japanese Americans* (Washington, D.C.: War Relocation Authority, 1947), p. 234.

45. See Shibutani, op. cit.

46. See the "History of the Midwest Buddhist Temple" in Munekata, op. cit.

47. Shibutani, op. cit., p. 18.

CHAPTER 5 | *Evolution of the American Buddhist Priesthood*

[handwritten annotations: "PRIESTS CAME to AMERICA to help ADHERENTS"]

Since 1899, more than 300 priests have served within the NABM or BCA.[1] Until the advent of the Nisei priests, they came from Japan to meet the spiritual needs of Japanese Buddhists who had already traveled across the Pacific. The priests first came to do missionary work, at the explicit request of the Japanese immigrants, and later, as the number of immigrants increased, to fill a continuing need as more temple structures were built and other priests returned to their homeland. At a time when most Japanese immigrants had not completed their high school education, almost all the priests had a university degree. These priests left their homeland, where most could have found a secure position in the religious order, to cross the Pacific when the trip was still an uncertain adventure, and to dedicate a part or all of their lives to their religious adherents in a strange land.

The Buddhist missionaries under the NABM and the BCA have occupied an important position in both the Jodo Shinshu religious institution and the Japanese communities where the member temples are located. Until the formation of the BCA, when the new constitution included lay Buddhist members within the elected board of directors, the priests and bishops of the NABM had firm control over virtually all facets of the organization. At the member temples, the priests were the spiritual and often administrative leaders, aiding in times of bereavement, stress, and joy. They were the acknowledged religious experts and teachers of Buddhist doctrine, as well as the recognized leaders in community affairs when there was a need for community spokesmen. Their duties thus transcended their religious obligations.

69

Like the organization as a whole, the ministry has shifted from Issei to Nisei and Sansei, and now includes an increasing number of non-Asian ministers. The clergy have been forced to adapt to the changing needs of the laymen as well as to the historical events impinging upon them and their organization.

Over the seventy-six years of its existence, the BCA has undergone constant change, as the priests have died or retired and as the membership has passed from Issei, to Nisei, to Sansei. This chapter explores the world of the ministers: their reasons for choosing this vocation, their role in the community, and the problems and rewards they all share. Two correlative topics, financial remuneration and the training of new ministers, are analyzed as sources of future change at all levels of the BCA.

The Jodo Shinshu Clergy

The Japanese Buddhist priests were products of an organized hierarchical ecclesiastical structure. They brought to America their religious terminology, rules of ordination, and patterns of action befitting their position as learned in Japan. As part of a foreign missionary program sanctioned and sustained by the Hongwanji, the early clergy depended upon the mother organization to supply and train new clergymen for the growing NABM.

The priests have in some cases altered practices or patterns of interaction found in Japan. For example, a Buddhist clergyman in Japan affiliated with Buddhist temples is commonly known as *jushoku, obosan, oterasan,* or *soryo.* [2] Other equivalent terms for a *soryo* (priest) may be *goinjusan* or *goingesan.* The individual temples in Japan usually belong to the *jushoku*'s (resident priest's) family. After the *jushoku*'s death or retirement, title to the property and building passes to his eldest son, if the latter has passed ordination rites in the Jodo Shinshu sect. [3]

The missionaries who came to America referred to themselves in English as reverends, ministers, or priests. These terms were taken as convenient labels to express the nature of their religious position to English-speaking persons, thus obviating the necessity to explain the more accurate Japanese terms. [4] "Reverend" is an apt term to capture the essence of the work undertaken by a Buddhist missionary, implying religious devotion and faith, an attitude of "reverence" toward the doctrines and teachings of the Jodo Shinshu sect, and the aid and comfort given to the adherents by the ministers and priests. Other terms that might have been used, such as "Father" or "elder," imply that the minister is responsible for the adherents, an implication not consonant with Shinshu Buddhist doctrine.

As mentioned earlier, the problem inherent in translating Japanese Buddhist words into English equivalents is that most of the latter have Judeo-Christian connotations. For example, the word "reverend" is associated with the Protestant movement, while "priest" is primarily Roman Catholic. The word "minister" has not only a religious sense, indicating a person authorized to conduct religious worship, but also a secular usage, as in "minister of state"; therefore, it is more acceptable in translation than the two other terms. However, since the *kaikyoshi* themselves utilize a variety of titles, their convention is also followed in this presentation.

The BCA Ministerial Research Committee has recently begun to study the appropriateness of certain English terms commonly used by the BCA.[5] The word "bishop" as the common translation for *socho*, was found to be acceptable: "Etymologically this term [bishop] originates in Greek EPISKOPOS (overseer). Through the metamorphoses of Latin EPISCOPUS, old English BISCOP, and Middle English BISSHOP, it has formed BISHOP. In Greek original EPISKOPOS appeared in literature many centuries [before] the birth of Christianity."[6]

Since the word "bishop" predates its present Christian connotations, is a common and neutral English noun, and describes the bishop as a spiritual leader, the proposed English title for the *socho* was slightly altered to "presiding bishop."[7]

The BCA priests have long been conscious of the difficulties in translating Buddhist terms and titles. When the adherents were predominantly Issei or Japanese-speaking Nisei, the need to find English equivalents was not as acute as when fluency in Japanese became less common. The first title generally used by American Jodo Shinshu adherents in reference to a minister was *sensei*, which literally translates as "teacher," and in Japan can refer to professors, medical doctors, dentists, judo instructors, etc. It is not common to use the term *sensei* when referring to a Buddhist priest in Japan, though if a priest is also a professor or an instructor or at a religious school, he may be called *sensei* by his congregation or by others within the religious order. *Sensei* is a flexible term indicating an honorific position and is used even today among the Sansei.

The ministers themselves seem to have no uniform word for addressing or describing their peers—although "reverend" is probably most frequently used in English. If the ministers are close in age, they will sometimes drop all titles in private conversation and call each other by their last names. If one is significantly older, the younger will address him more formally, employing the Japanese word *sensei* or *kaikyoshi* or the English "minister" or "reverend." For example, in the presence of minister *X* and a third party, the younger minister *Y* might say, "Isn't that right, X-*sensei*?, or *X-kaikyoshi*?" In an age peer situation, however, minister *Y* might say, "That's what you said, X."[8] The word "reverend" is generally used by the ministers when there is some reason to believe that the person spoken to would not understand a Japanese term.

The BCA has retained other terms not conducive to easy English translation: for example, sutras, *shoko* (offering of incense), *ojuzu* or *nenju* (Buddhist rosary or beads), *hoji* (memorial service), *soshiki* (funeral service), and *koromo* (Buddhist robe worn by the priests). Words associated with the ceremonies and rituals of the Jodo Shinshu, and others relating to Buddhist doctrines (such as "karma," "Dharma," "Sangha," "Nirvana," "Mahayana," "Hinayana," and so on), because they are intrinsically important to the denomination, will probably never have an acceptable one-word English translation.

There have been some attempts to incorporate Indian Buddhist terms into the BCA vernacular. The Indian words for "monk"—*bhikshu* (*bhikkhu*) for a male, and *bhikshuni* (*bhikkhunis*) for a female—were utilized by Ernest and Dorothy Hunt when they were active in the Hawaiian Buddhist institutions,[9] but they have not been adopted by the BCA or Nikkei Buddhists. The term *sangharaja*, from Theravada Buddhism, was even considered by the BCA as another translation for *socho*.[10] It was not accepted because it was unfamiliar to the BCA adherents, thus necessitating a long explanation, and because the word "bishop" was already adequate. The difficulty of translating Buddhist terms must be dealt with, since these Japanese or Indian words and concepts must be made understandable to a now English-speaking Buddhist populace. Otherwise, the BCA membership would be uncertain and uninformed about the basic nature of their religion.

Levels of Ordination in Jodo Shinshu Buddhism

The ministers of the NABM and BCA are ordained by the denomination's leading personage, the *gomonshu* or *gomonshusama* ("school" or "denomination chief"), or in English the lord or chief abbot.[11] There are various levels of ordination as well as of scholarly attainment in Buddhist knowledge. The missionaries coming to America and the present ministers of the BCA have all undergone extensive "seminary" training in Japan to preach the Buddhist doctrine in America. To understand their position within the Buddhist order, it is necessary to trace the various levels of ministerial rank within the Nishi Hongwanji.

The first level of ordination is called *tokudo*, a shortened form of *tokudocho*, which means "to receive one's enrollment in the books of the Law."[12] This lowest ordination may now be received at the age of fifteen, although most initiates are nearer to thirty.[13] The candidate is then recognized as an authorized minister of the Nishi Hongwanji Jodo Shinshu sect. The *tokudo* rites are held once a month on the sixteenth day—the day Shinran Shonin, the founder of the sect, died being January 16, the second year of Kocho (1262).[14] To receive the rights of *tokudo*, the candidate must pass examinations in at least the areas of Shinshu Buddhist doctrine, general Buddhism, Buddhist history, and comparative religion.[15] There are two gradations within the *tokudo*: the *soryo* and *jushoku*. A *soryo* is a qualified minister or priest; a *soryo*, who is a resident priest at a temple (*otera*), is called a *jushoku*. As to the position of the ministers: "The sole function of the clergy in Shin is to act as Teacher-friends (*Zenchishiki, kalyanamitra*) to their congregations, leading them in the paths of righteousness. The clergy are not distinct from the laity, and the Initiate Ordination does not create any special class or caste."[16]

The level above the *tokudo* is called the *kyoshi*. This rank, best translated as "docent," "might be considered as roughly equal to that of Monsignor in the Roman Church."[17] To qualify for the rites of *kyoshi*, the candidate must be over twenty-one years of age, and a graduate of an acceptable Buddhist "seminary"; he must also be able to pass both written and oral examinations and present himself in personal demonstrative areas.[18] The written examination covers six topics essentially the same as for the *tokudo*, but in more depth and including the history of Jodo Shinshu Buddhism and the rules and regulations of the sect. The demonstrative area covers the subjective field of proper attitude and personal presentation. After passing the examination, the candidate for *kyoshi* enters a special retreat center conducted by the Hongwanji and is later given his new rank.[19] The rank of *kyoshi* in Japan is held by the rectors of "fully established temples. The criterion for such qualification is a number of requirements dealing with the size and style of the temple building, the historical tradition of the congregation, and such."[20]

The number of ministers in the Nishi Hongwanji Jodo Shinshu sect is quite large. With an estimated seven million followers in Japan, the Hongwanji sect has around 23,000 ministers, of whom about 15,000 hold the rank of *kyoshi* in nearly 12,000 temples.[21]

After gaining from two to five years' experience, a person with a *kyoshi* may receive from the lord abbot the title of *fukyoshi* (literally, "gospel messenger"), with the right to lecture, preach, and do missionary service. There are special terms for a *fukyoshi* who lectures within Japan; for example, a prison chaplain is called a *kyokaishi* and a missionary traveling with the armed forces, a *jugunso*. For missionaries to a foreign land, the official term is *kaikyoshi* (literally, "open-teaching-messenger"). All missionaries from Japan to America are qualified *kaikyoshi*, which indicates that these persons have been given a missionary task by the Hongwanji. There are about 500 workers who devote themselves to missionary work in Japan, and about 200 other missionaries in foreign lands.[22] Thus, the ministers of the NABM and BCA are highly qualified for their positions, in comparison to the entire Jodo Shinshu clergy. A large measure of credit for perpetuating and sustaining the Buddhist institution in America must be given to the *kaikyoshi*. Their educational achievements, their endurance in the face of adversity, and their untiring efforts for their religious convictions have aided not only their temples and the BCA but also the general Buddhist community in America.

Although all NABM and BCA ministers are *kaikyoshi*, there are other differentiating titles denoting various duties or honorific positions. The highest title within the NABM was *kantoku* (literally, "director"), which was later changed to *socho* (literally, "chancellor"; usually translated "bishop"). Where there are *betsuins* (temples or churches with large congregations), or temples (with administrative responsibility for a cluster of branch temples), or "smaller" religious structures, the chief officer is called a *rimban* (literally, "wheel-taking turn"). The term *rimban* is an honorific title bestowed by the BCA for their long terms of service and for directing a physical structure with more than one minister. Any *kaikyoshi* can be a *rimban*. His responsibility is administrative, and his duties are the same as those of any other *kaikyoshi* who serves with him. At present there are five *rimbans* in the five *betsuins*— Sacramento, Fresno, Seattle, San Jose, and Los Angeles.[23]

The NABM and BCA Priests

The Nishi Hongwanji ministers arriving from Japan were missionaries who were sent to the foreign land to carry out the religious work of their faith among Japanese immigrants. Their main efforts have always been directed toward the Japanese population, and not toward converting racial or ethnic groups.

Most Nishi Hongwanji ministers are assigned to one of the fifty-nine member temples within the BCA. A few are attached to the BCA headquarters in San Francisco, while others serve at the Institute for Buddhist Studies in Berkeley. Most ministers are salaried functionaries serving the individual congregation at each temple location. Their main task is to propagate the teachings of the Jodo Shinshu faith (*shinjin*), a task that encompasses a wide variety of duties. They must preach, lead worship services, give counsel to their adherents, be administrators and leaders in the day-to-day activities of the temple, and involve themselves in community projects.[24] These five areas of responsibility are the general duties of every minister.

For several reasons, all temples have their own areas of emphasis. The views of the membership may vary sharply from temple to temple, as may the surrounding social environment, the size of the congregation, and their overall financial condition. In addition, all the individual ministers have their own personal interests, despite their common religious orientation. By necessity there is a continual, ongoing interaction between the ministers and their congregations. A minister's ideas must be tempered by his constituents' wishes and by the financial and social climate in which he finds himself. Because he is the recognized and responsible leader, the congregation and the minister must work together. In some cases, disharmony between the two has led to the reassignment of a minister to another temple.

Unlike their counterparts in Japan, where the priesthood is hereditary and the temples belong to the priests' families, ministers in the BCA are salaried officials. In effect, they are "hired" by the church board of directors, and ultimately by the members of the individual temples. As a consequence, their position, relative to what it would be in Japan, appears weak and tenuous.

As would be expected, some ministers do not like the changes from their traditional position in Japan. As one minister puts it:

> The things I don't like the most in reference to the Buddhist churches in America is the way they speak "to hire a minister." This represents the attitude of any employer to the minister looking down upon the minister. I assume that a minister cannot preach Buddhism if he is not treated with respect. I am not hired. I plan my activities according to my own idea in addition, to those tasks which are assigned by the church. Whenever I hear such remarks as "A minister is an employee," I clearly make corrections.[25]

This view of the ministers as hired persons, unfortunate as it is for them, is continually reinforced by their frequent transfers between temples. The frequency of these moves tends to validate the members' view that their ministers will stay for a finite time, only to be replaced.

Under the NABM, with the membership predominantly Issei, the ministers, in fact, were in strong leadership positions at the temples. The Buddhist adherents subscribed to Japanese tradition, whereby the priests' families controlled the temples. With their higher level of education and status, the ministers were able, in most instances, virtually to dictate the decisions and activities of the individual temples.[26]

Two other factors aid the ministers in their tenuous position. The first is the diversity of opinion at individual temples. Just as no minister can satisfy the needs and desires of all the membership, there will always be some members who support him. Removal of an established minister from a temple requires the moral agreement of a majority, if not a total consensus, of the membership. Such a consensus has always been very rare.[27] In the extremely unusual case where a minister is asked to leave a temple, the reason is generally his personal conduct; for example, he may have a problem with excessive drinking.

The second factor is the bishop, who has sole authority to transfer ministers within the BCA and arrange for their replacement. In making such a decision, he must consider a complex set of factors involving the temples, the ministers, and the BCA organization. Not only must the individual temples agree to release one minister, but they must also accept the replacement. The ministers must also accept the proposed transfer. For his part, the bishop must mediate, and then make decisions affecting all the personnel under his jurisdiction. Some ministers remain at a single temple for many years,[28] while others move about rather freely.

Occasionally, ministers leave the BCA as a result of problems within the churches and BCA. For instance, in 1972, to one California church, where the established Japanese members were predominantly from a single prefecture in Japan, came a sudden influx of new immigrants. The resident minister attempted to bring them into the church, but apparently the older members resisted their inclusion into the board of directors or any other part of the decision-making structure. The old residents saw them as a "threat" to the existing power structure and made their disagreement with the minister clearly known. At one board meeting, the minister became so emotional that he declared he would leave the church. The BCA headquarters personnel either could not or did not mediate, and apparently no one was sent to aid the church in resolving the dilemma. The minister left not only his church, but the BCA as well. He went to another area in California, where he recruited other Japanese members and started his own independent temple.[29] In similar situations, the bishop and BCA headquarters have attempted to find another position for the minister; but in this case, the extreme rancor and antagonism between the members and the minister apparently precluded an amicable solution.

Transfers are not always the product of disagreements between congregation and minister. Frequent transfer has always been the BCA's policy in order to allow them different locales and social environments and thereby facilitate changes and improvements in the church. A transfer is often a promotion, especially if it is to a temple with a large surrounding Japanese or Japanese American population. This insures a larger membership, which in turn provides a strong financial base to pay the ministerial salary and to sustain varied religious and community activities.

In overseeing the transfer of ministers, the bishop must deal with a number of problems that need the cooperation of the ministers and the membership: "In the reassignment of ministers numerous factors have to be considered: basic remuneration, fringe benefits, housing, transportation, location, size of Sangha (membership) etc. etc. Without the compromising attitude of both ministers and church leaders, ministerial appointments are impossible; but the parties concerned have displayed exceptional understanding."[30]

For the minister himself, the transfer or reassignment is relatively simple. Unless he has newly arrived from Japan, he will be somewhat familiar with the various problems of his new congregation from contacts with the previous ministers at the Buddhist conferences held throughout the year. The minister and his wife will usually make at least one visit to the prospective temple to become acquainted with the members. The members then report their impressions to the bishop, who becomes a neutral third party interceding and mediating points of differences between the prospective minister and the temple membership. If the bishop is successful in his mediation, the minister is assigned to the temple; if not, since the basic negotiation was accomplished through a third party, the possibility of conflict or loss of face is much reduced.

Under the NABM, the ministers' roles became increasingly varied and indefinite as more elaborate temple structures were built and membership increased.[31] The ministers were not only religious teachers but also administrators responsible for insuring a successful organization. The BCA Ministerial Association, recognizing the problem, submitted a set of guidelines defining the ministers' areas of responsibility.[32] These included the care of the altar, conduct of regular and special services, maintenance of temple records, study and teaching of Buddhist materials, counseling and visiting the members, rendering assistance to temple organizations, fund-raising, and involvement in the BCA organization and local community affairs.

In most temples, especially where there is only one resident minister, the membership expects the minister to be on call twenty-four hours a day. He usually has little time for himself or his family. He must not only prepare for the regular services and attend all temple-related meetings and activities, but he must also deal with whatever emergencies may arise among the members—such as death, sickness, financial difficulties, and marital problems. Such emergencies continually complicate his planning of tasks that are nontemple related.[33]

The Minister's Wife and Family

Especially important in the membership's definition of the minister's role is their inclusion of his wife and children. His wife is expected to enter completely into the spirit of service to the membership and community. She is also expected to participate and assume a leadership position in the women's organizations, to be continually at her husband's side on all ceremonial occasions, and to speak for him in his absence. Many ministers' wives aid the temple by serving as Sunday School teachers or instructors in the Japanese language school, playing the piano during religious services, making refreshments for the after-service socials, helping care for the temple grounds and building, and acting as secretary-receptionists and information officers for their husbands and temples.

The role of the minister's wife has never been explicitly defined, but she is generally viewed and treated as an extension of the minister. The usual assumption is that when she married a minister, she obligated herself to his life and duties. To do otherwise the wife would risk the criticism of the female membership, which would add to her husband's already numerous problems in running a complex temple organization. The women of the Buddhist temples, and especially the ministers' wives, are the unsung heroines of the Buddhist movement in America. The minister's clerical worker/piano player/wife assumes many responsibilities without adequate financial or status remuneration.

The wife comes with the minister to the temple. Whereas the minister is a *sensei* or *kaikyoshi*, his wife is simply the "Mrs." The Issei often call the *sensei*'s wife by the title *okusama* or *okusan* (literally, "madam"), although *okusan* can be and is used to address any married lady. The Nisei and many Sansei may address the Issei women as *obasan* ("aunt"), reserving the title *okusan* for the wife of a minister, doctor, professor, or the like. The title is honorific, yet it is not restricted to the particular constellation of duties and obligations inherent in her position, as is the title *kaikyoshi* for the priest.

With the priest deeply involved in temple affairs, the task of raising the children falls upon the wife. Following the patriarchal family system of Japan, the Issei ministerial family delegated responsibility for the children to the mother. The children were expected to lead exemplary moral lives, for deviations would result in gossip among the membership and add to the minister's problems. Among Nisei ministerial families, there appears to be more of an equal division of responsibility in rearing the children.[34] As among the Issei, the children are still expected to lead model lives. Thus, even they become an extension of the minister's role.

Generational Differences Among the BCA Priests

Within the NABM and the BCA, 308 officially registered ministers have served or are still serving. Within the *kaikyoshi* group[35] there are internal differences, which can best be understood by dividing the group into three segments: the Issei, the Nisei, and the Occidental priests. The Issei segment, including the Kibei,[36] are those ministers born and/or educated in Japan who profess better knowledge of Japanese than English.[37] The Nisei ministers are those born and educated in America, who thus feel competent in the English language. The Sansei ministers should be analyzed separately, but since there are at present only four of them, three of whom are not significantly different from the Nisei, they have been included with them.[38] Dividing the ministers into two even groups poses certain problems. First, some ministers were born in Japan and brought to America by their parents at an early age; these include Reverends Taitetsu Unno, Tetsuo Unno, and Akira Hata. Reverend Hata states that he is a Nisei; consequently, he and the other minister with similar backgrounds have been placed in the Nisei category. Second, some Nisei who are in the Kibei category, such as Reverend Shojo Honda of the Washington, D.C., Sangha, rate themselves more conversant in Japanese than in English. Other Kibei, like Reverend Kosho Yukawa of the Southern Alameda Buddhist Church, consider themselves equally conversant in English and Japanese. The linguistic difference is important, since the American Buddhists are rapidly becoming unable to understand or speak Japanese. Since these two ministers consider their Japanese better than their English, they and others in their category have been placed in the Issei group.[39]

The Occidental ministers, with a total of six in the BCA, only five of whom are still active, are a small group. Except for Reverend Alex S. White, who served from 1940 to 1941, the first took office in 1968: this was Reverend Phillip K. Eidmann, now with the Institute for Buddhist Studies at Berkeley. Most recently ordained, in 1973, was Rev-

erend June King, who has been assigned to the Fresno Betsuin.[40] These
six ministers were previously or are presently registered with the BCA.
However, since the 1930s some Occidental ministers not registered in
the BCA have aided the Jodo Shinshu Buddhist group—for example,
Reverend Julius Goldwater.

Table 1 lists the years of service within the BCA for all ministers
from 1899 to 1973.[41]

TABLE 1

**Length of Registered Priests' Service, in Years,
in NABM-BCA: 1899–1973**

	Number	Percent	Total Number of Years	Average Number of Years
Issei	272	88.31	3,317	12.21
Nisei/Sansei	30	9.74	347	11.57
Occidental	6	1.95	16	2.67
Total	308	100.00	3,680	11.95

SOURCES: Compiled from BCA, *Annual Report, 1970–1973*, Schedule A, "Ministers in Buddhist Churches of America Appreciation Fund, 1960," in BCA, *Annual Report, 1972.* See also Munekata, op. cit., pp. 118–137.

The largest group is, of course, the Issei, which comprises 88.31 percent
of the total; the Nisei/Sansei group is second, with 9.74 percent; and
the non-Asian group, with only 1.95 percent, is the smallest group. The
average years of service for the Issei group is 12.21; for the Nisei/Sansei,
11.57; and for the Occidental, 2.67. The total average length of service,
11.95 years, is deceptive, since thirty-two ministers have served over
thirty years, while many others served for less than five years before
they returned to Japan, resigned, or died.[42]

Table 2 presents the years of service of those ministers still active
within the BCA. The predominance of the Issei among the ministers is
still marked, yet their decrease from an overall 88.31 percent to 69.57
percent, and the increase of the Nisei group from an overall 9.74 percent to 26.09 percent of those on active service, indicate the growing
Nisei population since 1938. The active Occidental ministerial group is

TABLE 2

**Length of Service, in Years, of Priests
Still Active in the BCA to 1973**

	Number	Percent	Total Number of Years	Average Number of Years
Issei	64	69.57	1,130	17.66
Nisei/Sansei	24	26.09	296	12.33
Occidental	4	4.35	10	2.50
Total	92[1]	100.00	1,436	15.61

[1] This total is greater than the seventy-six questionnaires sent to the ministers. There are actually seventy-six full-time ministers on active service in temples, BCA headquarters, or at the Institute for Buddhist Studies. The remaining sixteen are on leave, working outside the BCA organizations (for example, in the Hawaii Buddhist organizations), etc.

SOURCE: BCA, *Annual Report, 1971, 1972, 1973.*

relatively late in its inception. Although Reverends S. Pratt and C. Paulson were aiding the BCA from the 1930s, they did not receive the *kyoshi* certificate until 1969.[43]

The Issei Priests

Reminiscing about the difficult early days of his fifty-seven years of ministry, Reverend Seikaku Mizutani states:

> I was 22 when I assumed my first assignment in Bakersfield. In those days the emigrants were all young men. They came with very little personal belongings and worked hard on farms and on railroads in an effort to attain financial security. Yet, they were not without their burning desire to follow their parents faith as manifested in the establishment of many sanctuaries of the Dharma. . . . In those early days the Issei commuted to work on wagons and horseback. . . . They either rented small residential homes as their temples or met at private homes. The early emigrants had very little personal belongings and were so engrossed

in making their meager living that they had difficulty financing their temples. Consequently, the life of the minister was extremely difficult also. They found it very difficult to educate their children let alone trying to save any money.[44]

Reverend Sensho Sasaki, who served forty-six years in the BCA, states:

> I came as a missionary in 1926. At that time the organization was not formally institutionalized and we were able to work freely. All weddings, funerals, and other festivities were conducted with the *fuho* [simple black robe] and *wagesa* [lapel-cloak] only. All social functions were informal also so that we were able to function without restrictions whatsoever.[45]

The temples and churches, the NABM and BCA, were created and constructed after the ministers arrived from Japan. The local temples have retained a general autonomy from the Buddhist headquarters in San Francisco, just as the individual ministers have remained independent of the central organization in Japan and of the San Francisco NABM. With their *kaikyoshi* status and with many temples physically isolated from observation and inspection by the *kantoku* or *socho*, the Issei ministers were in many cases virtually on their own. Thus, Reverend Sasaki could "function without restriction," as Reverend Mizutani could deal freely with the problems peculiar to his locale. This tradition of local autonomy, especially for the ministers, best characterizes the relationship of the individual temples to the BCA, and of the ministers to the bishop.

On Becoming a Kaikyoshi

Unlike most Japanese immigrants, who did not bring with them specific vocational or career choices,[46] the *kaikyoshi* were professionals; their career choices were made prior to their arrival in America.

The question "Why did you become a minister?" was asked of the BCA ministers.[47] Before examining their responses it should be cautioned that the Issei respondents, with an average of over twenty-one years of active service, may have had difficulty recollecting their exact motives for becoming ministers and for coming to America. Moreover, there may have been more than one reason for their decisions.

The Issei group's stated reasons for entering the ministry can be differentiated into three major categories. Out of twenty-three respondents, the largest group, with 52.2 percent, listed a religious commitment; the next largest group, with 30.4 percent, cited a family tradition of Buddhist priests; and the smallest group, with 17.4 percent, offered personal or individualistic reasons—for example, "I thought this is one way of working toward peace and harmony in the world."

Of these three categories, the reasons given by the first and last group are easiest to understand, for they revolve around a religious context. But the hereditary rationale cited by the second group must be understood in relation to the social environment in Japan. Many Issei families in Japan have a home temple: that is, a family-owned temple in which usually the first son receives religious training and later inherits his father's position.[48] From his childhood, the son is raised to become the resident *jushoku*, with his career expectation reinforced not only by the family but also by the community and the temple members. There is no need for this group to emphasize their religious commitment; they have been totally immersed in the Buddhist religion, both socially and psychologically. Thus, the second category, in effect, combines features of the other two categories.

Coming to America

Not all of the Issei ministers had originally planned to do missionary work in America. When asked their reasons for making the trip across the Pacific, three categories of responses again emerged: some desired to spread the Buddhist teachings (47.8 percent); some had prior ties with America (30.4 percent); and others had personal reasons (8.7 percent). One minister stated as a personal reason: "I decided to come to the United States where one's advancement is totally dependent upon one's ability, whereas in Japan it is mainly dependent upon nepotism."

The only element characterizing all of the individual responses was a sense of adventure. The Jodo Shinshu religion in Japan is a thoroughly entrenched Buddhist sect, replete with historical traditions. The NABM-BCA was a new institution requesting the service and talents of young ministers to meet the needs of Japanese immigrants and their children. The chance to break, for a few years at least, from the home temple and the ecclesiastical hierarchy in Japan, and to gain new experience and a sense of independence, have been important incentives for Issei missionaries. To this day, the independence of the ministry has been preserved within the BCA.

The Kibei, comprising 13 percent of the Issei, did not explain their reasons for returning to the United States. Because they were American citizens, it is probably safe to assume that they returned for the same reasons as the Nisei ministers: America was their home—not Japan.

There is perhaps some danger in generalizing these findings to the nonrespondent group. However, from impressions gained through personal interviews with the ministers, it can be concluded that the respondents are indeed representative. A large number of Issei ministers have returned to Japan after serving only a few years in the BCA. When some present ministers were asked[49] why these ministers returned, four main causes were suggested. (1) With the hereditary system of temple ownership in Japan, some ministers returned to assume their obligations to the family temple. (2) Some ministers encountered difficulty in preaching the Buddhist religion in a Western culture. (3) The many duties expected of a BCA minister were somewhat different from those expected of a priest in Japan. (4) Some ministers had come only to gain new experiences and to broaden their knowledge; once they had fulfilled whatever commitments they had made to the BCA, they were able to return to Japan.

The Issei ministers were always free to return to Japan; the only real stipulations upon their stay in America derived from their immigration status. After 1924, the Issei ministers came under the nonquota immigration category, with sponsorship from the NABM and later from the BCA. Until after the end of World War II, they could enter no occupation outside the BCA; otherwise, they would be subject to deportation. Since even today a change in occupation requires a change in immigration status, a number of ministers continually return to Japan. The Nisei ministers have never been under such a constraint. In cases where the salaries given by certain temples or churches are inadequate to meet the demands of a growing family, some Nisei ministers take positions in a university or other schools, while still retaining ties to the BCA.

Problems Facing the Issei Priest

The Issei ministers have, on the average, spent many years in America; this fact indicates their dedication not only to their religious beliefs but also to the Buddhist adherents. Once in America, they are confronted with problems and responsibilities largely different from those in Japan. (We have previously noted the multifaceted roles they were expected to assume.) When asked to name the greatest difficulties of Buddhist ministers in America, they listed four main categories.[50]

The greatest single problem cited by the Issei ministers (48 percent) was language. Their language difficulty is not easily solved, nor will it decrease as the number of Japanese-speaking Buddhists lessens. Some Issei ministers have attempted to overcome this problem by improving their English. For instance, just after his release from the Topaz relocation center, Reverend Tetsuro Kashima enrolled in English classes at Weber State College, Ogden, Utah. But as a result of pressing ministerial duties, he was forced to terminate his formal studies after only a few months. At other temples, the solution to the language problem has been to maintain two ministers, one Issei and the second an English-speaking reverend. Since only a few large temples are financially able to support two ministers, the practice is not widespread.

Regardless of language, the very teaching of Buddhism in a non-Buddhist environment was listed by 24 percent of the respondents as a major problem. The corollary difficulty of merely adjusting to the foreign environment was cited by another 8 percent. As one Issei phrased it: "The first difficult task is to catch up and become used to the American culture."

Finally, 20 percent of the Issei listed problems concerning their status and financial remuneration as the most difficult part of their missionary career. The monetary problem varies from temple to temple, since there is no uniform salary scale. Remuneration depends upon the temple's ability to support a minister and is a function of the size of the membership.

The Rewards of Being a Kaikyoshi

The life of a *kaikyoshi* is not without reward. When the Issei were asked about their greatest joys in being Buddhist ministers, 63.6 percent named a religious dimension. The following responses are representative:

> My greatest joy is that I'm surrounded by many Buddhists believing in the salvation of faith (*shinjin*).

I find the greatest joy in people listening to the sermons with sincerity and zeal.

To lead a Buddhist life together with the members. To see church halls, and Sunday Schools constructed. To have new members.

To see the teaching of Buddha-Dharma moving young people and to feel the *Nembutsu* working in people's minds on some occasions.

I found the greatest joy in those who are happy to be Buddhists. I feel this very strongly, especially when I conduct services to the bed stricken.

Another group, much smaller in number (13.6 percent), stated their greatest satisfaction came from helping others. For example:

As for being a Buddhist minister, people come to see me without any hesitation. They start treating me at once as if we were old friends. Therefore I become very well acquainted with them. This is my reward and joy of being a Buddhist minister.

A minister in the United States does not have to limit himself in the area of sacred vocation, but he can put his abilities for activities in all spheres of the society. While in Japan, a minister cannot engage in much other activities than in his religious domain.

Two ministers (9 percent) stated that their rewards came from the attitude of religious tolerance found in the United States:

One good thing about the United States is the emphasis on freedom of religion and the Buddhist ministers are as highly regarded as any other religious leaders. The public attitude toward religious leaders makes Buddhist preaching possible. This is why we have lasted so long. Americans are tolerant and wonderful.

To find the general public having great respect for religion.

Finally, three ministers (13.6 percent) emphasized the status of the ministers:

> To be respected and loved by the members and the general public.

> The respect given to the ministers by the members.

> Having been engaged in missionary work with good health, four temple structures were constructed while I was minister. Being unworthy myself, I had the great honor to be admitted to the ministry.

The comments of the Issei ministers speak for themselves. Most (seventeen of twenty-three) responses were in Japanese, and, unfortunately, the translations do not do full justice to their remarks. For example, the term *shinjin*, or the word *okagesama* (all is right), or the phrase *shuyo no tame* (to gain experience) can be literally translated, yet the associated Buddhistic meanings are thereby lost.

The frankness of the responses is also characteristic of the ministers; yet, to strangers or "outsiders," they may be somewhat less than open in revealing their thoughts about themselves and their organization. They are leaders in the church or temple, and often in the community. Their education, high status, and long experience in administering a complex temple has given most of them a background for making clear and definitive statements.

The BCA continues to receive new Issei ministers, and they will face many of the same problems that are troubling the present Issei ministers. To overcome the language problem, the new ministers undergo intensive training at the Institute for Buddhist Studies in Berkeley, and they are encouraged to become somewhat conversant in English before their arrival. Nonetheless, the process of acquiring facility in English is both long and arduous.

The Nisei/Sansei Priests

Since 1928, the NABM has recognized the need to recruit and train a Nisei ministry. At that time, the Issei members were predominant, but as the Nisei population grew, it became obvious that the NABM had to prepare for future religious needs. To divide the ministers into a generational framework as the Issei and Nisei/Sansei, separate from the non-Asian priests, requires some clarification. Still other distinctions could be drawn within the Asian group, by age or sex. Yet, it is because the Japanese members themselves use this classification system that generational distinctions are important.

The Japanese not only distinguish between those born in Japan and those born in America, but also impute particular personalities and behavioral patterns to each succeeding generation.[51] Issei consider the Nisei to be more "American" than themselves, and their grandchildren, the Sansei, to be even more like "Americans" than the Nisei; the Issei, meanwhile, are associated with the Japanese homeland in values, manners, and language. Thus, the Nisei are perceived as an intermediate group, retaining certain manners and values from their parents while receiving others from American culture. Certain Japanese values and behavioral traits, such as *enryo* (undue restraint), have been retained by the Sansei group; hence, there is a value and behavioral pattern continuum from the Issei to the Sansei.[52] But as certain values are retained by the succeeding generation, others fall into abeyance.

The Issei Buddhists were raised in an environment with strong Buddhist traditions fostered by the Issei in the home. Outside influences in America, however, were predominantly Christian. Whereas the prior tendency of the Buddhist religion had been to absorb or greatly alter the cultures to which it spread—from India to China, from China to Korea, from Korea to Japan—in America it found itself being absorbed. This is one important reason for the adaptations and changes of form that have been characteristic of the NABM and BCA.

The Nisei minister is likewise a product of this need to adapt and change. If the Nisei and Sansei Jodo Shinshu adherents had retained the Japanese fluency of the Issei, the NABM system, whereby the ministers were called from Japan, would not have been altered. The Nisei and Sansei Buddhist ministers do face a somewhat different and more complicated task than their Issei counterparts, especially in communicating Buddhist concepts, which even some Issei ministers cannot easily convey to Issei adherents. The Nisei ministers do not even have the advantage of using the original Japanese to help make these ideas meaningful. Since they cannot assume that Nisei or Sansei adherents are familiar with them, the Nisei/Sansei ministers are in the peculiar position of *introducing* the Buddhist religion to those who attend their churches.

Within the ministerial group, some disagreements based on generational difference have arisen, and language is and has been a key problem. For instance, in the BCA Ministerial Research Committee, a proposal was made in the late 1960s to compile a handbook to standardize the religious ceremonies and rituals. Initially, the project was to have been a joint venture between the Issei and Nisei/Sansei ministers, and the plans included a cross-translation procedure. But the group apparently was not able to reach unanimous agreement on the ceremonies. As a consequence, two versions of the handbook are now contemplated —one in Japanese, written by the Issei, and the other in English, written by the Nisei/Sansei ministers.[53]

The ministers' generational difference has been underscored by the formation of a Los Angeles-based Buddhist group called Kinnara, composed mainly of BCA Nisei and Sansei ministers and adherents, but autonomous of the BCA. An incorporated, nonprofit religious organization, Kinnara attempts to bring people to Buddhism through personal involvement. The Kinnara members refrain from, but do not entirely eschew, the "usual" BCA service format, where the emphasis is on ministerial sermons; instead, they emphasize meditation, sutra chanting, Japanese music, Japanese arts (tea ceremony, calligraphy, brush painting, and the like), and religious retreat centers. The individual is encouraged to concentrate on the essence and the spirit of Buddhism. As one Nisei minister involved with the Kinnara group states:

> It's just a question of just being; thinking in terms of more of the sense of maybe religious awareness, or just being human, and not so much in terms of conversion of having people understand it. It's sort of a natural flow. There's no pressure in the program. Those are the things we do, more or less. It's a spontaneously developed program. When we went there [to the retreat centers] we prepared something. We were going to have a lecture. We didn't have a lecture 'till the end when they really felt the need. But we didn't put the need right at the beginning which we thought would be very discouraging. It just didn't happen until the end. They said we should talk, we should have a little subject to talk about and then discuss it and that came toward the end of the meeting.[54]

The Kinnara group has succeeded in attracting the attention of young Nisei and Sansei Buddhists. The absence of a ritual format for their "services," and the emphasis on meditation and sutra chanting, have not gone unnoticed by the Issei ministers, one of whom expressed his thoughts on the group:

INT: I see the Nisei and Sansei [Jodo Shinshu] ministers bringing different forms of Buddhism into the Jodo Shinshu church. I wonder if . . . we had groups such as Kinnara or the return back to sutra chanting, is this acceptable in the Jodo Shinshu faith? . . . do you think that it is improper?

I: I think it is not satisfactory, you know. But I think we're readjusting or experimenting. So I don't think I blame them. They are just trying hard. Especially the Kinnara group.

INT: Obviously they learned this at a Jodo Shinshu University in Japan. Do you think if a group like Kinnara were [to be] successful, that the American Buddhist churches would follow this kind of success?

I: Yes, I guess if they find some proper or suitable way to propagate the Jodo Shinshu doctrine the right way, then the general headquarters would take it up and the followers some way or other. Because the United States and Japan are different countries with a different climate and different people, you know, so the outside roots must be in some way or other different, you know. But the content itself, in other words, the fundamental idea of Jodo Shinshu must not be changed. Otherwise it is not a missionary of Jodo Shinshu. It is a different religious mission.[55]

This Issei minister, not unlike others who were interviewed, was reluctant to give wholehearted support to the Kinnara; one reason was the type of change advocated by the Nisei and Sansei group. While the NABM and BCA have instituted many changes, the presentation format has not been drastically altered. Indeed, most churches have not changed the service format instituted by the prewar NABM. Recently, however, especially among younger ministers influenced by the Kinnara model and the urgings of the young Sansei, experiments have been made in modifying the format of services. For instance, at a 1972 Junior Young Buddhist conference, the religious services featured soft rock music, candlelight meditations, sermons by the laity, and ministers wearing ordinary business suits with only the *wagesa* (lapel-cloak) to indicate their religious status. As the conference prepublicity stated, "The services will not be the every-Sunday type but attempts to change the present types."[56] At the conference itself, many of the parents accompanying their children to the conference expressed their astonishment at the services. As one mother said, "I don't understand these kids!"

The older Issei members perceive the ministerial leaders of the young Nisei and Sansei to be different from their own. Reverend Arthur Takemoto, a leader in the Kinnara group, but also a Nisei minister at the West Los Angeles Buddhist Church, was at one time accused of being a radical for his espousal of change.[57] In most respects, the Nisei ministers truly are different from the Issei. The following comparison, derived from their mutual responses to the questionnaire, will suggest the more salient differences.

On Becoming a Priest

The Nisei[58] respondents listed three reasons for adopting the Buddhist ministry as their vocation: personal choice, desire to preach Buddhism, and willingness to follow a ministerial family tradition.

The largest category was personal choice; it was cited by 53.4 percent (eight ministers) of the Nisei/Sansei respondents. The six Nisei offered such explanations as:

> Just out of a personal need to know about Buddhism.

> Because I thought the ministry was most suited to my nature.

> To do something worthwhile with my life. To walk in step with truth and to lead others in that path is important to me.

The two Sansei respondents did not give a definite reason for becoming ministers:

Not sure yet.

No way of answering easily; only let me say that I wanted to (and my parents are not from a ministerial background).

Five Nisei respondents, or 33.4 percent, stated that they chose the ministry to preach Buddhism or for other religious reasons. Representative replies were:

Rather late in life I realized the need for a church worker who spoke English. When I was helping my father edit a thin quarterly called "Tri-ratna" and we received marvelous letters from all over the country from persons who were seeking the way and needed help.

Naive enough to think I could make Buddhism come alive for others as well as for me . . . and vain enough.

Finally, two Nisei ministers, or 13.4 percent, cited their ministerial background. The low percentage is not surprising, for of the fifteen respondents, only five, or 33.3 percent, were known to have been born into a Buddhist minister's family.[59] Neither of the Sansei ministers was in this group. Although it is difficult to ascertain the exact percentage of Issei ministers born into a family with a tradition of the ministry, the Issei clergy interviewed stated that most of them did come from this tradition. There is thus a growing tendency for Nikkei (Japanese Americans) to enter the Buddhist ministry without the role model they would have had if their fathers were reverends.

The role model of the Nikkei ministers derives from their image of the Issei clergy, from the lay members of the temple, and from their training in Japan. They see the demanding duties assumed by their Issei counterparts, in both religious and administrative areas, and they see the laity demanding that ministers be extraordinary men, without personal desires or touches of human frailty. As one Sansei minister said, "I think we've acquiesced in the image that has been given to us, because before I went to Japan [to receive ordination] my image was pretty much the same of what a priest should be as the laymen's."[60]

When the Nikkei ministers travel to Japan for their Buddhist studies and to receive the rites of ordination, they are exposed to other possible

behavioral patterns for a Jodo Shinshu priest. One minister described
the effects of his experience in Japan:

> I changed considerably in Japan, and coming back—I think that's
> one thing I wonder about. You see, if our kids are schooled here
> and ordained here, I wonder what their image of the ministry
> would be? Their role as a Jodo Shinshu priest, is a unique posi-
> tion. . . . I think we really lack almost totally the concept of
> *ondogondo*, the fellow-traveler type concept, where neither the
> priest nor the laymen are different: it's totally lacking. Because
> what we mean by it is that we're human. I mean ministers are
> only human, which is really a degrading thing to have said to you,
> because the assumption is that we aren't, in fact, and that we
> should be more than human, but not too much. Which is very
> Japanese I think. . . . At the same time you have somebody who
> is a symbolic leader; which is very unBuddhistic, I think.[61]

Two points should be raised here. First, the Buddhist members consider
their ministers to be spiritual as well as moral leaders, and they expect
them to behave as such. For instance, ministers must be careful not to
drink too much *sake* at a reception and they must guard against improper statements, maintaining an exemplary life at all times. Any
transgression would invite community gossip, and perhaps even reassignment.

Second, the trip to Japan will transform the Nikkei into Kibei. Their
stay in Japan, for a period of one to five years, in a culture where Buddhism is pervasive, forces them to reevaluate their image of the American Buddhist ministry from a Japanese cultural perspective.

> It's not so much what's taught in Japan, it's the fact of being
> there actually, and being close to people who are living there
> within this tradition. It's really just subconscious I think. All of
> a sudden you start questioning them after a while. You say the
> first two years are hell, it's very traumatic. Because fundamental
> things are very dear to you, you really can't let go. They are
> questioned every day, just by the fact of your being there. And
> I just wonder if that isn't really the most important experience
> to go through.[62]

Most Nisei Buddhists have never been to Japan and have never questioned the behavioral pattern of the Issei clergy. But Nisei ministers return with a new concept of the minister's role, quite different from that held by Nisei laymen.

With the number of Sansei members increasing, generational conflict may actually diminish. The Sansei, with their growing ethnic consciousness, are asking for a change in the institution and in the presentation of Buddhism. Precisely because the Sansei are questioning the Buddhist religion as understood by the Nisei laity, the newer ministers are achieving some success in instituting progressive religious protocols. One Nisei minister comments upon the Sansei as a force for a positive change:

> With the young people [innovation] is not going to be so much of a problem, because I think the ideas of institutionalization are drastically changed. And the attitude of formalism amongst the young is not there. And not so much in terms of pulpit ministry. Pulpit ministry will be . . . well, some people need this, it may supposedly be the thing although they don't show up. But . . . amongst the younger people, I don't think it's there. It's not whether you wear a tie and talk to them, but rather it's on [a religious] basis.[63]

Problems Facing the Nisei/Sansei Priest

The Nisei minister places different emphasis upon the tasks facing him than does his Issei counterpart. While the majority of the Issei listed language as the predominant problem, only one Nisei agreed. This respondent went on to list twelve other difficulties:

1. Must be bilingual
2. Difficulty of the Japanese language
3. Insufficient training in many fields
4. Young leaders all leave the area
5. Strong emphasis on financial things
6. BCA [organization] demands in finances
7. Narrow-mindedness of [the] Nisei
8. Acceptance of Jodo Shinshu versus general Buddhist teaching among the Nisei and Sansei

9. Money problems for the minister
10. Intrusions of the family life
11. No real day or days off. No real vacation time.
12. School makes great demands on youth. Not much time for church.
13. Lack proper propagation methods.

This catalogue of difficulties covers most of the problems listed by both the Issei and the Nisei/Sansei ministers. The first two difficulties concerning language have previously been discussed. The third problem, insufficient training in many fields, refers to the multirole obligations placed on the minister. For instance, he must not only perform religious services but also oversee fund-raising activities, administer a church organization, and prepare and write a periodic church bulletin. Ministers are most knowledgeable about their religion and receive no training in other areas, especially church administration. A Sansei minister states, "Well, think about the administrator's part: I mean, none of us are really qualified to be administrators. We certainly aren't trained in Japan."[64] The respondent's fourth and twelfth points are essentially that whenever young leaders leave the area, ministers must find and train new leaders, thus reinvolving youth in church projects. The fifth and sixth problems—money for church administration, dues to the BCA headquarters, remuneration of the minister, and so forth, are themselves tied to the size of the membership. The larger the membership, the more projects planned and the larger the temples and other structures required; thus, every temple has an ever-present concern about money. The seventh and eighth problems, "the narrow-mindedness [of the] Nisei" and the remark about Buddhism, are difficult to interpret; they may simply reflect some personal difficulty of this particular minister. The tenth and eleventh problems, concerning the minister's private life, are shared by many other Nisei ministers, as will soon be discussed. The last problem, the lack of adequate Buddhist materials, is related to the first point concerning language. The language base of the BCA has been Japanese; now that English is becoming more prominent, the problems of translation are increasingly evident in the shortage of written materials.

Twenty-four percent of the Issei ministers listed propagation of Buddhism as a difficult task. Five Nisei ministers (33.3 percent) cited this problem as the most difficult. The remaining ministers, including the two Sansei, gave personalistic responses to the question concerning their most difficult tasks. One Sansei went into more detail than the other ministers, emphasizing the fact that his age (under thirty) created a particular generation problem:

> Frustration at accomplishing anything. The spirituality of people has not been awakened; the awareness of the community needs to be expanded. Also because of age, there is a credibility gap, i.e., an image expectation by members is not fulfilled. Also the struggle to explain and to teach Buddhism in the English language is so difficult. The ignorance by the general public about even the existence of Buddhism in this area and related problems, etc., etc.

In contrast to the Issei respondents, the Nisei/Sansei made little mention of financial difficulties or problems encountered in spreading an Eastern religion within a Western social context. On the whole, the Nisei/Sansei ministers focused on problems between themselves and their adherents. They considered the members' lack of understanding about their religion and the unclear delineation of the minister's role as the most pressing issues.

The Rewards of Being a Priest

Nisei and Sansei assessments of the rewards of being a minister revolved around religious or personal fulfillment. Primarily because of this subjective dimension, it is difficult to make a clear separation among the respondents. All the responses involved a measure of personal satisfaction in being able to help the members, but two ministers included a parenthetical suggestion that their joys were somewhat less than complete:

> I think the greatest satisfaction lies in the close personal relationships that you establish with members of the congregation (not all members, of course).

> When members find Amida (very few really do).

One minister emphasized the personal religious rewards of Buddhism, while another discussed the social context in preaching the religion:

The joy of being free from neurosis.

I think the greatest reward for me is the freedom to experiment with different forms of Buddhism.

Overall, the Nisei/Sansei ministers are different from the Issei. As discussed above, the two groups exhibit generational differences in attitude toward the problems of the ministry and in reasons for choosing the ministry as a career. With the creation of the Institute of Buddhist Studies in Berkeley to train new personnel, there will be increasing numbers of Sansei and Occidental ministers. At the present time, the Sansei and the Occidentals are such a small group that generalizations are difficult to make. Since none of the four active Occidental ministers responded to the questionnaire, it will be necessary to rely upon other sources of information.

An Occidental Priest

From 1926 onward, one particular non-Asian priest has been notable within the BCA—Reverend Julius A. Goldwater. Although he was duly registered at the home temple in Kyoto, Japan, as a fully accredited clergyman with all rights and privileges, it appears that he was never registered as such with the BCA in San Francisco. He aided in the Buddhist movement in Hawaii and later on the mainland in the United States and in Canada just after the close of World War II. His relationship to Buddhism in America started with his association with Reverend Ernest H. Hunt of Hawaii:

G: You see, I made several trips to Hawaii as a child because my father was located there. . . . I [had] an elderly friend who said come with me to a Buddhist study class with an English reverend called Dr. Hunt. Well, I had been very much interested in the usual things of mysticisms and things as I thought I would. I never heard the word Buddhism before until that time and I was fourteen or fifteen;

so I finally went with the greatest of reluctance. . . . It was fascinating. I didn't understand a thing and he spoke in perfect English and I heard every word he said. I couldn't cognate his usage of words but it was very exciting you know and there were just a few people, about eight of us gathered, and of course I was their only kid. And gradually, this was in 1927 or 1926, a very long time ago . . . I became more and more seduced, caught . . . finally the group decided that they were going to take Pansil by this time. I said what was Pansil? To become publically the first group of Occidentals to become Buddhists under the American flag.[65]

INT: How did you come across to America then?

G: Bishop Yemyo Imamura (of Hawaii Hompa Hongwanji) together with the Venerable Reverend Ernest Hunt married Pearl and myself in 1931. Soon thereafter we returned to Los Angeles and some chap by the name of Robert Clifton looked me up . . . he made it known to me that there was a great need for some Occidental representative for both the youth amongst the Nisei (Busei) as well as Occidentals and would I please help. I agreed to function on a temporary basis until someone more suitable would come along. . . . I then accepted ordination in the Los Angeles Betsuin under the North American Bishop Masayama and with *Rimban* Sasaki and his assistant, Rev. Y. Yukawa, I was taken around to all of the various branch temples. Of course at that time I was used mainly to impress the kids that as an American Buddhist this area could not be used as an excuse to defect or not consider the teachings properly in their own right. And anyway I gave my childish talk. I was no longer a child, but I wasn't appreciably any wiser or knowledgeable or anything. Anyway, everyone was very kind and generous to me and ultimately I became included in all events of the family and community. Within a few years, I went together with the then *Rimban* Yukawa to Kyoto, Japan, where I became ordained in a tonsure ceremony with other like *bonsan* [priest]. Also, in China I became ordained in Hongchow . . .

by this time I felt that I was learning and deserved what I was becoming althou... still maintained that I was on a temporary basis and w... ing to step aside when someone better fitted became available. None appeared so I carried on and on. By this time there was a growing number of Caucasian and Occidental reverends of various sects; this is the general background.

The Buddhists experienced many personal and community problems both in Hawaii and the mainland states. One incident is very illustrative: "Oh, we had such troubles with the community. One woman came up to me and said, 'Are you Julius Goldwater?' I said, 'Yes.' She said, 'do you want to become a Buddhist?' I said, 'Yes,' and she spat in my face."

Later, in Los Angeles, Reverend Goldwater describes the life he led with the Nisei members just prior to the outbreak of World War II:

I was allowed an office at the Nishi Hongwanji, a little room; and more than that they asked me to join them at funerals and weddings, to be a party with the YBA youngsters, teach a class at Sunday school and so I was at the various events. I used to fight for the kids too, because to have a dance or to do other things wasn't acceptable by the Issei, but the young kids were Americans and didn't have any of the Japanese nationalistic limitations that the Issei thought should come through the blood, I guess. So gradually the young children observed me and thought I was a friendly, acceptable presence to have around and I had weekly classes at the temple in English and services in addition. With the outbreak of Pearl Harbor, I rushed right down and I had an idea of what we should do . . . and I told *Rimban* [successor to *Rimban* Yukawa] that I remembered the First World War because I'm of German extraction. My grandmother and the older folks spoke German and we had a hell of a time. . . . we had all these enemies around the neighborhood so I knew what could come of this. I thought I'd be of invaluable help to the *Rimban*. . . . so the *Rimban* says, "I didn't expect to see you anymore." . . . I explained what we had to do. The church has always accepted everything and if they didn't get enough they would ask for more. Now is the time for the church to give back to the people.

We had to open our doors, tell them to come here, they were safe
here, nobody's going to touch them here; we have to store their
belongings. We would secure things—everything like that and . . .
they brought in truckloads of possessions.

During the evacuation era, Reverend Goldwater was literally the resident minister at the Los Angeles Betsuin. Although all the members
were in assembly centers at first, he brought Buddhist books and port-
able shrines to the ministers in the centers while he was volunteer caretaker at the Betsuin. Reverend Goldwater was given power of attorney
and full control over three Los Angeles area temples: Gardena, Senshin,
and the Betsuin. Another minister[66] has stated that Reverend Goldwater's belief was that since the Japanese members had given their
money to the temples, in time of need they should be repaid in kind.
Therefore, when the members asked that their luggage or personal belongings be shipped back to the various concentration camps, he utilized temple funds for the postage fees without asking repayment from
the recipients. He also used some temple funds to print English Buddhist
service materials for the various camps. Some returning Buddhist ministers viewed these expenses as improper use of monies placed in Reverend Goldwater's trust, offsetting the goodwill that had arisen between
him and the other ministers before the war.

This delicate situation has not been previously discussed in the writings of the BCA. With the power of attorney given to Reverend Goldwater, all temple monies were in effect under his control. Had there
been any doubt as to his trustworthiness, such powers would never have
been offered to him, and because the funds were not used indiscrimin-
ately or for his personal gain, he cannot be faulted. A $10,000 law suit
was apparently filed against Reverend Goldwater by the Betsuin for
improper utilization of church monies, but the court ruled that he had
used them solely for the benefit of the people that the Betsuin considered their members. He himself never raised the topic of his disagreement with some of the Los Angeles ministers.

Reverend Goldwater's recollection of his relationship with the ministers is quite warm:

The *Kaikyoshi* and I were very chummy. We would go to each
others home, get drunk together. We would meditate together;

we would chant together, play together, fight against each other. But the main thing is when Rev. Yukawa became *Rimban* he dragged me around, introducing me to everybody personally as his brother . . . and they were very lovely and accepting to me, even when I guess in many instances . . . they resented me. And it was all so unnecessary, although I'm sure I never did anything to offend anybody, really. I may have done it during the war years inadvertently, but not consciously certainly.

After the evacuation and the start of resettlement back to the Pacific Coast, Reverend Goldwater was instrumental in refurbishing the temples as temporary hostels for the Japanese:

I found it necessary to create hostels here for the evacuees and so I asked if it would be possible for Arthur A. Takemoto (who has since become a much beloved and respected Reverend himself) to assist in this direction. . . . He was good enough to accept, and came. I asked at that time Reverend Kanmo Imamura (who has subsequently become a most honorable Bishop of the Hawaiian Islands) and his wife, Jane, to also come and assist, and so the four of us created the first Buddhist hostel. From that we . . . carried on the best that we could completely without training or background and transferred [operations to] one of the branches because the temple [Betsuin] was still full of luggage trunks and suitcases. . . . The area was also replaced by Negros that had been brought in from the deep South to work on the ships, the Liberty Ships . . . and the [Japanese] were timid to return to their area. So we began at Senshin [temple] on Normandie and 36th Place and we [carried] on from there.

Although Reverend Goldwater has kept his many friends in the Buddhist movement, he has not actively participated within the ministerial ranks of the BCA since the misunderstandings at the end of the war. Recently, however, through the West Los Angeles Buddhist Temple, he has become involved again, holding seminars, classes, and consultations.[67]

The role of the Occidental minister within the BCA is not clearly defined. Many problems arise since the members view their religious organization as a Japanese or Japanese American institution. Yet, to ask whether the problems that Reverend Goldwater faced with some Issei ministers would have occurred if he were of Japanese ancestry would be a misdirected question. The difference cannot be attributed to ethnicity, as even some Nisei and Sansei ministers have had difficulty instituting changes they see as desirable. Moreover, one Occidental, Reverend Sunya Pratt of the Tacoma Buddhist Temple, has successfully worked within the BCA since the 1930s—first as a lay person and now as a minister for a number of years. As the BCA continues to train and ordain new Occidental ministers, however, the problem of placement is becoming a more important issue. An Occidental minister cannot at this time be assigned as the sole minister of a temple that has large numbers of Issei. The communication problem is the obverse to that of a minister who cannot speak English.

Recently, a non-Japanese graduate of the Institute for Buddhist Studies returned from Japan and was offered a position as an assistant minister in a Buddhist temple. That he declined the position for personal reasons points to some interesting problems. First, the new ministers, both Occidental and Sansei, are now able to assert some independence from the desires of the bishop and BCA headquarters. Unlike the usual case wherein ministers first arriving from Japan were given little choice in their first assignment, the bishop must now consider the assignment's attractiveness to the minister, including such features as size of membership, locale, and ministerial salary. However, if all new ministers coming from the Institute of Buddhist Studies maintain complete independence from BCA headquarters, the Institute will have to adopt more stringent admissions criteria. Since the institute is dependent on monetary support from the BCA organization, an ongoing evaluative interaction continues to take place.

Occidental and Sansei ministers are limited in the temples or churches to which they can be assigned. Only at temples with relatively large memberships, and usually in an urban setting, are there enough Caucasians or English-speaking members to support more than a single minister. Thus, the newer ministers are found at the temples in Chicago, San Jose, Fresno, Gardena, Seattle, and Los Angeles. Because all BCA member churches pay to support the institute, and certain temples will not for some time, if ever, receive benefits from their dues assessment, increasing resistance from these churches may be forthcoming. The smaller temples, especially those in rural areas, are most likely to raise future objections.

The BCA has realized the need for English-speaking ministers, regardless of racial background, and the commitment of the institute, in personnel and funds, is clear. But the problems encountered by the new ministers are perhaps beyond the ability of any one group to solve because they involve the entire organization. As long as differences occur between the Issei and the Nisei/Sansei membership, they will affect the bishop, the BCA organization, the membership, and the ministers. One such pervasive difficulty for the BCA today concerns the ministers' financial remuneration.

Financial Remunerations

The actual salaries within the BCA vary widely, ranging from approximately $7,500 to $12,500.[68] Since the tasks and duties expected of all ministers are essentially the same, there is an inherent inequality in having the member churches independently determine the ministers' salaries. Length of time spent in the ministry appears to have little to do with actual salaries. The questionnaire distributed for this study reveals that the highest was earned by a minister with over thirty years of service, but the lowest was earned by a minister with from six to ten years' service. The main determinant of salary is the number of registered members at the individual temples; the largest temples pay the most, and the smallest pay the least.[69] Moreover, average annual salary does not significantly vary between districts, except for a lower salary scale in the Northwest.

Traditionally, the BCA member churches and temples have independently determined the ministers' financial and subsidiary remuneration, contingent upon dues paid by the membership and donations and revenues derived from property or fund-raising events. The member churches have usually allotted some income revenue to housing the minister and his family, supplying him with furniture and transportation, and paying his utilities, and recently they have contributed to the minister's Social Security fund and medical insurance.

The larger the minister's family, the more inadequate is the present salary scale. As we have noted, some Issei and Nisei ministers listed their financial situation as constituting a problem. In private conversations, many ministers discussed the inadequacy of their salaries, though they hesitated to make their feelings known to their members. They were, of course, more concerned about reaching and aiding their members through the teachings of the religion, but when discussing their families or homelife, they often mentioned financial difficulties.

The unequal salaries are a thorny and complex problem. Since at least 1969, the BCA bishop has attempted gently to focus attention on this topic by including the results of his annual ministerial salary survey in the *BCA Annual Reports*. In printing the various salary scales by district, with each reader cognizant of what his temple gives to his minister, the bishop can tactfully say, "I respectfully request the BCA and the local church Board of Directors to consider these [figures] in the reevaluation of their ministerial salaries, especially those districts in which the salaries are far below the national average."[70]

The bishop has no authority over the salary paid to the ministers. While he is quite concerned about the present system, he has only the power of persuasion at his disposal.[71] He, along with other ministers, has mentioned his wish to have a standardized salary scale dependent upon length of service and size of the minister's family. With a large membership, a church or temple may have little difficulty, but the temples with fewer members could be faced with a large financial burden.[72] In July 1973, a questionnaire was sent by the BCA Organizational Evaluation Committee to the forty-eight members of the BCA board of directors. Question seven reads, "There has been a study made by the Evaluation Committee regarding standardization of ministerial salaries. Would you favor such a move?"[73] Seventy-five percent of the respondents were in favor. The question has now been introduced into the BCA decision-making body; any further action will be raised in other committees for further study.

Question six has wider ramifications: "The Evaluation Committee has considered the possibility of the centralization of the payroll for all BCA ministers. Would you favor such a move?"[74] Again, 75 percent favored the motion. Centralization of monies would allow the member temples to send their ministers' salaries to the BCA, with dispersal power given to headquarters. Headquarters could standardize the salaries, thus obviating the need for the local temples to reach and obey a collective decision. The BCA could also subsidize the ministers not directly connected with a member temple. This change would permit the BCA, like other religious bodies, to send ministers wherever they are needed, regardless of local financial conditions.

However, the centralization of salaries would also remove much of the local autonomy now enjoyed by member temples. The control of these funds would undoubtedly remain with BCA headquarters, and the practice of raising a minister's salary to entice a desirable candidate or to retain a favorite minister could not as easily be implemented. Centralization would penalize the large member churches, as they would, in effect, be asked to subsidize the less affluent sectors of the organization. The ministers as a whole would gain by standardization, as would the smaller temples which are now barely able to meet minimal salary scales.

Whether salaries will in fact be standardized and/or centralized is an open question. There appears to be some support for both changes, as indicated by the response from the BCA board of directors. Standardization is the less radical change, with respect to its overall effect upon the BCA. Moreover, this motion had wide support among the ministers interviewed. Since the ministers also desire to maintain their independence from headquarters, which has already levied heavy assessments for the construction of a new BCA headquarters building, a new bishop's residence, and the like, some ministers feel that centralization of their salaries would make the San Francisco headquarters overpowerful in its ability to influence ministers at member temples. Whether there is sufficient support from the member temples for either change cannot at this time be determined. Until there are such changes, the impetus for salary equalization will lie in gentle and tactful persuasion and arguments presented by the minister and the bishop at each and every BCA temple.

We now return to the social history of the BCA. The focus of the next chapter will be on the organization's role in aiding in the ethnic adjustment of the Japanese Americans. In addition, consideration will be given to the difficulties of language, the suborganizations and ceremonies found in the BCA, and membership statistics.

Notes

1. BCA, *Annual Report, 1970*, mimeographed (San Francisco: 1971), pp. 1–4.
2. Personal interview with Reverend S. Sakow, Santa Barbara Bud-

dhist Church, on December 4, 1973. Much of this and the following section on the levels of ordination are derived from Reverend Sakow and Dr. Ryo Munekata. Dr. Munekata was a president of the board of directors and of the BCA. A *soryo* is a priest; when a *soryo* is a resident priest of a temple he is called a *jushoku*.

3. The rules of hereditary ownership of the priest's position and the temple are so important that if a *jushoku* does not have a son, a male relative or indeed in some cases any male willing to undergo religious training and willing to change his name to that of the temple family may inherit the title and property. When the *jushoku* has daughters and no sons, a daughter may request that her husband undergo religious training, change his family name, and enter into her family register. The succeeding *jushoku*, however, must request the change and receive approval from the headquarters in Kyoto, Japan. The approval is called a *haime*.

4. Personal interviews with Revered Sakow, *supra*, and Reverend Kakuyei Tada, February 24, 1973.

5. Fujitani, op. cit., pp. 1 and 2; and "BCA and the Buddhist Sangha of America," mimeographed, February 25, 1971, pp. 1, 2, in the personal possession of the author.

6. Fujitani, op. cit.

7. Ibid.

8. Personal observation during the BCA Minister's Conference, 1973, in Oakland, Calif., and other personal experience.

9. Buddhist Brotherhood of America, op. cit., p. 65.

10. Fujitani, "English Nomenclature of *So-Cho*," p. 1: *Sangharaja* means "overseer of a *Sangha*" (Buddhist gathering).

11. The chief abbot's position is held hereditarily by descendants of the founder of the sect, Shinran Shonin.

12. Reverend Philipp K. Eidmann (ed.), "The Lion's Roar," St. Paul, Minn., October 1957, p. 7. The section on the levels of ordination was also derived from personal interviews with Reverend S. Sakow, Dr. and Mrs. Munekata, and Reverend K. Tada, as cited above.

13. Eidmann, "The Lion's Roar," p. 9. In 1937, the lowest acceptable age for *tokudo* was nine, since that was the age at which Shinran Shonin first entered the Buddhist order. See Utsuki, op. cit., p. 40.

14. Utsuki, op. cit., pp. 26, 40.

15. Eidmann, "The Lion's Roar, p. 9.

16. Ibid., p. 12.

17. Ibid., p. 9.

18. The following material is excerpted from the *Hongwanji Hoki*

Jodo Shinshu Hongwanji-ha Shu Sei [Rules and regulations of the Jodo Shinshu Hongwanji]. The candidate is required to attain a score of 60 out of 100 on each subject, and the examinations are to be of a university level of difficulty. I am indebted to Katsuhiko Abe for his help in the translation.

19. Eidmann, "The Lion's Roar," pp. 9, 12.

20. Ibid., p. 9.

21. Eidmann, *Young People's Introduction*, p. 59.

22. Ibid.

23. The Los Angeles Betsuin also has a *fuku-rimban* (vice-rimban) with seven *kaikyoshi*. Sacramento has two *kaikyoshi*, Seattle three, San Jose three, and Fresno two. BCA, *1972-1973 Directory* (San Francisco: 1972), pp. 4-9.

24. Reverend Kosho Yukawa, et al., "Role of the Minister," in *BCA, Annual Report, 1972*, pp. 148-150, and from personal observations.

25. From the response to the Minister's Questionnaire. See Appendix 2.

26. Interview with some Issei ministers. Manimai Ratanamani, "History of Shin Buddhism in the United States," Master's Thesis, College of the Pacific, Stockton, Calif., January 1960, p. 35, also states that during the pre-World War II era, "In some churches, the board always accepted the minister's demands and submitted to his financial management."

27. Personal interviews with some Issei ministers.

28. For instance, Reverend Sensho Sasaki served the Sacramento [Betsuin] for twenty-one years; Reverend Sadamaro Ouchi served the Tacoma Buddhist Church for twelve years; Reverend Enryo Unno served the Senshin Buddhist Church (in Los Angeles) for ten years; Reverend Eryo Terao served the Spokane Buddhist Church for sixteen years and the Alameda Buddhist Church for thirteen years.

29. Interview with active BCA ministers on February 24, 1973. Subsequent to that time, this minister has reentered the BCA organization but has been assigned to another temple.

30. Bishop Kenryu Tsuji, "Office of the Bishop," in BCA, *Annual Report, 1972*, p. 5.

31. Yukawa, et al., "Role of the Minister," op. cit., pp. 148-152.

32. Ibid.

33. Personal interviews with BCA ministers, and other personal observations.

34. Personal observations in the home of Nisei priests.

35. A Minister's Questionnaire plus two followup letters in 1973–1974 were sent to seventy-six full-time ministers at the temples, headquarters, and Institute for Buddhist Studies and to twenty-five other Jodo Shinshu ministers not presently active in the BCA. Fifteen formal interviews and numerous personal interviews were also obtained throughout 1973–1974 at various BCA conferences. The ministers' listing was obtained from the BCA, *1972–1973 Directory.* There was a total of forty responses, with thirty-seven ministers presently active at the various temples, headquarters, or the Institute for Buddhist Studies. See Appendix 2 for the questionnaire.

A total of 311 names are listed as official BCA registered priests from 1899 to 1973 in BCA, *Annual Report, 1970–1974.* See "Ministers in Buddhist Churches of America, Appreciation Fund," in BCA, *Annual Report, 1970.* The names of three priests were duplicated in the official roster; they were registered with different names (see Chapter 5, note 41). Information concerning the three priests was obtained from Dr. Ryo Munekata, Los Angeles, Calif., November 3, 1974.

36. A Kibei is a person born in and returning to America after spending part or much of his early life in Japan. This practice was especially prevalent from the late 1920s through the 1930s. See Thomas, op. cit., pp. 17, 63–65.

37. The priests were asked to rate themselves on their ability to speak Japanese and English.

	Fluent	*Good*	*Passable*	*Poor*	*Unable*
Issei:					
Japanese	15	6	2	0	0
English	0	4	8	8	3
Nisei/Sansei:					
Japanese	4	3	6	1	0
English	9	3	2	0	0

Two Issei priests rated their speaking ability in Japanese as "passable" and their English as "poor." Both are very conversant in Japanese and their questionnaire was completed in Japanese. All the Nisei/Sansei responses were in English. The two ministers rating themselves "passable" in English were a Sansei and a Nisei. Having talked with this particular Nisei priest, I would rate his English-speaking ability as "fluent." The Japanese concept of *enryo* (undue reticence or restraint) may in part explain the personal ratings. For a discussion of *enryo*, see Harry Kitano,

Japanese Americans: Evolution of a Subculture (Englewood Cliffs, N.J.: Prentice-Hall, 1969), pp. 103–105.

38. The four ministers are Reverends Masao Kodani, Senshin Buddhist Church, Los Angeles; Ronald Miyamura, Midwest Buddhist Temple, Chicago; Jimmy Yanagihara, Gardena Buddhist Church, Gardena, Calif.; and William Masuda, Los Angeles Betsuin.

39. Generational categories are not concrete and inflexible. Stanford Lyman has correctly analyzed the social definitional nature of the classification: "Age and situation may modify the strictness of membership. . . . In practice they tend to demonstrate the sociological rule that status is as status does; that is, they enjoy the classification which social relations and personal behavior assign to them and which they assign to themselves." Lyman, op. cit., p. 84.

40. Besides those mentioned, the present ministers include Reverends Sunya Pratt and Kenneth O'Neill. Reverend Charles Paulson served from 1969 until he passed away in 1970.

41. Determination as to generation was derived from self-labeling on the Minister's Questionnaire, question 25d, and from various other ministers within the BCA.

BCA, *Annual Report, 1970–1973*, reports 311 official priests registered. Three individuals were duplicated with different names: Tassho Noryo, 1920–1923, was also Tassho Yuge, 1920–1925; Seikai Sasaki, 1927–1934, was Kazuo Toyooka, 1927–1934; and Hiteki Kuwabara, 1934–1937, was Hifumi Kuwahara, 1931–1938. All were Issei. The name changes reflect a Japanese custom whereby a priest can be taken into another priest's family to continue a family line where a male heir is absent. The custom is called *yoshi*. Interview with Ryo Munekata, Los Angeles, November 3, 1974.

42. The record for active service was held by Reverend Seikaku Mizutani—from 1916 to his death in 1972, for a total of fifty-six years.

43. BCA, *Annual Report, 1970*, p. 4.

44. "Discussion on Early Missionary Work," p. 3.

45. Ibid.

46. See Ichihashi, op. cit., pp. 66–68.

47. With seventy-six ministers, the response rate was 48.68 percent (thirty-seven responses). The breakdown by generation for all those on active duty, compared to those who responded, was: Issei, 69.57 percent to 62.5 percent; Nisei/Sansei, 26.09 percent to 37.5 percent; non-Asian, 4.4 percent to 0 percent. Thus, there was an overrepresentation of Nisei/Sansei responses and an underrepresentation of the Issei and non-Asian ministerial group. Furthermore, the respondent Issei group

had, on the average, longer active service than the total active group: 21.17 years for the respondents, and 17.66 years for the total still active group. The Nisei group was about equal: 12.14 to 12.33 years.

48. For instance, in the town of Edo, Yamaguchi Prefecture, the Kashima family have been priests for over three centuries. On one wall of the Kashima temple are placed the names of all the preceding priests written on small wooden slates, and these fill nearly all the available space.

49. Personal interviews, especially with Reverend S. Sakow and K. Tada, op. cit.

50. Of twenty-three Issei respondents, two gave multiple responses. The percentages are therefore based on twenty-five responses.

51. For a detailed discussion, see Lyman, *Asians in the West*, pp. 81–97.

52. See Tetsuden Kashima, "Japanese American Patterns of Interaction: *Amaeru* and *Enryo*," unpublished paper.

53. Personal interview with an Issei minister within the BCA Ministerial Research Committee, January 1, 1974.

54. Interview with Reverend Arthur Takemoto, Los Angeles, February 26, 1972.

55. Interview with Issei minister; see n. 53.

56. Bay District Junior Young Buddhist Conference, Oakland, Calif., July 29, 1972.

57. Personal interview, Los Angeles, February 26, 1972.

58. There are twenty-four active Nisei ministers. Of the fifteen respondents, fourteen are still active, giving a 58.3 percent response rate.

59. The five are Reverends A. Hata, Y. Kyoguku, S. Oi, L. Sasaki, and G. Shibata.

60. Interview with Reverend M. Kodani, Los Angeles, February 26, 1972.

61. Ibid.

62. Ibid.

63. Interview with Reverend A. Takemoto, February 26, 1973.

64. Ibid.

65. Interview with Reverend J. Goldwater, May 12, 1972, Los Angeles. G = Goldwater; INT = Interviewer. Further information provided through personal correspondence with Reverend Goldwater on November 22, 1974.

66. Interview on May 12, 1972, in Los Angeles.

67. He has maintained ties with the Buddhist movement. For example, he appeared at the Kinnara Spring Lecture, held at the Senshin

Temple, Los Angeles, on April 6, 1974. The topic concerned the Buddhists during the war years.

68. BCA, *Annual Report, 1971*, pp. 8a, 8b.

69. Ibid., p. 8b.

70. BCA, *Annual Report, 1972*, p. 8.

71. Interview with Bishop K. Tsuji in San Francisco, June 25, 1971.

72. The minister's salary is not the only problem. Other financial encumbrances are placed upon the temples; e.g., BCA dues, Institute for Buddhist Studies dues, and various calls for donations.

73. BCA, *Annual Report, 1973*, p. 121.

74. Ibid., p. 120.

San Jose Buddhist Church, Betsuin, California

Los Angeles Hompa Hongwanji Buddhist Temple, Betsuin, California

Stockton Buddhist Church, California

Senshin Buddhist Church, Los Angeles, California

CHAPTER 6 | *The Role of the Buddhist Church in the Ethnic Adjustment of the Japanese American*

As noted in Chapter 1, not all the Japanese who came to America in the late 1900s espoused Eastern religions; some were Christians. There were obvious differences between the two groups, in terms of cultural continuity and adaptation to the new social environment. The Buddhist missionaries who began arriving in 1899 were able to offer the immigrants a cultural tie to the world they had left behind, in a way the missionary Christian church could not. In any case, social intercourse with the American populace was as limited for the Japanese Christians as for the Japanese Buddhists:

> Not only the Buddhist but also the Methodist churches were strictly for Japanese and services were conducted in the Japanese language. Of the two religions, Buddhism provided an important link with Japan in ways Christianity did not. Buddhism was the religion of the ancestors of the Japanese immigrants, and when a man died, his ashes were preserved in the church until ready to be taken back to Japan by one of his relatives or friends.[1]

To offset some of the inevitable "sociological death,"[2] the Japanese created or modified their processes and organizations within the United States. It does not come as a surprise that as the numerically stronger Japanese religious institution, Jodo Shinshu Buddhism was able to retain its Japanese adherents and to attain an importance that far surpassed its original position in Japan. In Japan, the temples in the community are viewed predominantly as religious organizations; in America, the NABM served as a place not only for religious solace, but also for social gatherings that preserved communal ethnic ties.

Life for the early immigrant was full of hardships. Without a surrounding social support to aid and bolster the young men living and working in a foreign environment, such conditions could easily have lead to alienation and loneliness. The following description of the relationship of the church to the immigrants suggests the importance of the social aspects of the religious organization:

> Instead of trying to drown out their unhappiness with mere pleasure seeking, they [the young immigrants] turn to the church and religion to afford them comfort and relief from their economic and social misery, and they hold a cheaply optimistic, goody-goody idea that if they stay in their place, work hard and please the Americans and remain happy in the position where God has placed them, surely the Christian Americans, out of the generosity of their hearts, will throw out to them a few more crumbs to ease their condition.[3]

The important point here is that the church was able to offer this necessary spiritual and social solace for those immigrants who desired it.

Most of the elements within the NABM and BCA were brought to America and utilized by the Buddhists, but certain inimical events made it more tactful and judicious to downplay or suppress various constituent parts of the organization that could become controversial or injurious to the Buddhist religion. The story of the Buddhist swastika is one example of a social change within the Buddhist institution in America.

The sauvastika or swastika[4] has long been a traditional Indian symbol for Buddhism. In most Buddhist temples and churches before World War II, the swastika was exhibited ornamentally. The Buddhist church in Seattle, Washington, for example, displayed the symbol on an archway above the front entrance upon a temple building built in 1906.[5]

It is clear today that the sign of the swastika, constructed either in a counterclockwise Buddhist fashion or clockwise as used in Nazi Germany, remains a symbol of Nazism for most Americans. Long before the 1940s, however, the swastika was regarded as a symbol representing a foreign tradition.

One might pass the Buddhist temple in Portland a hundred times a day, and unless one's eyes were quick to spy the modest Swastika 卍 on the door glass, and the neat gold letters BUDDHIST CHURCH on the transom, one would never suspect the square brick house of being other than an old-time domicile, or a present-day rooming house; but there it is, a heathen temple on American soil.[6]

Madden described the swastika as the symbol of Buddhism in America. Her main objection as a non-Buddhist was the presence and threat of this religion to America: "Who shall rule America, Christ or Buddha? Just outside your church door is the sign of the Swastika, what will you do about it?"[7]

Despite anti-Japanese sentiment in America during the 1920s, the swastika did not become as overt an issue at that time as it did in the 1940s. Until the advent of World War II, the Buddhist churches continued to utilize and to display the swastika as a religious emblem. Then, just after the attack on Pearl Harbor, not only things Japanese, but especially Buddhist artifacts and writings, became immediately suspect in the minds of Americans. Some Japanese Americans, cognizant of the suspicions generated by war hysteria, attempted to divest themselves of their Buddhist religious possessions.

Those who had little confidence in their own religious beliefs believed that any association with a Buddhist organization would be to their disadvantage. Possession of Japanese writings became suspect and a source of concern; thus, the fearful ones removed their Buddhist altars, destroyed their sutra books and burned their family albums containing photos of relatives or friends in uniform.[8]

The use of the Buddhist swastika as a symbol was repressed during the war. The attendant meanings that non-Buddhists could attach to the swastika created a crisis for the Buddhists. Hence, from that time, other Buddhist symbols were given more emphasis: the "Wheel of Law," an eight-spoked wheel representing the "eightfold noble path," became, and remained, the accepted logo for the American Buddhists.

However, one recently formed Jodo Shinshu Buddhist group in Los Angeles, the Kinnara, now utilizes the swastika as its logo.[9]

The BCA as a Cohesive Force: 1945–1975

To be sure, the swastika is a mere symbol, and the resemblance between the Buddhist and Nazi emblems was ultimately a historical accident. But the repression and degradation inflicted upon all Japanese Americans during World War II was not an accident of history.

The immediate problem after the relocation of the Japanese was the reopening of the dormant temple structures. Most temples were initially used as hostels, with all available space converted to makeshift bedrooms, except the kitchens, which were used to prepare communal food. These hostels also served as job placement offices and community centers for all Japanese and Japanese Americans.

Upon their return, many ministers found that their temples had been vandalized and religious articles destroyed or stolen.[10] Religious services were at first given secondary consideration, since the personal needs of the Japanese Americans were paramount and acute. The ordeal inherent in their return, especially with regard to employment and housing, became another complete dislocation process for the returnees.

Along the West Coast, people of Japanese descent did not return to precisely the places they had left. Before the war, the Bakersfield Buddhist Church had a membership of approximately fifty families, with a resident minister; the only Japanese who returned were those who owned agricultural lands. With only a handful of families to support it, the temple was forced to close. The Guadalupe Buddhist Church also lost many members, although a sufficient number did return eventually to support a resident minister and an active church organization. The Buddhist Church of Salinas lost about a third of its previous membership families, but it retained enough members to continue supporting a resident minister. The Oakland Buddhist Church, an urban temple that had once enjoyed a large membership, also experienced a large decrease. The Placer Buddhist Church and the West Los Angeles Buddhist Church had stable membership numbers only because new families moved in to replace those who did not return.

On the other hand, churches and temples in Berkeley, Palo Alto, Reedley, Gardena, San Diego, Oxnard, and San Jose, and in Denver,

Colorado (Tri-State Buddhist Church), experienced a small to large increase in membership. Many new churches or temples were constructed to meet the needs of the new Japanese population; by December 1946, organizations were established in Cleveland, Ohio; Detroit, Michigan; Idaho-Oregon (Ontario, Oregon); Spokane, Washington; Minneapolis, Minnesota (Twin Cities); and Monterey, California. From 1950 to 1971, seven new churches or temples were constructed: at Mountain View, Union City (Southern Alameda County Buddhist Church), Anaheim (Orange County Buddhist Church), Marin, and Fowler, California; Seabrook, New Jersey; and Honeyville, Utah. The last church to become independent was Venice, California, on March 1, 1976.

Since 1945, the Issei population has grown older and fewer in number, while the Nisei and Sansei population has increased. Because the Nisei have continued to move into nonagricultural occupations, rural Buddhist churches have suffered the most from resettlement. Although some ministers who would have returned with their adherents to the West Coast took over the new temples and churches in the Midwest and on the Eastern seaboard, from 1948 onward a continuous flow of new ministers, both Nisei and native Japanese, has entered the BCA.[11]

Conflicts between the Issei and Nisei, within the temples, continued after the war. The Issei and Nisei both desired decision-making powers within the church organization. Most temples had their own constitutions and eventually incorporated under the laws of their respective states whereby the elected board of directors controlled their finances. The Issei ministers with their bishop continued to dominate the BCA, but at the local temples the Nisei continued to gain in ascendancy. Income was difficult to generate since the members were readjusting to life outside the camps. The prewar language schools, which had augmented the salaries of the ministers and temples, were not immediately reestablished to any large extent. Only after the BCA Buddhist adherents started to overcome their financial losses from the evacuation, in the late 1950s, were the churches and temples able to provide substantial increases in the ministers' salaries and other necessary church expenditures. During the readjustment period, large-scale financial projects such as the NABM *Zaidan* (Endowment Fund) were tabled because of insufficient funds; however, two important centers were created to fill the need for more English-speaking ministers.

A Ministerial Training Fund was emphasized through a BCA Special

Project Fund in 1966 to further the training of Nisei ministers, through scholarships for prospective ministerial candidates studying here or in Japan, and to aid active ministers desiring to continue their study of English.[12] The BCA established a Ministerial Training Center at the Hompa (Nishi) Hongwanji in Kyoto, Japan. A plan to initiate the training of the priests in the United States resulted in the American Buddhist Academy in 1948 under the Reverend Hozen Seki and the New York Buddhist Church; and the Berkeley Study Center in 1965 under the BCA Bishop Enryo Shigefuji, the Reverend Kanmo Imamura, and the Berkeley Buddhist Church.

The period from 1945 to 1965, with the start of the Institute of Buddhist Studies in Berkeley, can be characterized as a consolidation era, with the BCA reevaluating the Issei priorities and anticipating the changing needs of Buddhists. However, the Buddhist religion remained tied to those of Japanese ancestry, in the Nishi Hongwanji sect as embodied in the BCA.

The Present Crisis

Changes in the BCA in the 1960s have resulted in a more vocal organization than previously existed. An important issue entered into by the BCA concerned the California State Curriculum Committee's approval of a textbook entitled *Japanese Americans: The Untold Story*.[13] The textbook, aimed at the third to fifth grade grammar school level, was written by a team of twelve authors (Nikkei school teachers and citizens) forming the Japanese American Curriculum Project (JACP). The JACP had previously produced a television program in San Francisco on Japanese Americans, which had drawn criticism from some individuals who felt it made "inaccurate representations of the Japanese American Community."[14] After writing the short book in four months, the JACP submitted it to various Japanese organizations for prepublication approval. Instead, the textbook was overwhelmingly denounced by the Japanese American Citizens League, the Southern California Buddhist-Christian Clergy Fellowship, and various Asian American student organizations, as well as parents, educators, and ministers.

On October 7, 1970, in a letter signed by the bishop, the president of the board of directors, and the chairman of the Ministerial Research

Committee, the BCA stated that there were "overtones to the book which were racial, consistently anti-Buddhist and pro-Christian biased, and a gross misrepresentation of the true picture of the lives of Japanese Americans. . . . The preface of the book is written as though the authors have acquired the endorsement of the Buddhist Churches of America, but actually the Buddhist Churches of America have not endorsed the book, whatsoever."[15] Through a series of meetings and public presentations, the BCA and other organizations and individuals were able to convince the California State Curriculum Committee to reject the book. The authors now have plans to rewrite some portions of the text and to submit the revised version for reconsideration.

Regardless of the outcome of the television program and textbook controversies, the BCA in 1970 clearly stepped out of what many had considered an insular, conservative community position. The BCA perceived the book to be a threat to the future Buddhists of America. In an unsigned but BCA-sponsored letter distributed to the members of the Buddhist churches to elicit written support of the BCA's position, the concern for the Buddhist child's self-image is very apparent:

> This book reflects unfavorably upon the Japanese American Buddhists and has a pervading religious bias. We feel that this religious bias could be very detrimental to the Buddhist identity of our children. It can only serve to make our children feel insecure about being Buddhists, but also can serve to make a critical change in their thoughts and minds about their Buddhist identity and heritage. How it will affect the thinking of others about Buddhists and Japanese Americans is an equally disturbing thought.[16]

The BCA's and their adherents' willingness to come forward to speak in defense of their position had a precedent in Bishop Uchida's testimony at the Immigration Commission meetings in the 1920s. The crisis concerning the textbook was a perceived threat to the image of Buddhism presented to the adherents' children. It was important enough to involve the headquarters and the member churches and temples in a lobbying and letter-writing campaign to help avert the State Education Committee's adoption of the book.

Another issue on which the BCA took an active position concerned the inclusion of the Divine Creation Theory in California public school textbooks.[17] The Reverend Hogen Fujimoto, director of the Bureau of Buddhist Education, BCA, testified before the State Board of Education that this "Divine Creation" represented a religious interpretation; it was therefore a subject for churches—not schools. Reverend Fujimoto quoted from various sources and explained that Buddhists did not subscribe to the ideas inherent in the theory: "According to Buddhism, human beings and all living things are self created or self creating. The universe is not homocentric, it is a creation of all beings. Buddhism does not believe that all things come from one cause, but holds that everything is inevitably created out of more than two causes."[18]

Thus, by 1972 the BCA was willing to enter into debates in secular areas, utilizing its religious doctrines in defense of its stand on public issues. The YBA has demonstrated a similar initiative by passing an antiwar resolution deploring the destruction of human life in the Vietnam conflict[19] and by giving Buddhists guidelines for becoming more involved in protest against racism and other forms of social oppression.[20]

The BCA and some BCA member churches have also sponsored housing projects to assist the elderly Issei. With the cooperation of the San Francisco Redevelopment Agency and the Japanese community, the Japanese American Religious Federation (JARF) has begun construction of a thirteen-story, 272-unit apartment building for low-income residents.[21] This joint undertaking of the BCA, the Buddhist Church of San Francisco, and nine other Japanese and Japanese American member churches[22] is but one example of the ability of religious organizations to work together on a project of mutual benefit.

The 1970s has been explicitly proclaimed a period for broadening Sansei involvement in the BCA. As the past president of the BCA board of directors has stated, "With the coming of the 75th Anniversary, we must begin the new era of American Buddhism. The area of youth is a challenging area."[23] The Sansei represent the important problems of the present and the future. There is some reason to suppose that some Sansei perceive themselves as outside the mainstream of American life.[24] Many are now, in one sense, returning to their Japanese cultural and associational roots, refusing to forget their Asian past. Of the third generation Marcus Lee Hansen has written that "what the son wishes to forget, the grandson wishes to remember."[25] The creation of Asian American Studies Centers, Yellow Brotherhood, and Asian American Anti-

Drug Groups, as well as the Relevant American Buddhists and Kinnara groups within the Buddhists of America, indicates that the Sansei are not only willing to stay in the Buddhist religion, but also to form new organizations tailored to their needs.

To facilitate communication with the Sansei, the BCA board of directors authorized the creation of the Relevant American Buddhists (RAB), with eight youth coordinators' positions within the BCA districts to aid the YBA and their programs and to insure that the youths' needs and demands would be given an official channel of communication to the BCA ruling bodies. Since the older YBA members, parents of the third generation, have now formed the Adult Buddhist Association (ABA), the Sansei have desired to expand their activities to aid the aging Issei, allow other racial groups within the Junior and Senior YBA, become involved in social and political issues, and initiate changes in the presentation of their religion.

The Kinnara, a Southern California-based Buddhist organization, was formed, in the main, by a group of Nisei and Sansei BCA ministers and the Sansei membership to change the format of religious teachings. The Kinnara group, as was mentioned previously, has incorporated traditional Japanese music (*gagaku*), sutra chanting, and meditation techniques to allow for a diversity of methods in Buddhist services and ceremonies. For instance, the group has instituted Buddhist retreats, daylong celebrations of important Buddhist days of reverence, and interchurch gatherings to sustain and generate new interest in Buddhism among the Nisei's children. It would be premature at this time to estimate the longevity of this new organization. However, it can be stated that the membership is growing. Moreover, since more Nisei and Sansei ministers are entering, while maintaining their particular churches for the Issei and Nisei, there is reason to believe that the Kinnara group represents one vital and important alternative to the existing BCA organization.

There is some evidence too that some of the Sansei are returning to their Buddhist religion.[26] They are still young, in their teens and twenties. The BCA ministers have had difficulty attracting them to existing church organizations[27] primarily because the ministers are still largely Issei, the member churches are controlled by a Nisei board of directors, and the Sansei have not clearly communicated the type of changes they desire.

The Sansei would appreciate a stronger voice in the activities of the church or temple organizations, but they have not yet articulated a positive program that the churches could accept or reject. Most churches have included sports and other social activities, but Buddhist study groups or religious-oriented activities have not met with overwhelming success in attracting the Sansei.[28] The future of the Sansei in the BCA is still uncertain. Programs and activities will continue to be modified to attract the Sansei and non-Japanese; upon their success or failure rests the future of the BCA.

The Continuity of Buddhism and the Problem of Language

The strongest force for continuity in the member temples has, of course, been the Jodo Shinshu Buddhist religion itself. Throughout its history, the basic religious tenets, practices, and ceremonies have constituted the major continuous and unchanging focal point for the membership. An Issei minister was asked in an interview:

INT: What is the difference between Issei Buddhism and Nisei Buddhism, and then Sansei Buddhism?

RESP: That definition would be based on majority membership, and so, of course, [on the] accompanying psychological or other cultural differences.

INT: But they are all Buddhist?

RESP: All Buddhists, yes.

INT: Now, is Jodo Shinshu Buddhism different between the Issei, Nisei and Sansei?

RESP: I don't think so, and the doctrine, of course, never changes. Buddhism you know consists of the triple jewels: [the Buddha], the teaching of the Buddha, and the Sangha [brotherhood of Buddhists].... The Sangha may be changing. Even many of the vocabularies must be carefully used. This is a funny example, but the lady's breast is a symbol of mother's love in Japan. So we often refer to *Ochichi o nomaseru* [literally: to allow someone to drink from the breast], but some Issei ministers came to this country and explained [this concept] pointing [to the breast region] causing laughter among the [non-Japanese speaking] audience. So we have to adapt ourselves to this particular situation even linguistically. So from that standpoint, maybe our way of presentation must be changed.

INT: But not the doctrine.

RESP: Not the doctrine.

INT: What are the purposes of the Buddhist church for the Issei?

RESP: Of course, to retain, to keep the Jodo Shinshu [for] themselves and also through their capacity as the leader of the family to transmit the teaching to the children, the grandchildren. . . .

INT: What is the purpose of the Buddhist Church for the Nisei?

RESP: Niseis of course accept this precious gift of Dharma of Buddha from their parents and transfer [it] to their children. So nowadays, Issei and Nisei are not young anymore. So in spite of linguistic differences, language differences, from their chronological experiences they are becoming closer to the Issei. . . .

INT: Now what is the purpose of the Buddhist church for the Sansei?

RESP: Not very much difference from Issei, Nisei propagation. But if I [could] add a point, it is [that it] makes them missionary agents to all other non-Japanese Americans, because they are at a good position to do that. . . . They have the same language as the American people in general, so they are in a good position to introduce Buddhism, explain Buddhism to others.[29]

This Issei minister, like many others, emphasized the continuity of religious doctrine within a modified form of presentation. The most important modification is the use of English, with the attendant problem of adequately translating Buddhist terminology to make the religious concepts understandable to the membership.

Another minister, a Nisei, seconds the points raised by the Issei *kaikyoshi*:

INT: What do you think are the purposes of the Buddhist Churches in America?

RESP: The first purpose is to keep on propagating the Jodo Shinshu to the Nisei and Sansei and Yonsei and Gosei.[30]

All ministers appear to agree that the roots of the Buddhist tree have been kept healthy in America. They also agree that there are many methods of presentation:

INT: It has been said that the BCA and North American Buddhist Mission stem traditionally from Japan. Can you name some things that are purely Japanese that are still carried on in the 1970's?

RESP: Oh yes, the teaching of the *Nembutsu* (Dharma), the Jodo Shinshu teaching has been the same all the way through, and lately, we have realized that, in some ways, the presentation has to be changed to compromise with our younger youngsters.

INT: What do you mean by compromise?

RESP: Well, in, not to compromise with their wishes all along, but to make them understand, have them enjoy our religion.

INT: Although the Buddhist doctrine comes from Japan, has it changed because we've had to use English as the main language for the Japanese Americans?

RESP: Yes, we have had a language barrier there. The translation of Buddhist teaching into English is very difficult. That is, sometimes we lose the essence of the teaching.

INT: And how is that being counteracted, or is it being counteracted?

RESP: Well it has been brought out by the Sansei and the Nisei. However, I don't think we have found a solution to that yet.[31]

The problem of adequate English translations has yet to be resolved. Thus far, the translations have been handled on a utilitarian or expedient basis—a past course presently undergoing criticism by ministers and lay members alike. There has been no attempt to change the basic doctrines or precepts of Buddhism. Instead, the adaptations have been made to render Buddhism more comprehensible to an English-speaking audience. Transmission and preservation of the tenets of Buddhism has been the paramount goal of the Buddhist institution.

Services and Ceremonies

The most important components of any religious organization are the religious services and ceremonies. From the start of Jodo Shinshu Buddhism in America to the present, important religious observances have continued. Although the format of the religious services may have changed in varying degrees over the years, especially with the prevalent use of English in the services, consistency and continuity in the content of the services are very apparent in the observances of Buddhist religious ceremonial days.

There are eleven important days and ceremonies within the Jodo Shinshu sect. The BCA ritually observes these occasions:

Shusho-E: January 1 (New Year's Service). A dedication service for the start of the new year.

Ho onko: January 16 (Shinran Shonin's Memorial Day). A special service to honor the founder of the Jodo Shinshu sect of Buddhism.

Nehan-E: February 15 (Nirvana Day). A service to memorialize the passing away of Sakyamuni Buddha.

Higan-E: March 21 *and* September 23 (Spring and Autumn Equinox). The equinox day, where the nights and days are of equal length, symbolizes the harmony pervading the universe. "Therefore we gather before the sacred shrine of Amida Buddha and meditate on the harmony of nature and devote ourselves to the realization of this harmony in our inner lives."[32]

Hanamatsuri: April 8 (Wesak Day). A day to commemorate the birth of Sakyamuni Buddha.

Gotan-E: May 21 (Shinran Shonin's Birthday). Commemoration to honor the birth of Shinran Shonin.

Ura Bon-E: July 15 (Obon Festival). A Buddhist memorial day for all who have passed away.

Beikoku Bukkyo Kaiyo Kinenbu: September 1 (BCA Founding Day). September 1, 1899, is accepted by the BCA as the date of its inception, and a service is held to honor the occasion.

Jodo-E: December 8 (Bodhi Day). A special service to commemorate the day that Sakyamuni Buddha finished his meditation under the Bodhi tree and became enlightened.

Joya-E: December 31 (New Year's Eve Service). A service to meditate on the events of the past year.

These eleven special ceremonies (*Higan-E* is observed twice a year) are observed by the member churches of the BCA. Except for the BCA Founding Day, the services have always been a part of Jodo Shinshu services in America. Most temples and churches have taken a very flexible attitude toward the actual date for these observances. Many schedule the ceremonies for the "usual" weekly services or observe them on a more convenient day close to the ritually prescribed date. For instance, the observance of *Ura Bon-E*, or *Obon* for short, usually includes not only a religious service, but also a "dance for the deceased." This celebration is inspired by a legend concerning a disciple of Buddha who performed a dance of joy when his mother was given entrance into Nirvana after her death. The entire congregation, dressed in traditional Japanese attire, enters into the *Obon* dance; it is a time for gaiety and enjoyment. Since *Obon* is very colorful, in many locales the event draws both Buddhists and non-Buddhists as onlookers and as participants. Besides the *Obon* dance, many churches feature booths and counters to sell Japanese foods and other refreshments. For many churches, the revenue generated by the booths augments regular income. In areas where there are many geographically close Buddhist churches, the individual churches will space out the observance of the event over a month's time, so that participants from one church may attend another's celebration. Scheduling also allows for guest speakers in the area to give special sermons at several churches.

At other ceremonies the bishop, as well as other speakers, may be asked to participate. These occasions are reserved for the more important services such as *Shusho-E, Ho onko, Nehan-E,* or *Hanamatsuri.* In order to make his presence available to as many temples as possible, the celebration days are often negotiated with the bishop or other church dignitaries. The spacing of the special services is an example of one form of change within the BCA. Where the special observance days in the Buddhist temples in Japan are more ritually followed, the absence of a large pool of available guest speakers or Buddhist priests outside the BCA has required that the temples accommodate the dates of observances to coincide with the availability of desired speakers. The priests within the BCA often travel to other temples to give guest lectures. This allows each church to hear priests other than the resident minister. However, for the special services, prior coordination must be accomplished with the minister to preclude conflicting engagements.

Aside from these ceremonial occasions, each temple or church conducts funeral, memorial, and wedding services. Among the most important of these services is the *hoji* or memorial service for the departed, which is observed in a very formal manner. For example, just after the death, a *makura-gyo* or bedside service may be held at the home of the deceased. Then an *otsuya* or wake service is held one day prior to the funeral service for the family of the deceased. At the *soshiki* or funeral service, a posthumous Buddhist name (*homyo*) may be given to the deceased if he or she has not previously been granted one. The officiating priest will place the Buddhist name inside the casket, and another copy is given to the family to keep within their family shrine. Family memorial services (*hoji*) are then held on the seventh day after the death, and if the family is very devout, also on the fourteenth, twenty-first, twenty-eighth, thirty-fifth, and forty-ninth day. Ceremonies after the forty-ninth day service are observed on the hundredth day, then on the first anniversary, and thereafter in the seventh, thirteenth, seventeenth, twenty-fifth, thirty-third, and fiftieth year. At most temples and churches, a collective monthly memorial service (*shotsuki hoyo*) is held, and the names of those families with relatives who have passed away during that month are printed in the church bulletin.

Each church or temple also has regularly scheduled services. These include the children's Sunday Schools and the adult services on a weekly, biweekly, or monthly basis, depending upon the number of adherents. The typical adult service may start with an opening address by the chairman. "Meditation" follows, in which the members bow their heads, placing an *ojuzu* (a Buddhist rosary) over their hands with palms together, while the priest gives a Buddhist invocation. The meditation concludes with a thrice-given recitation of an homage to the Buddha, "Namu Amida Butsu." Then a sutra (Buddhist scripture) is chanted by all, followed by the singing of a Buddhist *gatha* or hymn. The minister then gives a sermon, after which another *gatha* may be sung. The conclusion of the service includes another meditation, followed by an "incense offering," where the members may go to the front of the altar to bow, offer incense, recite the homage to the Buddha, and return to their seats. If there are any announcements they are given here; otherwise, the members leave the worship hall (*hondo*) by bowing to the shrine and departing.

The sermons given by the priests are usually of an emotional or analytic type. In the former, the priest starts with a story, usually of a personal nature, introducing an appropriate Buddhist interpretation, and usually concludes with the thought that all human events, be they tragic or comic, can be understood from the Buddhist perspective. The analytic sermon generally starts with a Buddhist concept such as *karma* or *shinjin* (faith). This is exemplified, expounded upon, and interpreted in everyday language. One priest has stated that priests can be typified according to the type of sermon they give. The Issei congregation prefers an emotional appeal, but the sermons given to the Nisei and Sansei vary.[33] For a Sansei audience from a university community, the analytic approach is most common; in an agricultural area, the emotional sermon may be better received. For a regular service, the priest's everyday activities apparently serve as a source for his sermons. The topics may range from mercury poisoning in a village in Japan[34] to the deathbed statements of an eighty-year-old Issei lady.

For special ceremonies, the sermon topic usually revolves around the reasons for the service. For example, *Hanamatsuri* sermons often discuss events surrounding the birth of the Buddha, and *Joya-E* or year-end service may recount the events of the past year as they have affected the temple or its members. For these ceremonies an outside priest or speaker is invited to give a sermon. Having a visiting priest always signals a special event for any temple, for he gives his most effective sermon, having pretested it at his home temple. Thus, there is usually a larger than average attendance during these occasions.

Buddhist Weddings

Another important service conducted by the Buddhist priests in America is the Buddhist wedding ceremony. The wedding ceremony in Japan is traditionally performed by the Shinto priests; however, the Jodo Shinshu sect of Buddhism has had a long history of performing weddings—both in Japan and in America.[35] When a marriage occurred within the family of a Buddhist priest in Japan, the wedding ceremony was almost always performed by another Buddhist official.[36] Reverend Koju Terada stated that the marriage ceremony conducted in front of the Buddhist altar was not an uncommon occurrence, especially if the participating families were strong believers in Buddhism. He also stated that the prevalent view that weddings in Japan are performed solely by Shinto priests is an idea that has developed in America since World War II.[37]

The Buddhist wedding ceremony in Japan is rather uncomplicated. The nuptial couple appears before the family Buddhist shrine, performs a *gassho* (bow) before the shrine, and recites the *Nembutsu*. A sutra may or may not be chanted, although usually there is an exchange of *ojuzu* (Buddhist rosary) between the couple. The name of the new bride is then recorded in the groom's family register. Finally, the couple goes to the reception, where part of the ceremony is to sip *sake* three times each (called *sansankudo*).[38]

The American Buddhist wedding ceremony is somewhat more complex. As in Euro-American ceremonies, the American ceremony includes the use of wedding gowns, the playing of a wedding march (Mendelssohn's "Wedding March"), the exchange of rings, and the witnessing of a wedding license. All officiating ministers must be sanctioned by the respective state legal body and empowered to perform a ceremony binding to the laws concerning the rights, privileges, and responsibilities inherent in the marriage contract. The groom wears a formal tuxedo, especially for the picture-taking portion of the wedding ceremony. (This custom, by the way, has been followed in Japan since the Meiji era and was utilized by the Japanese prior to the arrival of the Jodo Shinshu institution in America.) The marriage license is also a part of the Japanese wedding ceremony; the erasure of the bride's name from her family register and the recording of her name in the groom's register is in effect a legal sanction of the marriage ceremony.

Despite all the Western innovations, the American Buddhist wedding ceremony does retain some elements peculiar to the Buddhist faith. The couple offers incense at the Buddhist altar, affirms their faith in the Buddhist religion, and have placed over their hands the *ojuzu*, the string of beads symbolic of the Buddhist faith. The *ojuzu* is given to both participants as an affirmation of their partnership and of their commitment to the Buddhist "way of life."

An important part of the wedding is the postceremony reception. At many of the receptions, a thrice-called salute to the couple (*"Banzai"*) is often given by the guests. The reception features the singing of Japanese *No* songs (*yokyoku* or *utai*) by the guests, along with felicitations in both Japanese and English. There was a time when the nuptial couple would toast each other with *sake*, a custom similar to the *sansankudo*; however, this practice is now less frequently seen at the Sansei weddings.

The social forms of the wedding ceremony in America are now undergoing some changes. For example, some of the young have their ceremonies outside of the temples—in a wooded glen or at home; the guitar is sometimes played instead of the piano; and wedding gowns and tuxedos are becoming optional items of apparel. Such changes will undoubtedly continue in the future.

Sutras and Appurtenances

Other elements besides the religious ceremonies, services, and weddings are intrinsic to Buddhism in America. The most important of these concerns the religious sutras, the sermons of the Buddha. The sutras used by the BCA are in Chinese with Japanese pronunciations. The members chant with the priest. Only a few sutras are used in the Buddhist churches today, although the collection of the original sermons of the Buddha has been estimated at about thirty volumes.[39] The most important for the BCA are: *Shoshin-ge* (the Hymn of Faith), *San Sei-ge* (the Three Sacred Vows), *San Butsu-ge* (the Praises of the Buddha), and *Junirai* (the Twelve Adorations).[40] In a technical sense these four are not sutras since they are not authored by the Buddha. However, the Nikkei Buddhists call them sutras, and we will follow their convention. The sutras are not comprehensible to the American-born Japanese, although they have been translated into English.[41] They are still chanted in the traditional language, however. No service or ceremony is conducted without the chanting of at least one sutra. Although there have been attempts to chant them in English, the cadence and intonations have not been successfully adapted to this idiom.

Besides the sutras, elements that have persisted since the start of Buddhism in America include the shrine (*onaijin*), candles, incense, floral offerings, and gongs, bells, and drums. The shrines are often ornate gold-gilt, elaborate structures. In the center is a statue or picture of the image of the Buddha or a scroll with the sacred writings ("*Namu Amida Butsu*"). The candles are used both to symbolize the impermanence of all material objects and to shed light upon the teachings of Buddha. The incense, which symbolizes a technique of purification, is used to expunge unfavorable odors and to burn and extinguish impure thoughts. The flowers also symbolize the impermanence of living things. The gongs and bells are used to punctuate pauses within the sutras, but the fading tones also symbolize the impermanence of all material beings. All of these appurtenances have been part of the services and ceremonies of the Buddhist churches and temples both in Japan and America. All have continued throughout the years of the NABM and BCA, and have not been altered in content to adapt to a non-Buddhist environment. The Buddhist services, ceremonies, sutras, and appurtenances have remained unchanged for Jodo Shinshu adherents in America.

Problems of Ethnicity

Aside from teaching the precepts and practices of Buddhism, the NABM and BCA have attempted to sustain ethnic community solidarity —for the creation and enjoyment of group cohesiveness through racial, ethnic, and religious ties. Throughout its history, the BCA has been predominantly an organization by and for the Japanese and Japanese Americans.[42] As one Nisei father stated, "The Buddhist church is a place for the Japanese to meet other Japanese." The pressures created by prejudice and oppression during the early 1920s, and especially during the relocation in World War II, drove the Japanese to look to their own group for solace and companionship. The NABM and BCA have been religious institutions, for all Japanese and Japanese Americans, and together with the Japanese Association, the *kenjinkais* (prefectural associations), and the Japanese American Citizens' League, they have offered their members a social haven in a hostile environment.

In 1945, even the Japanese Christians were subjected to anti-Oriental prejudices, the roots of which are traceable to the early 1920s: "The Japanese feel that they are not wanted in the American churches. . . . Some who have attended the Occidental churches have experienced a warm reception, only to find later, as their numbers increased, that they were no longer welcome. Apparently, their presence in white American churches, arouses opposition as soon as there is danger of a Japanese invasion."[43] Thus, since the Japanese Christians also felt the effects of anti-Oriental sentiment, it can be stated that the basis for the prejudice was racial and only partly religious or cultural in origin.

A problem of religious differences between the Japanese and Caucasians occurred even in the 1960s. Situated in an agricultural community near the coast above Los Angeles County, which has a sizable Japanese American population, is a town with both a Nikkei Christian (Methodist) and a Buddhist church. The Methodist organization had a Japanese minister, a predominantly Japanese congregation, and a

Japanese-dominated board of directors. A nearby Caucasian Methodist church approached the Japanese Methodist church with a proposal to merge the two churches for their mutual benefit. Part of the benefit involved selling the Japanese church building, making $45,000 available for the downpayment on a new structure. The agreement which was accepted included integration of the membership, combination of the boards of directors, and retention of the Japanese American minister in the combined church. The retention of the Japanese American minister, which later caused some concern, was the result of an informal agreement:

> It was an understanding that a Japanese minister would be employed at the merger church. The assumption was [for] forever, I think. Nothing was written on paper. Being a church, I think things were done in "good faith." . . . I think the Japanese never raised this issue [of who would be head minister] but accepted whatever the Caucasians said. There is an interesting followup on this when the confrontation occurred on the head minister position. It was not raised by the Japanese members. It was raised by the second Japanese minister (by second, I mean the one succeeding the first). He was quickly reassigned to a small church in Piru [California], largely a migrant labor community. There were no more ministers of Japanese extraction thereafter. (I suppose that Caucasians here didn't think a Japanese could service their needs.)[44]

A new church building was financed, with substantial monetary contributions from the Japanese and the Nikkei. After the structure was completed in 1963, for a number of years the social relations within the church continued without incident. H. Kajihara explains the nature of the interaction: "I don't feel that there was any harmonious or disharmonious social relationship after the merger. You just went to church. You didn't have in-depth socialization which is common in all-Buddhist or all-Japanese membership church. In fact, the Japanese-Americans formed the Nisei Fellowship. To some Caucasians and Japanese this was strange, because the purpose of the merger was to integrate, so why have a segregated organization?"[45]

A series of events soon disturbed the existing relationship. The initial event was the transfer of the second Japanese American Methodist minister, which was followed by discussions as to his replacement. Although the initial church board had been composed of both Japanese and Caucasians, most decisions were now being made by the Caucasians because the Japanese were outnumbered (by twenty to three)—and apparently because the Japanese were reticent in making their position known. The Asian board members began to skip the board meetings. The general Japanese membership also declined to attend, although they generally never resisted openly, nor did they bring the disagreement into the open. Instead, person by person, they began to drop out of the church. The replacement minister was a Caucasian, and in time the board of directors also became a Caucasian-dominated group.

Subsequent board decisions had further effects on the Japanese and Nisei congregation. For example, the social hall had been reserved for some time, on one Saturday night per month, for meetings or social activities for the Japanese. Suddenly they found that that night was filled with social activities for the Caucasian Methodist Youth Fellowship. A "*shikataganai*" (literally, "cannot be helped") or stoical attitude prevailed among the Japanese Americans, and they expressed few words of protest. One Japanese American board member approached the bishop of the southern district with a plea to improve the situation— but to no avail. The Caucasian church members made no direct attempts to change the deteriorating interracial relationship. The Japanese American congregation gave up and stopped participating in church activities; they perceived the situation as an attempt to give them second-class membership status and to drive them out of the church. Since the Caucasian group had originally introduced the idea of a merger, and since the Japanese had donated funds for the construction of the new structure, the Japanese were troubled. Nonetheless they meekly accepted the situation.

Many Nisei left the church and attended no other religious institution. Others left the church and started to participate in the activities of the nearby Buddhist temple; this group was especially interested in maintaining some institutional ties with a Japanese American religious organization. They apparently believed that the retention of ethnic ties was of paramount importance, since the Caucasians, as a group, had indicated the unacceptability of the Japanese Americans as full members of their religious institution. One member who came from the Methodist church stated: "I started to attend the Buddhist temple for the sake of my children. There, they could meet other Japanese Americans and meet other boys and girls with whom they could play and eventually date. And then I started to learn about Buddhism. It has really been a great help to me and my family."

Racial differences between the Caucasians and Nikkei have not occurred in many other instances, perhaps because the Japanese Americans have been able to retain control over all facets of church organizations, monies, and programs in other churches.

Ethnic Community Solidarity

Ethnic community solidarity is defined not only in terms of affective ties; the BCA has instituted practices to maintain group cohesiveness along racial and religious lines as well. The members of the Buddhist churches have encouraged racial and religious intramarriage, attendance at Japanese language schools, community picnics, sports activities, and religious conferences. These practices not only ensure the continued ties of members or possible members to their religious institution, but they also allow the Japanese to congregate and socialize within a homogeneous group.[46]

Ethnic community solidarity has been a persistent feature of the NABM and BCA. The basis of the organization's structure, the role and recruitment of ministers, and the preponderance of Japanese and Nikkei members have all kept the BCA remarkably identifiable as an American ethnic institution.

One central example of ethnicity is the food bazaar. Most Japanese American organizations, especially the Buddhist churches, feature a yearly food sale or bazaar where barbecued teriyaki chicken is an important customer-drawing item. Chicken is relatively inexpensive and ensures a higher profit than other foodstuffs. A teriyaki chicken dinner is quite similar from church to church: a quarter to half a chicken; rice, either plain white or *sushi* style; a fruit, with a decided preference for an orange or apple; something sweet, a cupcake or Asian cookie (*senbei*); and the inevitable parsley for garnish and color. There is often also teriyaki beef and noodles (*udon*) at the food bazaars, and for those who prefer them, hamburgers and hot dogs. But the overwhelming volume of sales to both the Asian and Caucasian customers is of Japanese foods.

Most of those who attend the food bazaars are Japanese or Japanese Americans, members of the sponsoring church, or others in the surrounding Japanese communities, primarily because most publicity is by word of mouth or posters hung in establishments with a Japanese or Nikkei clientele. The bazaars are held on a regular basis, and community members can come to renew friendships, socialize, and have a family meal outside the home. Whatever outside publicity may be available, such as newspapers, television, or radio announcements, is usually not extensively exploited.

The food sales or food bazaars emphasize ethnic heritage. The Japanese Americans sell foods that are their national specialties, and that Caucasians generally do not prepare at all. Furthermore, the sales are a sort of Japanese "gathering of the clans," emphasizing a particular place and time where Japanese Americans have created their own territory;[47] any non-Japanese may feel that he is in the minority, or even an interloper. While the primarily economic motive for the food bazaars cannot be overlooked, the intragroup camaraderie and the opportunity to socialize with like people aid in understanding why these events persist. After all, most of the Japanese and Nikkei who attend the bazaars could well prepare the dishes themselves. That they continue to support the bazaars and do not extensively alter the menu indicates the extent to which ethnic community solidarity operates among the Japanese Americans.

A few observations concerning the food sales should be mentioned. First, since the profits of the bazaar go to maintain the church, many people, if not most, attend not only to buy food but also to aid the organization. In this case, sustaining an ethnic religious organization becomes a primary motive. Second, although many Japanese are able to make their own teriyaki chicken, the churches, after years of trial and error, have perfected a teriyaki recipe that may be more tasty than one prepared at home. At one church, for example, the cooks buy a prepared sauce from the city's best Japanese restaurant to insure a tasty chicken. Except in this latter case, the recipe can usually be obtained from the food committee and thus can be easily duplicated at home; yet people still come to purchase the dinner. Third, some non-Japanese food has been introduced in the food sales: boiled corn, pies, tamales, and tacos. The addition of these foodstuffs depends upon the capacity of the church to prepare them, and they are usually donated to the church bazaar.[48] These foods are served to give the Nisei, and especially the Sansei, a variety of choices; they are never given primary importance and are merely used to supplement the main attractions.

Every Buddhist church maintains some type of social function, either to benefit its members or to raise funds to sustain Buddhist activities. These functions also help defray the cost of supporting a church with a resident *kaikyoshi.* Many churches maintain a large activities program in addition to the regular religious-oriented services. Placer Buddhist Church, Penryn, California, for example, "keeps the [Japanese] community together"[49] and "serves as the Japanese social life center."[50] Furthermore, this church has a number of activities that aid in identifying the Buddhist church as a social center:

> The church as a social center is well illustrated by numerous activities affiliated with it. A Japanese language school is held at the church. The Sierra Bonsai Club holds its meeting at the church. Various women's groups and youth organizations are also part of the many social events of the church. Basketball, baseball and volleyball teams are organized for the younger members of the church. Japanese benefit movies are also frequently held at the church so non-Japanese people can better understand the Japanese culture and people.[51]

In many cases, unless the social event is sponsored directly by the church, the organizers are asked to give a donation for the use of the church building. Thus, the Bonsai Club or a private language school may utilize the space, and while the church gives service to its members, it also receives monetary support.[52]

The present social activities can be seen as a result of the relationship of the church to the members and of the members to the wider social environment. Historically, the Japanese in America were excluded from full participation in the mainstream of American life, especially in the period from the late 1800s to 1924, and again in the 1942 to 1945 evacuation. The church has attempted to meet this problem by offering its members and the surrounding Japanese community a program of religious and social activities. Thus, within the church, the *Fujinkai* was the social center for the Issei woman. The purpose of the *Fujinkai* was to aid the church in preparing refreshments or food, conducting the bazaars, helping needy families, and other such necessary activities. In addition, the women's groups allowed Issei women to gather together and socialize in a racially homogeneous surrounding. The YBA, as well as the Junior YBA, cater to the Nisei and now the Sansei by holding dances or sports activities under the direct sponsorship of the church.

At any one church, the differing auxiliary organizations depend upon the constituency. Where there are many young members, a large number of youth-oriented organizations will be found. For example, Orange County Buddhist Church, Anaheim, California, was started in the 1920s[53] with a minister commuting from the Los Angeles Betsuin. A Sunday School and a Japanese language school were established in the late 1920s along with a Young Women's Buddhist Association and a Young Men's Buddhist Association in the 1930s. With the rapid postwar increase of the Nikkei population in Orange County, by 1971, the Youth Department was created. The Youth Department, with its own budget and director, coordinates the social, athletic, and religious activities of the various age groups. For girls from six to twelve years of age, the Golden Chain Club, which meets after Sunday School, not only takes part in the religious services but also learns cooking and baking, visits other churches, and aids in a senior citizens' project. The Dharma Wheel Club, for boys from ten to twelve years of age, emphasizes sports activities. For the youth from thirteen to fifteen, the Sangha Teens aids the church through various service projects while also sponsoring their own social activities. For youths from fifteen to nineteen years, the Junior YBA also combines services to the church (aiding in the church festivals, helping in church bazaars, and sponsoring social events, such as athletics) with religious-oriented activities (church youth conferences or religious seminars). The Senior YBA , open to those twenty years of age and older, offers the same religious and social activities as its junior equivalent.

This particular church also offers a broad range of activities for adults. The Adult Buddhist Association, composed mainly of Nisei, provides services and leadership for the youth organization as well as for the church itself. The church also has a *Fujinkai* and a Junior Matrons group. Their respectively Japanese and English titles are significant: although the terms are sometimes used interchangeably, they often imply an Issei/Nisei division. At churches where there are many active women, there may be two groups, the Junior Matrons association being composed of Nisei women and the senior *Fujinkai* group of Issei. The Junior Matrons of Orange County, formed in 1957, aids the church in the same capacity as the senior *Fujinkai* at other churches.

Thus, from early youth through adulthood, there is an active social and recreational program that serves as an adjunct to the age-graded religious activities, from Sunday Schools to the adult services. The emphasis on youth activities is strong. In 1972, the Golden Chain Club had sixty members; the Dharma Wheel Club, thirteen; the Sangha Teens, forty-four; the Junior YBA, fifty-six; and the Senior YBA, thirty, for a combined total of 147. There were only 164 paid members in 1972, with the Sunday School population at ninety-nine.[54]

The age group breakdowns at any one church will largely dictate the type of organizations that the church will sponsor. In Orange County, there is also a probability, for the near future at least, that more young Nikkei couples and their children will migrate to the area. Other Buddhist churches nearer the central Los Angeles basin will retain settled families, while losing the more mobile younger ones. The suburbs of Los Angeles offer a better climate, less smog, and less overpopulation; with the increase of tract home construction in the area and the increasing mobility of the Nikkei, the Orange County Buddhist Church has been gaining many new members.

This church is new to the BCA. Although it was established in the early 1920s, with a church building constructed in 1936, it operated as a branch of the Los Angeles Betsuin until 1965. A new church building was erected in 1964, and in 1965 the organization requested and received new status as an independent church with a permanent resident minister. The membership in 1965 totaled eighty-five families; by 1972, there were ninety-three member families with 164 paying members.

Southern Alameda County Buddhist Church, located between Oakland and San Jose, California, is another organization that has gained in Nikkei population since World War II. The area covered by this church includes Fremont and Hayward, California. From the 1920s until 1954, ministerial assistance was provided on an infrequent basis by Alameda Buddhist Church, Alameda, California. From 1955 onward, with rapid commercial development and the construction of suburban tract housing, has come an influx of younger married couples working in the nearby metropolitan San Francisco Bay area and San Jose. By 1964, a new church building was completed in Union City, California, with a large Japanese language school student body (109 students in 1964)[55] and Dharma School (Sunday School, with seventy-eight students in 1972)[56] already in progress. Here, as elsewhere where there are many young children, there are a Junior YBA, a Sunday School, and the Athletic Association which coordinates a basketball league and volleyball games. From forty-one member families in 1961, membership had grown to seventy-seven families by 1972.[57]

Other churches have not fared so well since the end of the war. For example, the Santa Barbara Buddhist Church, established in 1912, had eighty member families by 1930 with a Sunday School of seventy-five pupils; by 1972,[58] it had sixty-eight member families with forty-eight students in Sunday School.[59] The Vacaville Buddhist Church has terminated independent operation altogether; a fire destroyed the church building in 1951, and membership had been declining for years.[60] Established in 1909, the Vacaville church in 1931 had a total of 175 member families with a Sunday School enrollment of fifty-five.[61] The church members are now under the jurisdiction and ministership of the Sacramento Betsuin.

Membership Statistics

By 1931, the NABM had 11,852 member families:

> Almost all of these are the first generation immigrants. Here, however, another fact must be taken into consideration in estimating the actual influence of Buddhism in the United States and Canada. In Japan, by the very nature of the family life, which is strongly patriarchal, the religion of the father is believed in by the wife and children. Although this custom may not apply strictly to the families of Japanese immigrants in North America, it is a safe estimate, the writer believes, to consider [that] three-fifths of the family members [share] the beliefs of the patriarchs. Supposing there are five in each family, which is very conservative number, there must be at least thirty-five thousand Buddhists under the NABM.[62]

Although Ogura's figure of 35,000 Buddhists under the NABM in 1931 is an estimate, it is as reliable as could be expected from the data available to him.

The NABM used various methods to compute its membership. In most temples or churches, the membership count was by number of families, with the head of the family representing the rest. This method allowed a relatively stable count, as individual family sizes change with births or deaths, or as individuals depart for work or school and leave the family's church. The BCA recognizes the fact that as the children grow into their late teens or early twenties, and until they marry and start their own families, because of attendance at schools or service in the armed forces, they may not participate in church functions or aid in the various church financial programs. The family membership system, utilized in Japan, allows the church to obtain a reasonable estimate of church membership dues and to project a realistic budget. However, some churches do count their membership by individuals, while others utilize a combination of family membership and individual membership to arrive at an aggregate listing.

It is not unusual to find a family with from five to eight members counted as "one," and it is therefore difficult to ascertain the total number of Buddhists in America. The situation is further complicated in that many Buddhists do not belong to an individual temple, although they may sporadically attend church services and functions. Yet, the church leaders have long recognized the importance of reliable statistics on the actual number of members. From 1957 to 1975, except in two instances, there has been a continual increase in the budget of BCA headquarters, which depends upon contributions from the member temples.[63] With a growth in the actual income of BCA headquarters from $25,456 in 1937 to $312,673 in 1975, the importance of membership statistics for planning projects and disbursing monies according to the needs of the entire membership became apparent.

Several attempts have been made to gather reliable population statistics for the NABM and BCA. The most accurate data were collected by the War Relocation Authority during the incarceration period 1942–1945 and by the membership census conducted by the BCA in 1972 (see Table 3).

Before commenting on the implications of these data, a brief discussion of their reliability is in order. For the 1930 family membership figure, Ogura obtained his data from the NABM; he then estimated that,

TABLE 3

NABM–BCA Membership Statistics, 1931–1972

	1930[1]	1936[2]	1942[3]	1960[4]	1972[5]
Family Membership	11,852	14,388	Not available	10,000	14,008
Estimated total Membership	35,000	43,164	46,289	50,000	43,476

1. Ogura, op. cit., p. 13.
2. Freed and Luomala, op. cit. Their source was the census of Religious Bodies, 1936.
3. War Relocation Authority, *The Evacuated People,* Table 24, p. 79. The WRA lists the number of Buddhists as 61,719. However, Freed and Luomala estimate that 75 percent of the Buddhists are Jodo Shinshu Buddhists. (Seventy-five percent of 61,719 is 46,289.) For further clarification, see the text.
4. Dorothy A. Stroup, "The Role of the Japanese American Press in Its Community," Master's Thesis, University of California, Los Angeles, 1960, p. 85.
5. Reverend J. Tsumura and George Aoki, BCA Census Committee, BCA census, September 1, 1972.

with five persons in each family, a multiple of three-fifths would give a conservative figure. The 1936 figure covered all Jodo Shinshu Buddhists, with an "estimated average of three members of each Buddhist family (belonging) to the church . . . (for) a total of 43,164 members."[64] The 1942 figure represents a 25 percent sample survey of the 111,170 incarcerated Japanese and Japanese Americans. The Buddhist category was not broken down into the various denominations:

> Of the eight major Buddhist sects found in Japan, six are represented in the United States and Hawaii. The six are Shin, Shingon, Zen, Nichiren, Tendai and Jodo. Only the first four named are numerically important in the United States, and of them the Shin is by far the strongest, having a membership that is estimated to include three-fourths of the Buddhists in this country. . . . Though the Shin denomination has ten subsects in Japan, only two are represented in the United States. They are the Nishi Hongwanji

and the Higashi Hongwanji, and of them the Nishi subsect has by far the greater number of members.[65]

Thus, religious census data from the camps do not adequately separate the Nishi Hongwanji from the Higashi Hongwanji sects of Jodo Shinshu. The WRA census for 1942 lists 61,719 respondents as Buddhists, but a WRA researcher estimates that 75 percent of that number are actually Jodo Shinshu Buddhists.[66] Thus, the conservative figure of 46,289 is given in Table 3. The best organized Buddhist religious order was the NABM, with programs and ministers at every camp. The non-Jodo Shinshu Buddhist groups were less organized, and their members joined in the NABM religious services and activities. In the Jodo Shinshu religious body itself, some camps had joint services for the Nishi Hongwanji and the Higashi Hongwanji or NABM-BCA, and the figure 46,289 is almost certainly an underrepresentation from the camp population. Also, the total camp population is given as 111,170, even though the total Japanese and Japanese American population according to 1940 United States census was 126,947. The difference between the two statistics suggests some degree of underrepresentation of the total number of Buddhists in the United States. Those Buddhists residing on the East Coast, or in the southern or midwestern states, as well as those in hospitals, could not be counted, since most did not enter the camps. The 1960 figure of 50,000 members is an estimate from BCA headquarters, but the sheer roundness of the number makes it suspect.

The 1972 population figure is the most complete attempt at tabulation conducted by the BCA. Each church was asked to designate a census chairman to coordinate information by families. Each family was asked to complete a form which named the head of the family, spouse, and all children with their respective ages. There were again significant instances of under- and overrepresentation. For the former, the census committee co-chairman estimates over 30 percent underreport the members.[67] Not all churches fully cooperated in the count.[68] There were apparently two main reasons: first, many churches believed that a large family membership might be reflected in future increases in the assessment of church dues to be forwarded to BCA headquarters. Second, the churches with large memberships had difficulty in contacting all their members. This problem was compounded at churches that had branch temples some distance from the main temple. For example, the

Tri-State Buddhist Church, located in Denver, has jurisdiction over the entire state of Colorado, plus Scottsbluff, Nebraska. The Fresno Betsuin, as another example, handles eleven separate subtemples with at least 2,216 members.

The 1972 census also contains a slight overrepresentation. Some individuals were counted as members of churches where they once paid dues, even though they had not paid for the past year or two. These persons may still be considered active members, if they still attend the church services and take part in the social functions; but since they do not pay dues, they should be listed as nonmembers.

NABM membership increased from 1930 to 1942. The increase actually began prior to the 1930s. As Ogura states, "Since the passage of the immigration law of 1924, the members of the Buddhist churches showed a rapid increase."[69] Although data for the 1936 and 1960 computations are probably less reliable than those for 1930, 1942, and 1972, the trend for Buddhist membership is not unlike that for all churches in the United States: "Growth of American church membership, which soared in the 1950's and slowed in the 1960's, now has come to a virtual standstill."[70] The adjusted 1972 BCA census figure of 43,476 represents a decrease from the 1942 and 1960 estimates, and is close to the 43,164 figure estimated for 1936.

When the estimated BCA constituency is compared to the Japanese American population of the continental United States, the problem of membership is further highlighted. The Japanese American population, 126,947 in 1940, had increased to 373,983 by 1970.[71] With a decrease in BCA members from 1960 to 1972, the BCA has not only been unable to maintain a constant ratio in relation to the total population, but it has also been unable to retain even its potential membership. One reason for this loss is obvious. The Issei have historically been the strongest supporters in both attendance and monetary contributions; they constituted 34.6 percent of the Japanese American population in 1942, while the Nisei and a few Sansei accounted for 66.4 percent.[72] At the same time, 68.5 percent of the Issei gave their religion as Buddhist, as compared to 48.7 percent of the Nisei.[73] The average age of the Issei and Nisei male in 1941 was, respectively, fifty-five and nineteen.[74] Thus, by 1972, the surviving Issei males would be perhaps eighty-six, and the Nisei, perhaps fifty. The Issei no longer have control of the BCA; since the 1950s, the Nisei have come to accept the responsibilities left to them by their parents.

Another probable reason for the loss in membership is a negative one. The BCA as an organization has never systematically attempted to proselytize. Instead, it has sought to retain the existing membership and to encourage the young children of the members to remain within the Jodo Shinshu religion. Six programs lately instituted by the BCA to hold onto their members are the Soldier's Identification Kit, the Sangha and Karuna awards, the Sarana Affirmation Ceremony, the Relevant American Buddhist (RAB) program, visits to prisons, the BCA correspondence program, and the lay speakers program. The objective of the first three programs is to retain the Buddhists in the BCA, while that of the latter three is oriented toward service and information dissemination.

The Soldier's Identification Kit was instituted in 1951 for those Buddhists entering or serving in the armed forces.[75] The kit consists of a bronze Buddhist medallion and various Buddhist written materials. Two years prior to the development of the kit, the Hawaiian and continental United States YBA were successful in their negotiations with the U.S. Army to identify those Buddhist servicemen desiring recognition of their religious preference. Henceforth, the letter "B" or the word "Buddhist" would be included on the individual's dog-tag identification if he so desired.

The Sangha and Karuna awards are recognized religious awards for deserving Boy Scouts and Camp Fire Girls. The Sangha award committee was organized in October 1954 to:

> give the scouts of Buddhist faith a practical guidance in achieving the spiritual pledge made in the Scout Oath and Law, thereby developing a boy whose views and actions in life would stem from the highest of Buddhist thought. . . . Further, the Award program duly recognizes the twelfth point of the Scout Law that the scout "is faithful in his religious duties and respects the convictions of others in matters of custom and religion." The scout is expected to receive religious training and participate actively in his temple program.[76]

To receive the award, the Boy Scout must be a first-class scout or an Explorer Scout for one year; he must understand the precepts of Buddhism and actively participate and aid in temple activities. By 1972, ninety-one

Sangha awards were presented. Nineteen churches sponsor a Boy Scout program, and the BCA has authorized several ministers to serve as Buddhist chaplains at various Scout Jamborees since 1957.[77] The Sangha award is not exclusively a BCA program. It is presented and approved by four other, though numerically smaller, Buddhist subdivisions and sects: Koyasan, Higashi Hongwanji, Jodo Shu, and Zen Shu. But the most active participating organization is the BCA. The award is seen as an important step toward maintaining Buddhist ties in a boy's life.[78] The Camp Fire Karuna (literally, "kindness") award is the girl's equivalent to the boy's Sangha award. Approved by the BCA and other Buddhist institutions, the award has also received the sanction of the Camp Fire Girls organization.

The Confirmation Ceremony (*Kikyoshiku*) is a rite for Buddhists who wish to pledge themselves as life-long adherents to the faith. The *Kikyoshiku* is open to all, regardless of age, and is traditionally performed in Japan by the lord abbot of the Nishi Hongwanji. It includes a service, tonsuring (to symbolize entrance into the religious order), and the bestowal of a Buddhist name. In America, this rite usually awaited the sporadic visits of the lord abbot, but in April 1962, Shinsho Hanayama, then BCA bishop, conducted the service for sixty-eight persons at the San Jose Betsuin.[79] The *Kikyoshiku* has a continuous history from the time of the Shakamuni Buddha[80] in India, but it is infrequently practiced in America. On very rare occasions the ceremony, called the Sarana Affirmation Ceremony, has been performed for newborn children, where the parents pledge "before Buddha that the child will be nurtured in the Buddhist tradition to the best of (their) ability."[81]

The RAB program was briefly discussed earlier in this chapter. The national YBA and the BCA recognize that the future of their religion and their organization depends on the youth:

> The young adults in this age group [from high school juniors to 25 years of age] are highly predisposed to search [for] identity, purpose, and religious conviction. Therefore, every possible means must be garnered to cater to these precious aspirations and allow full maturity. *Only in this way can these young adults be kept within the religious or spiritual "arena," thereby maintaining their affiliation to the church.*[82] (Emphasis added)

The emphasis indicates the BCA's overt recognition of the membership problem. The RAB program, officially approved in December 1971, was established to serve as a conduit for information and guidance. Eight RAB field workers were designated to provide speakers, ideas, and pro-grams; coordinate youth groups and activities; organize religious sem-inars and community projects; and offer programs for college students. At many churches—for example, the Berkeley Buddhist Church, and the San Diego Buddhist Church—the youth organizations of the late 1960s, especially the Junior YBA, languished for lack of youth partici-pation and support. It is still too soon to estimate the success or failure of this program. However, some RAB representatives report a growing enthusiasm among Sansei and ministers for effecting changes in church youth programs and activities.[83]

The RAB coordinators are predominantly Sansei (a recent RAB co-ordinator is Caucasian) and have an extensive history of participation in their temples and in BCA-sponsored conferences. They see their po-sition as one of mediator between the BCA administration and the youth organizations. These coordinators act as spokesmen within the various temples; since the creation of the RAB, the latent schism be-tween old and young has become overt. Many Nisei parents apparently feel that they cannot communicate with the younger members of the church, and the coordinators are used as the medium of reconciliation. For instance, at one temple when the Sansei desired an interracial dance, the coordinator was used to explain the situation to the parents. The parents may still disagree with the desires of the young, but with the BCA sanction given to the RAB, the coordinators are able to speak to them with some degree of authority and respectability.

As a result of the lack of communication and understanding between many parents and their children, many youths do not participate in church activities. By bringing back the teenaged and college-aged youth through various temple programs, the BCA hopes to alleviate the grow-ing problem of membership decline.

The BCA Bureau of Buddhist Education directs and houses corres-pondence courses, the prison inmate project, and the lay speakers pro-grams. The BCA receives many letters from persons across the United States seeking information about Buddhism. Although it does not so-licit these letters, the significance of the correspondence has not been overlooked: "These people can become potential members if they can be reached through correspondence courses."[84] Some English-speaking ministers and members are endeavoring to institute a detailed course of instruction in Buddhist philosophy and literature.

Following the tradition of Japan, where Jodo Shinshu missionaries have aided Buddhists in penal institutions, the BCA has encouraged their ministers to visit American prisons. Since 1967, monthly Buddhist services have been conducted for about twenty inmates of the California State Correctional Facility, Soledad, and since 1970, Buddhism has been offered as part of the San Quentin religious classes. Buddhist services are also offered at the Federal Correctional Institution, Lompoc, California, and the California Men's Colony at San Luis Obispo.[85] Not all the inmates who attend are Japanese Americans. Besides the regular services, special visitations have been made throughout the correctional institutions in California and at the Nevada State Prison, Carson City, while a continual program of correspondence is maintained throughout the United States with inmates requesting information about the religion.[86]

The Buddhist Education Department has also instituted public lectures, with noted Buddhist scholars as speakers; presented speeches at various educational institutions upon request; and instituted a lay speakers program to aid Buddhist conferences and outside groups requesting information about Buddhism.

The purposes of all of the above, from the Soldier's Identification Kit through the RAB program to the lay speakers program, are (1) to retain the Buddhist membership who, for a variety of reasons, may decline to be active church supporters or (2) to educate other individuals who desire to learn about the religion. The active recruitment of new members—that is, a concerted effort to encourage individuals to join the BCA—is noticeably absent. At the individual temples, the minister may pay visits to families who were once supporters of the temple or to other Japanese Americans known to be from Buddhist families, but there has been no concerted membership drive at any level of the BCA.

The six programs were created to meet the needs of the changing population of the BCA. For the Issei, continuation of the religious practices they knew in Japan was sufficient; but with the birth of the Nisei, religious education for the children was instituted, in the form of Sunday Schools and YBAs. The Sansei participate in both organizations and the RAB program.

The 1972 BCA census reflects not only the important position of the youth but also the decline in membership from the 1940s and 1950s. Table 4 indicates the membership breakdown by age within the BCA.

TABLE 4

1972 BCA Membership Statistics, by Age Group

Age in Years	Male	Female	Total	Category
0–9	1,234	1,151	2,385	*Youth* (0–19 yrs.) (8,998) 28.92%
10–19	3,391	3,222	6,613	
20–29	2,237	1,886	4,123	*Young Adult* (20–39 yrs.) (6,238) 20.05%
30–39	914	1,201	2,115	
40–49	2,239	2,664	4,903	*Adult* (40–59 yrs.) (10,251) 32.95%
50–59	2,814	2,534	5,348	
60–69	1,076	1,043	2,119	*Elderly* (60–99 yrs.) (5,626) 18.08%
70–79	789	1,526	2,315	
80–89	502	505	1,007	
90–99	132	53	185	
Subtotal	15,328	15,785	31,113	
Nonreport of Age			2,330	
Subtotal			33,443	
Plus 30% Underreport[1]			10,033	
Total			43,476	
Family Head (10,783 + 30% underreport)			14,018	

[1] Personal correspondence with George Aoki, October 25, 1972. Aoki estimates that there is over 30 percent underreporting.

SOURCE: BCA Census, September 1, 1972, Reverend J. Tsumura and George Aoki, BCA Census Committee.

The census gives 33,443 members actually counted. This figure does not include an estimated 30 percent underreporting, but does include 2,330 persons who did not report their age. The remainder, 31,113, indicates that the Issei group, with 18.08 percent, is the smallest, and the Nisei group, with 32.9 percent, the next smallest. The Sansei group (although the thirty to thirty-nine year age group includes a small number of Nisei) is the largest, with 48.9 percent of the reported population.

The Nisei membership's recognition of the youth has come relatively late. The reason is clear. After resettlement from the camps, the ministers and the Nisei members were, by necessity, preoccupied with reestablishing their churches and temples on a sound fiscal foundation. The members themselves were occupied with gaining or regaining their means of livelihood. The Sansei from zero to nineteen years of age were not yet born; and there were, conversely, more Issei still actively supporting the church. In the 1950s, the Nisei became numerically important, as the Issei group diminished and more children were born.

The NABM was obviously cognizant of the Buddhist youth, as discussed earlier, since it introduced the Sunday Schools and encouraged the training of Nisei ministers. In 1963, the BCA instituted the Youth Department within the Bureau of Buddhist Education, with a Nisei minister, Reverend Hogen Fujimoto, as the director. The Youth Department aids organizations such as the YBA and Junior YBA with their religious workshops, conferences, awards, scholarships, and publications. Given this recognition of the importance of youth within the BCA, it is only reasonable to predict increasing emphasis and encouragement of activities oriented toward that age group.

Over 32 percent of the BCA's membership falls within the forty to fifty-nine year age category. This adult group constitutes the present leadership stratum. Most Issei, those now in the sixty and over age category, have passed on to the Nisei the responsibilities for fund-raising and church social activities (such as movies, picnics, and bazaars), and have given up their positions on the various church boards of directors. While the Sansei are most important to the future of the church, and the Issei were important to its genesis, the Nisei now hold sway.

The Nisei group was responsible for the suborganizations now being utilized by the Sansei—the Junior and Senior YBA. Since they have passed from the age appropriate to these two organizations, the Nisei have created two new suborganizations suited to their needs. The

Western Adult Buddhist League was formed in 1949 by those YBA leaders active during World War II. Initially the Young Adult Buddhist League (YABL), the organization was formed to retain former YBA members who had married and were in the process of raising a family. The goals of YABL were to aid the churches or temples, support the BCA and its activities, and assist in the Sunday Schools and YBA activities at the various churches. The name YABL was changed to the Western Adult Buddhist League in 1965, as an indication that it encompassed all territory bordering on the Pacific Coast. The YABL has been particularly helpful in financial activities designed to sustain the BCA.

At the individual temples, the members also have the Adult Buddhist Association (ABA). The members of ABA are usually parents of YBA and Junior YBA members, and/or of children attending Sunday Schools. ABA groups therefore direct much of their energy toward sustaining these programs by raising money and sponsoring parties and outings. Most of the funds they raise are used to augment the minister's salary and to maintain or renovate temple buildings.

The National Federation of Buddhist Women's Associations was created in 1952 as a general forum for women's groups at the various local temples or churches. The predominantly Issei *Fujinkai*, as well as their Nisei counterparts, the Matrons, send delegates to the National Federation's annual conference. In this way, the individual women's groups, originally formed as social and charitable organizations with a purely local focus, have attained national scope.

For the elderly men and women, who comprise 18 percent of the BCA population, the only essential active and churchwide organization is the *Fujinkai*. Issei males infrequently become presidents of their churches or other elected officials. More often they are elder statesmen or advisers to the Nisei leaders on any long-range plans, such as relocating a church structure or constructing a new Sunday School building. The active participation of the elderly, except through attendance at the religious services, has greatly diminished in the past few years.

Thus, the problem of membership, with reference to generation, has resulted in the adoption or creation of suborganizations that aid the constituency. From RAB for the Sansei to the *Fujinkai* for the Issei women, there has been a genesis and a continuity; for the Issei, there has been a diminution of the population, and thus a consequent lessening of activity and impact on the member temples and the BCA.

The Buddhist Sunday Schools

The Buddhist Sunday Schools are an important part of the NABM-BCA organization. Along with the Buddhist services, the Sunday Schools have been a strong factor in keeping Japanese American children within the Buddhist religion.

With the start of the Nisei births in the 1920s, the members and ministers of the NABM experienced a crisis that would remain a continuing problem. This crisis concerned the proper education of the Nisei to insure their adherence to Buddhism. The Buddhist Sunday School was thus created, "to make Buddhism an American religion by educating the children of the church members in the ideas and atmosphere of Buddhism; to insure a happy religious life for the individual and the family."[87] The continual problem of perpetuating Buddhism in America was long ago recognized by Ogura: "As the future of Buddhism in the United States depends almost entirely upon the second generation Japanese, the Sunday Schools fill an important position in the work of the Buddhist mission."[88]

Creating and sustaining this educational portion of the NABM was recognized as vitally important to the organization. The Sunday Schools, though, were not without precedent in Japan *prior* to their incorporation within the temples in America. Contrary to other researchers' writings on the BCA, the Buddhist Sunday Schools did not originate in the United States after the arrival of the Japanese immigrants.[89] The Sunday Schools, Young Men's Buddhist Associations, and other such institutions were already in Japan by the late nineteenth and early twentieth centuries. The reasons for the adoption of the Euro-American forms of religious propagation are instructive.

Even before the Jodo Shinshu Buddhist religion was established in America, Japan's Buddhist leaders had sent priests to Europe to study Western religions and their activities. Other Buddhist priests visited the United States to observe religious conditions there through the 1870s, as a result of which changes within the Japanese religious institution occurred.[90] After the Tokugawa era (1601–1868), the Meiji authorities attempted to suppress Buddhism and to make Shintoism the state religion. This move could have resulted in the "complete expulsion of Buddhism from Japan."[91] Aided by reports and observations about the West, the lord abbots of the Nishi and Higashi Hongwanji petitioned the Meiji authorities to allow the Japanese people the right to practice any religion they chose. This petition was accepted in 1876, and as a result the Jodo Shinshu sect, in particular, was able to reassert itself in Japanese national life. Freedom of worship, coupled with the insights brought back from Europe and America, helped revitalize and reorganize Buddhism in Japan.

The Jodo Shinshu Buddhists in Japan adopted certain European and American techniques of religious dissemination. Thus, in the late 1800s and early 1900s, not only the Sunday Schools, but also Buddhist women's societies, orphanages, and Buddhist homes for ex-convicts were instituted. During this phase of Japanese infatuation with Western ideas, some Buddhist sects inaugurated street preaching, "evangelical" campaigns, sermonizing, and hymnals along "Christian" lines.[92] The changes were made primarily to resolve problems that Buddhist organizations were having with the Meiji authorities. For one thing, the government then favored Occidental ideas and practices, and for another, the changes alleviated the problem of membership losses resulting from the apparent complacency of the Buddhist leaders during the Tokugawa era.

The Japanese model was resurrected in the United States with the birth of the Nisei, when the need for some form of educational institution became apparent. As Ogura states, "All the Sunday Schools are modeled after those of Japan, which are conducted by the Shin sect."[93] The first Sunday School in America was established in 1913 by the San Francisco headquarters.[94] The early teachers were the *kaikyoshi* and their wives; later, with more students attending the classes, YMBA and YWBA members were trained and assisted the priests in conducting classes. The various Sunday Schools from the early 1920s to the middle 1930s were affected by conditions at the member temples. The programs and quality of instruction varied according to the talents of resident ministers and interested lay leaders. Mrs. Kiyo Kyogoku gives her impression of the early Sunday Schools: "I was disappointed in the first Sunday School session I attended on my arrival [from Japan] forty years ago [1912]. It consisted of practicing a few secular songs and listening to fairy tales."[95] At that time, the lessons and tales were given in Japanese and were apparently copied from the Jodo Shinshu Sunday Schools of Japan.

For the Buddhist churches in America and for the Buddhists themselves, the designation of Sunday as the day to hold services has no religious significance. Sunday was chosen as a matter of convenience, since in the United States most individuals and families do not work on that day. However, at some churches, the term *Sunday School* is a misnomer. Localities where the members were predominantly agricultural workers often held their services on Saturdays. Sunday was a workday for these people, as they prepared farming produce for distribution to the urban markets for Monday sales.[96]

Aware of the possibility that the Buddhist Sunday Schools might be mistaken for Christian Sunday Schools, some Buddhist churches have changed the old designation to Dharma Schools.[97] Others have instituted monthly Saturday night family services[98] to encourage the children and their parents to attend services together. The Sunday Schools, like many other activities and programs in the Buddhist churches, are best understood as having arisen to meet the demands of the Buddhist members.

The Sunday School was the first organization under the NABM to be directly affected by transplantation to America. The Buddhist education of the Nisei was an immediate challenge to the Issei because the Nisei manifested the immediate influence of their new homeland. As K. Kyogoku states:

> The strongest reason all of us tried to build up the Sunday School came from a remark my husband overheard at a non-religious function of leaders of the Japanese community. At the meeting, a non-Buddhist minister chanced to say, "Oh, Buddhism will quietly fade away." My husband asked, "Why do you think so?" He replied, "The Issei may be members of your church, but they're sending their children to our Sunday Schools." My husband made a survey right away and was awestruck at the discovery that what the minister said was true."[99]

The Buddhist institution recognized this possibility in the 1920s with reference to the Nisei. The immediate problem concerned the appropriate method of education to counteract the loss of future members. The initial approach was to examine American religious educational techniques to ascertain those methods most suitable and adaptable for the NABM. One important source of information in the 1920s was a group of four ministers studying at the University of Southern California.[100] A few were majoring in religious education, and all helped the Southern

California Buddhist churches on weekends, especially in developing the embryonic Sunday Schools.

Beginning in the middle 1930s, English became the primary means of communication within the Sunday Schools, although the *kaikyoshi* continued to give sermons to the children in Japanese. Sunday School lesson cards, initially printed in Japanese, were later modified for the English-speaking children. The cards, of varying sophistication based on an age-graded system, had religious pictures that the preschool children could color and paste into books. For the advanced children, religious stories were used for instruction and discussion.

An annual NABM summer workshop (*kaki koshukai*) was inaugurated in about 1924 to coordinate and train Sunday School teachers more systematically. The workshops, held throughout California until the outbreak of the war in 1941, were attended by YMBA and YWBA members. The YMWBA teachers were taught by a team of resident area ministers. After the war, the use of picture cards and the more centralized training centers resulted in the development of a BCA Sunday School Department to coordinate most aspects of the religious education of Buddhist children.

By 1959, the training of the young was regarded as important enough to warrant a Bureau of Buddhist Education (BBE). Created by the BCA in 1959, the BBE became an umbrella bureau supervising the Youth Department, Sales Department (e.g., bookstore), Audio-Visual Departments, Boy Scout Committee, and public programs. The Sunday School Department came under the Bureau in 1963; until that time, it had been supervised by the Ministerial Association. This responsibility had been vested in the ministers because the Sunday Schools were primarily viewed as places for religious services. As more sophisticated educational methods were introduced, there was an increasing need to centralize control of the Sunday Schools for more efficient dissemination of materials such as films. Thus, in 1963, a full-time minister-director position was created to oversee the program; this resulted in a cohesive and integrated educational system for preschool to college-aged students.

The importance of youth to the BCA is reflected in the continually increasing annual budget of the BCA Sunday Schools. Whereas the first Sunday Schools were staffed and paid for, in the main, by the individual member temples, the BCA Sunday School budget had grown to $3,725 by 1948 and $7,000 by 1957.[101] Table 5 shows the current budget.

TABLE 5

Finances of the BCA Sunday School Department, 1970–1975

Year	Income	Expenditure
1970	$13,207.71	$12,674.93
1971	16,104.09	10,100.08
1972	15,703.93	21,344.49
1973	14,875.32	15,078.81
1974	13,691.42	13,705.68
1975	19,936.23	18,965.91

SOURCES: BCA, *Annual Report, 1970*, p. 38; *1971*, p. 41; *1972*, p. 42; *1973*, p. 35; *1974*, p. 35; *1975*, p. 27.

The BCA Sunday School Department gets its income from BCA member dues, donations for the national *Fujinkai* and the Western Adult Buddhist League, and sales of Sunday School curriculum materials and yearly BCA calendars. These funds are used to print curriculum materials, defray travel expenses, purchase office equipment supplies, and pay part of the BCA assistant's salary. Most Sunday Schools at the member temples or churches are staffed by volunteer superintendents and teachers; many also utilize Nisei and Sansei primary or secondary school teachers. The latter receive no financial remuneration except for a year-end *oseibo* ("thank-you" envelope) with from five to twenty or more dollars plus a bishop's Recognition Certificate Award for those teachers serving ten years or more. Gifts such as a plaque or pen are often given, but these are only small tokens of appreciation.

The Sunday School Department has various subdivisions, each with its own set of responsibilities: the Card Division, to produce lesson cards; the Music Division, to develop new *gathas* (hymns); the Research Division, to coordinate and produce age-graded lessons; the Slide and Story Division, to relate Buddhist stories through the use of various media; the Textbook Division, to compile a Buddhist textbook suitable for children; and the Creative Arts and Crafts program, to explore other multimedia approaches to Buddhist instruction.

The BCA Sunday School program attempts to use all available techniques and resources for the most effective presentation of Buddhist materials to the children. Innovations have often come through the personal efforts of Sunday School leaders. For example, Reverends Kyogoku, in the late 1940s, and Daisho Tana, from 1928, worked extensively to develop the paste-on lesson cards utilized until the middle 1950s. In 1960, Reverend Ensei Nekoda, director of the department, advocated a multi-resource approach, combining audio-visual, arts and crafts, and an age-graded thematic approach to the presentation of the Buddhist lessons. The themes utilized were geared to the various grade levels; for example, for the grade school children, the themes "Caring for Amida's children," "Interdependence," and "Appreciation of our Buddhist heritage" were stressed.

The effectiveness of the department cannot be measured by the number of students it serves. The department has very little to do with the recruitment of students and teachers; this is still the responsibility of the temples or churches. However, the 1972 BCA census reveals a decrease in the actual number of students as compared to an estimate for 1940 (see Table 6).

The decrease in Sunday School attendance from 1940 to 1972, coupled with the increase in the total Japanese American population

TABLE 6

Number of BCA-NABM Sunday School Students, 1913–1972
(Selected Years)

Year	Number of Churches with Sunday Schools	Number of Students
1913	1	Not available
1930	56	6,969
1940	65	7,500
1972	82[1]	6,209

1. Includes branch temples or churches.
SOURCES: for 1913, North American Buddhist Mission, op. cit., p. 48; for 1930, Ogura, op. cit., p. 18; for 1940, Spencer, op. cit., p. 81; and for 1972, BCA census.

during this same period, indicates a very substantial loss. Because Sunday School-aged children represent 28.9 percent of the BCA population, the decline in attendance has become a pressing concern for the BCA. BCA headquarters and individual temples had once hoped that the Sunday Schools would soon be overrun with children, provided entertaining and sophisticated teaching techniques were used. This has not proven to be the case. One tentative explanation might be that children attend the Sunday Schools not out of personal interest, but because of threats and pleadings from parents. The children enjoy playing with other children once they come to the temple but are less interested in the religious teachings, however attractively presented.

In interviews, many reverends and lay leaders indicated that the future of the Buddhist churches lies in the children. Despite this view, the Sunday Schools and Junior YBA are often given secondary consideration in the face of economic issues confronting individual temples. For example, the annual food bazaar at one small (198-member) southern California Buddhist church,[102] with a gross receipt of about $5,400 in 1974 and a net gain of about $3,000, is discussed at the board meetings for four months prior to the event, and in the last month before the bazaar is held it almost monopolizes the attention of the temple's leaders and members. The bazaar is important to the financial stability of the church; consequently, the Sunday School, with forty-eight students, is left solely to the Sunday School superintendent, the minister, and the teachers. The future members of the church are often given less consideration than present needs.

The problems of the smaller churches in sustaining an active Sunday School program are different from those of large churches. With fewer members, there are fewer volunteer-teachers, a smaller pool from which new teachers can be recruited, and fewer financial resources to subsidize new methods and techniques of presenting Buddhist materials. If the children are forced to attend Sunday Schools, the atmosphere will hardly be conducive to effective religious training. The first issue that must be resolved is the children's apparent disinclination to attend Sunday services; resolution of this problem will probably necessitate the closer attention of BCA leaders, member ministers, and interested family members. If, as the church leaders state, the future of the church depends upon these youngsters in the Sunday Schools, then the BCA as it is known today faces a bleak and uncertain prospect.

Notes

1. Befu, op. cit., p. 212.

2. The term *sociological death* was used to describe the process whereby blacks attempted to portray themselves as white. "For the negro to pass socially means sociological death and rebirth. It is extremely difficult, as one loses in the process his educational standing (if he has gone to a Negro school), intimate friends, family and work references." St. Clair Drake and Horace Cayton, *Black Metropolis* (New York: Harper and Row, 1945), p. 163.

3. Kazuo Kawai, "Three Roads and None Easy: An American Born Japanese Looks at Life," *Survey Graphics* (May 1, 1926): 165.

4. The Buddhist swastika extends in a counterclockwise fashion 卍, while the symbol associated with Nazi Germany extends clockwise 卐.

5. Munekata, op. cit., p. 166. The swastika is noticeable on the older structures, either embedded within the structure (see Los Angeles Betsuin, constructed in 1925), on the front windows as in San Francisco (Munekata, p. 145), or as a design on the front wall as in Sacramento (Munekata, p. 151).

6. Maude W. Madden, *When the East Is in the West* (New York: Fleming H. Revell Co., 1923; reprint ed., San Francisco: R and E Research Associates, 1971), p. 120.

7. Ibid., p. 128.

8. Reverend Arthur Takemoto, "The War Years," in Munekata, op. cit., p. 61.

9. *Kinnara Newsletter*, Los Angeles, September 1972.

10. "Part of the loss the evacuees suffered during their detention in camps was in communal religious property. Of the twenty-eight temples in Los Angeles, twenty-two were damaged, some almost beyond repair; in Seattle the Navy took over the temple for its use." William Petersen, *Japanese Americans* (New York: Random House, 1971), p. 178.

11. From 1948 to 1971, eighty-five new priests entered the BCA. Of that number, twenty-one have subsequently withdrawn, leaving sixty-four priests still active. There were, in addition, nineteen priests in active service from before 1948. BCA, *Annual Report, 1970*, pp. 1–4; the figures do not reflect changes since 1970.

12. Manimai Ratanamani, op. cit., p. 86.

13. Japanese American Curriculum Project, *Japanese Americans: The Untold Story* (New York: Holt, Rinehart and Winston, 1971).

14. Ethnic Studies Committee, Asian American Alliance, Stanford University, "Critical Reviews of *Japanese Americans: The Untold Story*," mimeographed, March 1971, p. 1; also a letter written to the San Francisco Station (KQED) objecting to the telecast, signed by the bishop of the BCA, the president of the board of directors, and the chairman of the Ministerial Research Committee, dated October 5, 1970, in the personal possession of the author.

15. Ethnic Studies Committee, op. cit., "Documentary Appendices," p. 10. Critiques by the other organizations did not always focus on religious bias, but on the pro-Japanese, anti-Chinese, Anglo-conformity, "model-minority" perspective.

16. Mimeographed letter dated October 6, 1970, in possession of the author.

17. "State Textbook Body Hears Buddhist Viewpoint Concerning 'Divine Creation,'" San Francisco *Hokubei Mainichi*, November 14, 1972, p. 1.

18. Ibid.

19. "Young Buddhists Pass Anti-War Resolution," Los Angeles *Kashu Mainichi*, May 25, 1971, p. 1.

20. The Reverend LaVerne Senyo Sasaki, "Buddhism and Social Activism," a lecture presented at the Western Young Buddhist League Conference, March 31, 1973, Los Angeles.

21. "JARF Gets Federal Approval for Apartment Construction," San Francisco *Hokubei Mainichi*, December 2, 1972. The Parlier Buddhist Church has also started a housing project for low-income persons.

22. The other participating churches are: Christ Episcopal Mission, San Francisco Independent Church, Konko Church, Nichiren Church. St. Xavier Mission, Zen Sokoji Mission, Seventh Day Adventist Church, Pine United Methodist Church, and Christ United Presbyterian Church.

23. "New Era of American Buddhism with Youth in Focus Emphasized," San Francisco *Hokubei Mainichi*, February 29, 1972, p. 1.

24. See Amy Tachiki, et al., *Roots: An Asian American Reader* (Los Angeles: UCLA Asian American Studies Center, 1971); and Joe R. Feagan and Nancy Fujitaki, "On the Assimilation of Japanese Americans," *Amerasia Journal* 1, no. 4 (February 1972): 13–31.

25. Marcus Lee Hansen, "The Third Generation in America," *Commentary* 14 (November 1952).

26. Yuki Yanagita, "Familial, Occupational, and Social Characteristics of Three Generations of Japanese Americans," Master's thesis, University of Southern California, Los Angeles, June 1968, pp. 35–37. "On the other hand, among the Sansei generation the percentage of Buddhists has increased, and the percentage of Protestants has decreased."

27. Most conferences on the ministerial and affiliated Buddhist organizational levels have included topics on the problem of the Sansei. Author's personal observation from 1970 to 1974.

28. Personal interview with BCA ministers.

29. Interview with Reverend Masami Fujitani, Oxnard Buddhist Church, Calif., June 14, 1974.

30. Interview with the Reverend Seiko Okahashi, Santa Barbara, June 6, 1974. Reverend Okahashi was formerly with the Seattle Buddhist Church and is one of three active women ministers in the BCA. Yonsei refers to the fourth generation or great-grandchildren of the Issei; Gosei are the fifth-generation Japanese Americans.

31. Ibid.

32. Reverend Osamu Fujimoto, "Nembutsu," in BCA, *Shin Buddhist Handbook*, p. 118.

33. Personal interview with Reverend S. Sakow, Santa Barbara, December 4, 1973.

34. Reverend J. Yanagihara, sermon given at a Buddhist conference, October 21, 1973, Los Angeles.

35. One researcher is in error when he states, "We can conclude that Buddhism as an indigenous religion from Japan had no formal experience with performing weddings in Japan." Isao Horinouchi, "Americanized Buddhism: A Sociological Analysis of a Protestantized Japanese Religion," Ph.D. dissertation, University of California, Davis, 1973, p. 164.

36. Personal interview with Reverends S. Sakow, December 4, 1973, Santa Barbara, and K. Terada, January 1, 1974, San Diego. Both Reverends Sakow and Terada had their marriage ceremonies performed in a Buddhist temple in Japan.

37. Interview with Reverend Terada.

38. Ibid.

39. Eidmann, *Young People's Introduction*, p. 40.

40. BCA, *Shin Buddhist Handbook*, pp. 125–136; and BCA, *Buddhism and Jodo Shinshu* (San Francisco, 1955), pp. 179–186.

41. Ibid., and Shoyu Hanayama, op. cit., pp. 12–29.

42. There have been a few non-Japanese members and ministers. The non-Asian membership has always been very small, however, usu-

ally limited to isolated but dedicated individuals and the spouses of Asian members. The non-Asian Buddhist priests have played an important role, especially in influencing the Nisei priests. Within the non-Japanese membership and ministerial group, Caucasians are most widely represented. There are few black, Chicano or native American Buddhists within the BCA, although at the 1972 BCA ministers' conference, three blacks did address the ministers, at least one of whom was singled out as a Buddhist. See "Black Buddhists Speak at BCA Ministers' Seminar," San Francisco *Hokubei Mainichi*, August 28, 1972, p. 1.

43. Forrest E. La Violette, *Americans of Japanese Ancestry: A Study of Assimilation in the American Community* (Toronto: Canadian Institute of International Affairs, 1945), p. 48.

44. Interview with Mr. and Mrs. Harry Kajihara, May 11, 1974; and personal correspondence, June 29, 1974. I am indebted to Mr. and Mrs. Kajihara for this example and for their observations about the Japanese American reactions to the situation.

45. Ibid.

46. Non-Japanese persons are encouraged to attend a church-sponsored function primarily when fund-raising or sports events are involved. At church bazaars, cookouts, and so forth, the intent is usually to raise funds. The youths have a variety of sports activities at member temples. Friends of the members are often encouraged to join basketball, volleyball, bowling, and baseball leagues in order to field a more competent team. Especially in interchurch games, one may find Chinese American, Filipino American, and Caucasian youngsters aiding one church to bring home the honor or the trophy.

At other places, sports activity transcends religion: one finds an occasional all-Sansei team, but some team members are usually Christian or otherwise non-Buddhist.

The pressures against a non-Japanese attending or becoming a member of the Buddhist church are often subtle. The BCA has never taken a discriminatory stand against any group because of race; however, at the member temples, non-Japanese are usually met with less than overwhelming cordiality. The seemingly subtle hostility from the Issei can be explained by their inability to communicate in English; they leave the hospitality to the minister. Among the Nisei, the Japanese cultural trait of *enryo*, or excessive restraint in social interaction, may initially give the impression of noncordiality. If the non-Japanese perseveres in his attendance and inquiry, he will meet with some of the more open Buddhist membership. For a discussion of *enryo* as a Japanese American interactional concept, see Kitano, op. cit., pp. 103–105.

47. For an analysis of territory, see Stanford M. Lyman and Marvin Scott, *The Sociology of the Absurd* (New York: Appleton-Century-Crofts, 1970), pp. 89–110.

48. At the San Diego Buddhist Church during the mid-1950s, a Mrs. Hosaka was noted within the community for her cooking ability. Her tamales were especially well received, and she was prevailed upon to donate her time and expertise in making large quantities of them for sale at the bazaar. Personal observations.

49. Ken Kitada, "Field Assignment: Placer Buddhist Church," San Francisco *Hokubei Mainichi*, March 19, 1973, p. 2. Interview with Reverend Tanryo Hata.

50. Ibid.

51. Ibid.

52. At the Santa Barbara Buddhist Church, there is neither a youth organization nor any basketball or volleyball team because of the limited membership in the appropriate age category. A language class on Saturdays, a flower arrangement class, and a *kendo* (Japanese fencing) group meeting are held at the church, but are not under its direct sponsorship.

53. Munekata, "Orange County Buddhist Church," op. cit., pp. 441–445. From May 1936 to February 1965, this church was a branch of the Los Angeles Betsuin; in 1965, it received its independent church status.

54. Compiled from BCA census, September 1, 1972. Reverend J. Tsumura and G. Aoki, BCA Census Committee.

55. George Kato, "Southern Alameda County Buddhist Church," in Munekata, op. cit., pp. 437–440.

56. BCA census, loc. cit.

57. Ibid.

58. Ogura, op. cit., pp. 12–13.

59. BCA census, loc. cit.

60. Mickey Matsumoto, "Buddhist Church of Sacramento, Betsuin," in Munekata, op. cit., p. 152, and Roy Nakamura, "Vacaville Buddhist Church," in Munekata, op. cit., pp. 234–236.

61. Ogura, op. cit., pp. 12–13.

62. Ibid., p. 13.

63. BCA, *Annual Report, 1975*, p. 156.

64. Freed and Luomala, op. cit.

65. Ibid., pp. 3, 4.

66. Ibid., p. 3.

67. Personal correspondence with G. Aoki, October 25, 1972.

68. Interview with Dr. Ryo Munekata, Los Angeles, on July 22, 1974.

69. Ogura, op. cit., p. 13.

70. "U.S. Church Growth Comes to Standstill," Los Angeles *Times*, March 20, 1972, Part I, pp. 1, 9. See also "Church Attendance Decline Continues," Santa Barbara *News-Press*, January 9, 1972, p. A–12.

71. U.S. Bureau of the Census, op. cit. Excluding Hawaii and Alaska, the census reports that the Japanese and Japanese American population for 1930 was 138,834; 1940, 126,947; 1950, 168,773; 1960, 260,195; and 1970, 373,983.

72. War Relocation Authority, *The Evacuated People*, p. 79.

73. Ibid.

74. Girdner and Loftis, op. cit. Dorothy S. Thomas (op. cit., p. 19) lists the median age twenty-six as a separate category.

75. Munekata, op. cit., p. 69.

76. Eidmann, *Young People's Introduction*, p. 129.

77. Munekata, op. cit., p. 100.

78. Recognition is also given to boys and girls from twelve to eighteen years of age, who are not scouts but who complete the study and activities outlined in achieving the Sangha award. This recognition is called the Dharma award.

79. Munekata, op. cit., p. 74. When the lord abbot or his deputy performs the rite, it is called *Kikyoshiku*; when conducted by the BCA bishop, it is called *Kieshiki* (or Sarana Affirmation Ceremony).

80. BCA, *Shin Buddhist Handbook*, p. 116.

81. Ibid.

82. BCA, *Annual Report, 1971*, p. 149.

83. Interview with Marshall Kido and Roy Hirabayashi, present and past Bay area RAB coordinators. Kido was interviewed in 1973 and Hirabayashi in 1974.

84. BCA, *Annual Report, 1973*, p. 20.

85. Ibid., p. 17, and BCA, *Annual Report, 1970*, p. 26.

86. BCA, *Annual Report*, 1970.

87. Ogura, op. cit., p. 19.

88. Ibid.

89. Both Spencer and Horinouchi appear to be in historical error on this point. Spencer has stated, "As a means of maintaining a Nisei interest in Buddhism, the Sunday School was inaugurated. It is of interest to note that this concept spread back to Japan from America, the Buddhist Sunday Schools or its equivalent now having become part of the organizational program of the Shin sect there." Spencer, op. cit., p. 212.

Horinouchi states that "Sunday schools were created like the Christian Sunday Schools" and credits a Hawaiian Buddhist adoption of the Christian educational format. Horinouchi, op. cit., p. 100.

90. Hideo Kishimoto, *Japanese Religion in the Meiji Era* (Tokyo: Obusha, 1956), p. 137.

91. Utsuki, op. cit., p. 34.

92. August K. Reischauer, *Studies in Japanese Buddhism* (New York: AMS Press, 1917, 1970), p. 154.

93. Ogura, op. cit., p. 19.

94. Chonen Terakawa (ed.), *Hokubei Kaikyo Enkakushi* [History of the North American Buddhist Mission], (San Francisco: North American Buddhist Mission Publication, 1936), p. 48.

95. Munekata, "BCA Sunday School Department," op. cit., p. 101.

96. Thus, prior to 1942 and after 1946, the Orange County Buddhist Church held its Sunday School on Saturdays, until the population changed from an agricultural occupational base to a suburban housing area in the late 1950s. Munekata, "Orange County Buddhist Church," op. cit., p. 44.

97. The term *Dharma School* is used, for instance, by the Southern Alameda Buddhist Church, Union City, Calif., and the Oxnard Buddhist Church, Oxnard, Calif.

98. Title used by the San Diego Buddhist Church.

99. Munekata, "BCA Sunday School Department," op. cit., p. 101.

100. Reverends Kenjo Kurokawa, Ryugyo Fujimoto, Nishi Utsuji, and Ryuchi Fujii. From Munekata, op. cit.

101. Munekata, "BCA Sunday School Department," op. cit.

102. BCA census, 1972.

CHAPTER 7 | *Pressure on the American Buddhist Church Toward Denominationalism*

The organizational model for the BCA is the Japanese Buddhist temple in Japan. The basic model has not altered very much in the last seventy-six years, and whatever changes have occurred have been closely patterned on changes in the structure of the Japanese organization.

As soon as the NABM had more than one temple under the jurisdiction of the San Francisco headquarters, institutionalization of the religious body began. The present BCA structure has its roots in the organizational pattern of the NABM, whose structure in turn comes from the sect headquarters, Hongwanji-ha Hongwanji (abbreviated Hompa Hongwanji or Nishi Hongwanji), in Kyoto, Japan. In order to understand the organizational structure of the NABM and BCA, it is necessary to explore the organization of the Nishi Hongwanji headquarters.

Throughout the history of the Nishi Hongwanji sect, the *monshu* (the lord or chief abbot) has held the highest office in the sect. Although the organizational structure under the lord abbot has changed with time, his position as the sect's spiritual leader has remained constant. He is always an hereditary descendant of the founder of the sect, Shinran, a lineage unbroken since the thirteenth century. The Japanese structure is divided into "ecclesiastical" and "legislative" bodies with formal demarcated areas of responsibility (see Figures 1 and 2). The ecclesiastical body is responsible for the religious and ceremonial duties. The legislative body represents the temples and adherents through the election of a *jushoku* (resident priest at a temple) from nineteen districts to serve in the *Shu-e*. (The *Shu-e* is a collective body of forty-five

Figure 1
Ecclesiastical Headquarters, Kyoto, 1937

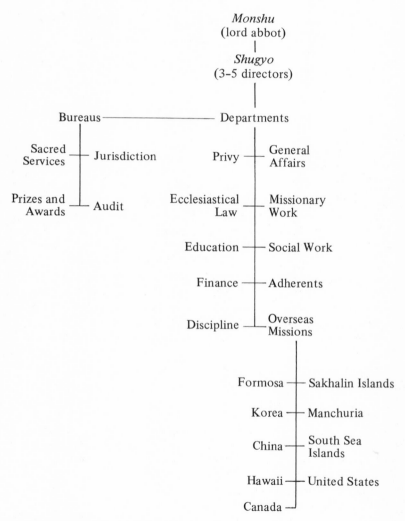

SOURCE: Utsuki, op. cit., pp. 39–41.

Figure 2
Legislative Body, Kyoto, 1937

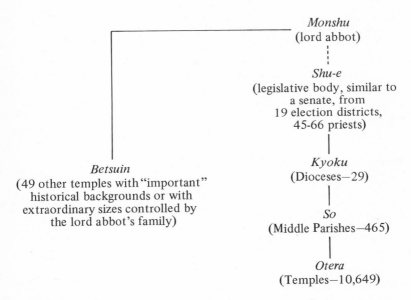

Monshu
(lord abbot)

Shu-e
(legislative body, similar to
a senate, from
19 election districts,
45-66 priests)

Betsuin
(49 other temples with "important"
historical backgrounds or with
extraordinary sizes controlled by
the lord abbot's family)

Kyoku
(Dioceses—29)

So
(Middle Parishes—465)

Otera
(Temples—10,649)

SOURCES: Utsuki, op. cit., p. 40; and an interview with Reverend
Masami Fujitani, October 26, 1974.

to sixty-six elected priests from nineteen districts throughout Japan.)
The *Shu-e* legislates on fiscal and district-related matters outside the
purview of the ecclesiastical body. ⌋

During the 1930s, the ecclesiastical organization was under the operational control of the directors of the sect, the *shugyo.* This is an administrative cabinet, which includes the chief administrator or *socho* of
the Jodo Shinshu sect. The decisions within the ecclesiastical body are
made by the *shugyo,* although they are theoretically responsible to the
lord abbot.[1]

The *monshu* is the spiritual leader, and as such, in his official capacity as the supreme authority, he is expected to reign but not rule. The
monshu is to the Nishi Hongwanji sect what the emperor is to the present

Japanese government. The *monshu*'s presence is necessary for all official ceremonies and especially for the investiture of new priests, but he does not take a direct part in the administrative affairs of the sect. That does not mean that he cannot rule; for instance, *Monshu* Myonyo Shonin (1850–1903) sent priests to study various religions in foreign countries and directed the missionary priests to the United States.[2] However, such direct actions are very rare.[3] The philosophy of the religious order is such that the spiritual leader would demean his position and his honored status by involving himself in mundane affairs. As one priest stated, "The Lord Abbot is not supposed to lead except by being a great spiritual example." The division between ruling and reigning has been kept from the early 1900s to the present day.

Under the *shugyo* are various departments such as Education and Ecclesiastical Law, chaired by department heads who coordinate and aid Nishi Hongwanji activities throughout Japan. The bureaus under the *shugyo* maintained the ceremonial features of Nishi Hongwanji. The *monshu*'s responsibility lies in legitimizing activities such as the presentation of prizes and awards.

The Overseas Mission Department, which supervised the NABM until the start of World War II, is also the responsibility of the *shugyo*. Prior to the war, the organization maintained nine overseas missions (Formosa, Korea, China, Sakhalin Islands, Manchuria, South Sea Islands, Hawaii, Canada, and the continental United States). Presently, there are only five mission organizations (South America, Office of Okinawa Affairs, Hawaii, Canada, and mainland United States). Prior to World War II, the ties between the Kyoto headquarters and the NABM were very strong; the director (*kantoku*) of the NABM was selected by the Kyoto headquarters, and his salary was augmented by the headquarters in Japan.[4] All missionary priests to America were also assigned from their department.

The powers of the legislative body before World War II resided in the *Shu-e*. Only the *soryo* or *jushoku* were eligible to stand as candidates. They controlled fiscal and legislative matters concerning the many Jodo Shinshu temples not directly controlled by the ecclesiastical headquarters. The *otera* (temples) in Japan are usually the property of the residential minister's family. They are independent of the direct control of the ecclesiastical organization; however, there is a connection to the *monshu* through the elected body, the *Shu-e*.

Also under the legislative body is the *betsuin* (literally, a branch temple) which is under the direct authority of the *monshu*'s family. However, the *monshu* appoints a caretaker priest, called the *rimban*, to oversee the *betsuin*. The term *betsuin* has been utilized by the BCA for some of the larger membership temples as an honorific designation; the American *betsuin* is not part of the *monshu*'s family holdings.

Between the pre-World War II era and the present time, an important change occurred in the legislative organization. Just after the end of the war, the *Shu-e* was expanded from forty-five to sixty-six priests to one hundred members. The *Shu-e* was renamed the *Shukai* (see Figures 3 and 4) and is now composed of fifty priests and fifty lay members. With the inclusion of nonpriests within the legislative council, the once monolithic control by the priests was abolished. The lay members attained representation, according to Reverend M. Fujitani, because of the influence of American democratic ideals introduced into Japan with the termination of the war.[5] Other than this change, the essential model of both the legislative and ecclesiastical structure remained unchanged.[6]

The past organizational structure resembles the prewar ecclesiastical structure of the Japan headquarters (see Figure 5). All priests and the *kantoku* of the NABM were assigned by the Overseas Mission Department within the ecclesiastical body of the Hompa Hongwanji. The *kantoku* was assisted by an executive secretary (*shuji*) and their counselors (*sanji*). The *sanji* were priests usually from temples geographically close to the NABM headquarters in San Francisco. They were elected on an annual basis at the priest's conference. The *kantoku*'s administrative responsibility as the head of the NABM included the authority to assign and transfer priests, once they were assigned to the NABM. He had no power to invest or deny priesthood; such powers resided solely with the *monshu*.

One important duty of the *kantoku* was a yearly inspection and visitation tour to each church or temple. Each temple or church was and still is independently incorporated, although they are also members of the inclusive incorporated organization, the BCA. Thus, the *kantoku* had no direct authority over the temples or churches. His authority was over the assigned priests. However, the yearly visitation gave him the opportunity to understand local problems and to coordinate the headquarters' activities needs. While this duty is still carried out today,

Figure 3
Legislative Headquarters, Hompa Hongwanji,
Kyoto, Present

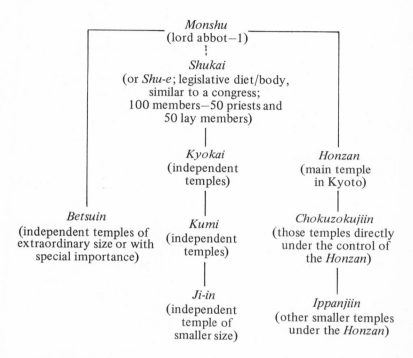

SOURCES: Personal interview with Reverend S. Sakow, December 3, 1973, and M. Fujitani, October 26, 1974; and the *Hongwanji Hoki, Jodo Shinshu Hongwanji-ha Shu Sei* [Rules and Regulations of the Jodo Shinshu Religious Sect], n.d., n.p.

Figure 4
Ecclesiastical Headquarters, Hompa Hongwanji, Kyoto, Present

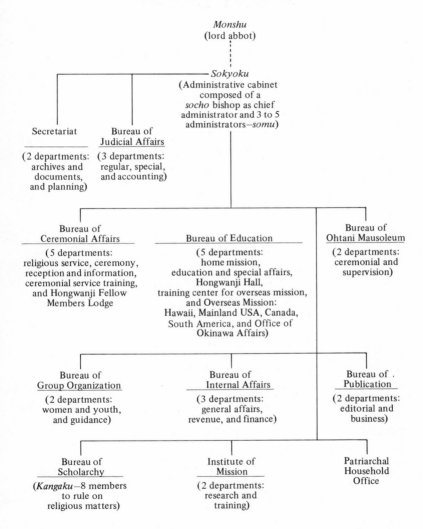

Monshu
(lord abbot)

Sokyoku
(Administrative cabinet
composed of a
socho bishop as chief
administrator and 3 to 5
administrators—*somu*)

Secretariat

(2 departments:
archives and
documents,
and planning)

Bureau of
Judicial Affairs

(3 departments:
regular, special,
and accounting)

Bureau of
Ceremonial Affairs

(5 departments:
religious service, ceremony,
reception and information,
ceremonial service training,
and Hongwanji Fellow
Members Lodge

Bureau of Education

(5 departments:
home mission,
education and special affairs,
Hongwanji Hall,
training center for overseas mission,
and Overseas Mission:
Hawaii, Mainland USA, Canada,
South America, and Office of
Okinawa Affairs)

Bureau of
Ohtani Mausoleum

(2 departments:
ceremonial and
supervision)

Bureau of
Group Organization

(2 departments:
women and youth,
and guidance)

Bureau of
Internal Affairs

(3 departments:
general affairs,
revenue, and finance)

Bureau of
Publication

(2 departments:
editorial and
business)

Bureau of
Scholarchy

(*Kangaku*—8 members
to rule on
religious matters)

Institute of
Mission

(2 departments:
research and
training)

Patriarchal
Household
Office

SOURCES: Interview with Reverend S. Sakow, December 3, 1973;
and the *Hongwanji Hoki.*

Figure 5
Buddhist Mission of North America,
Organizational Structure, pre-1944

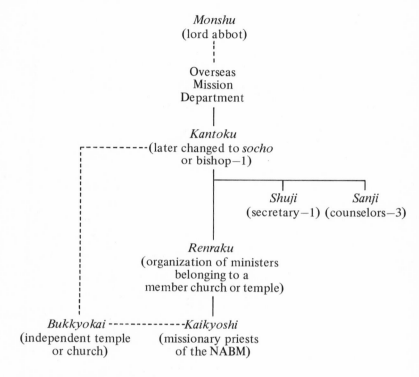

Monshu
(lord abbot)

Overseas
Mission
Department

Kantoku
(later changed to *socho*
or bishop—1)

Shuji   *Sanji*
(secretary—1) (counselors—3)

Renraku
(organization of ministers
belonging to a
member church or temple)

Bukkyokai ------------- *Kaikyoshi*
(independent temple   (missionary priests
or church)   of the NABM)

SOURCE: Terakawa, op. cit., pp. 9–10.

the number of visitations has greatly increased. In 1935, there were only thirty-five churches and temples in the continental United States and Canada; there are now fifty-nine independent structures, with thirty-nine separate branch temples in the continental United States alone.

The title of *kantoku* was elevated to *socho* (bishop) in 1918. *Socho* is literally translated as "chancellor" or "president." The occupant of this office within the *shukai*, Nishi Hongwanji in Japan, is in effect the chief executive. The Buddhist literature does not explain the title change in America. One priest interviewed has suggested that it was an honorific title change given to the members and priests of the NABM, a gesture symbolic of the considered importance of the overseas mission to the Nishi Hongwanji sect in Japan. Another probable assumption would be that with the increasing number of Buddhist members, temples, and priests that took place within the NABM from 1899 to 1918, the responsibilities of the *kantoku* were increasing. For instance, from 1899 to 1918, twenty-three new Buddhist churches and temples were created, with sixteen constructed between 1905 and 1918.[7] Not all overseas missions at that time had a *socho*. Even in Japan, with an estimated 7,500,000[8] followers in 1937, there was, and still is, but one *socho*, although the present administrative leaders of the Hawaiian, Canadian, and American Buddhist churches have that designation. As one priest commented, "There is no comparison with the *socho* office in Japan and in America. Here it is only an office for a small number of followers."[9]

Under the NABM, the *kantoku* headed the *Renraku Bukkyo Dan* (the *Renraku* Buddhist Association), which was composed of all missionary priests (*kaikyoshi*) assigned to the NABM member churches or temples. Little formal authority was given to nonpriests within the NABM, although each individual church or temple had lay members on the board of directors. The NABM supervised the *kaikyoshi*, arranged for lectures and visitations from Japan, convened the annual priests' conference, supervised and coordinated interchurch activities, and published material relevant to Buddhism and to the various temples.[10]

The present BCA structure came into existence just after World War II and resembles the organizational pattern of the present Hompa Hongwanji (see Figures 6 and 7). As was discussed earlier, in 1944, the name Buddhist Mission of North America was changed to the Buddhist Churches of America, and the inclusion of a legislative structure within the BCA dramatically altered the older existing structure. The BCA National Council, predominantly composed of lay persons, is very similar to that found in the Hompa Hongwanji. The two major areas of activity, the religious, and the financial and secular spheres, are assigned to the bishop's office and the legislative body, respectively.

Figure 6
Present BCA Headquarters

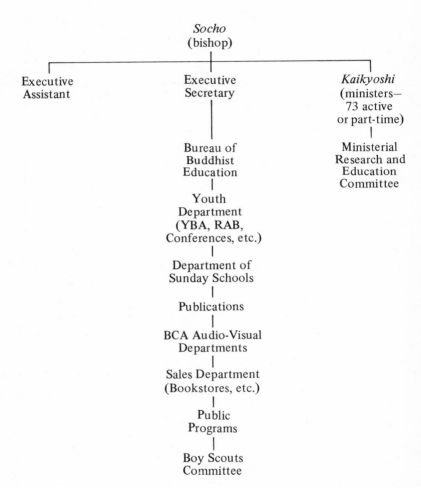

SOURCES: BCA, *Annual Report, 1973*, pp. 17–44; and interview with Dr. Ryo Munekata, Los Angeles, May 1974.

Figure 7
Present BCA Legislative Body

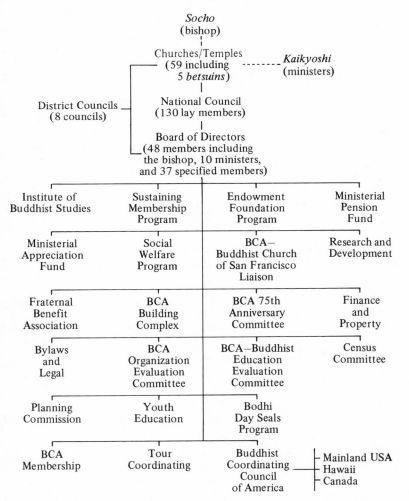

SOURCES: BCA, *Annual Report, 1973*, pp. 45–157; By-Laws of the Buddhist Churches of America; and an interview with Dr. Ryo Munekata, Los Angeles, May 1974.

In the BCA legislative body, the National Council is composed of two lay representatives from each member church or temple. Under the National Council is the board of directors. The board is composed of forty-eight members; twenty-four lay members (three each from eight BCA districts); the bishop; eight priests elected from each of the eight BCA districts; one priest who is the chairman of the BCA Ministerial Association; four lay members from BCA affiliated organizations (Adult Buddhist Association, National Young Buddhist Association, National Buddhist Women's Association, and Sunday School Teacher's Federation); nine directors-at-large elected from the National Council; and the immediate past president of the board of directors of the BCA. Like the *Shukai* in Japan, the National Council is responsible for legislation regarding the secular activities of the BCA and the financing of the various projects under its jurisdiction. The board of directors is the operational working body of the BCA; it has the power to call special meetings of the National Council, appoint committees and personnel, collect and assess dues when necessary, and incur indebtedness or accept donations.

In the BCA headquarters, as in the ecclesiastical headquarters in Kyoto, the *socho* is the executive superintendent. He is aided by the executive assistant to the bishop, an executive secretary, and a staff composed of priests and lay members for the various departments under the Bureau of Buddhist Education. As in Japan, the bishop has direct authority in the bureau as well as the authority to assign and transfer priests within the BCA.

The bishop's authority over an individual temple or church is twofold: the most important influence is in the assignment of priests; second, he oversees matters of concern to all the churches. In addition, the suggestions he makes during his yearly visits can have important indirect influence on the temple's board of directors.

It is clear that there are similarities between the Kyoto and NABM-BCA headquarters. Both headquarters have a similar division between ecclesiastical and legislative organization, and both had a policy of noninclusion of lay members within the legislative organization before World War II and inclusion after the war. A comparison between the two headquarters makes one point very clear: the essential model for the organizational structure of the NABM was the Hompa Hongwanji. Since the NABM provided the BCA model, the present organization in America has its roots in Kyoto. This conclusion is further strengthened by the fact that all *kantoku* and priests before World War II came from or were trained in Japan. Their organizational experiences were based in the Japanese Nishi Hongwanji sect. Furthermore, until World War II the lord abbot and his staff had immense direct influence on the NABM. Presently, the influence is less strong, although formal ties are still maintained. Even after World War II, most priests, except for the Nisei, Sansei, and a few Caucasian priests, came from Japan. Until the creation of the Institute for Buddhist Studies in America in 1966, all priests received their training in Japan.

Although the basic organizational model for the BCA has come from Japan, some modifications have taken place. Many of the programs under the legislative body, such as the BCA Endowment Foundation Program, the Ministerial Appreciation Fund, and the Institute for Buddhist Studies, are endemic to the United States. These programs are best understood as modifications and additions arising from the specific needs of the membership or priests. For example, the 75th Anniversary Committee was created to coordinate projects such as the BCA history book for the anniversary celebration. Other programs, however, do derive from the Kyoto headquarters organization (for example, the Social Welfare Committee, Finance and Property Committee, and Bylaws and Legal Committee). Thus, although there have been changes within the organization in America, there is also a strong continuous link with the parent organization in Japan.

The Training of New Priests

Traditionally, the BCA has had a policy of training, ordaining, and certifying Nishi Hongwanji ministers in Japan. The Kyoto headquarters has retained primary control of their overseas mission by selecting the bishop or overseers, and by sending missionaries they deem suitable. But this situation has changed drastically.

The new constitution which created the BCA in 1944 also provided for the election of the bishop from within the American-based organization. Bishop Ryotai Matsukage, having served the NABM-BCA from February 1938 through the difficult evacuation years, passed away in June 1948. As his successor, the BCA ministers selected Reverend Enryo Shigefuji, who had previously served the Fresno Buddhist Betsuin. This group, in turn, submitted Reverend Shigefuji's name to the lord abbot in Japan for formal approval. This method of the bishop's selection is a historic change from the previous system; it gives the BCA ministers, as well as the BCA members, a significant degree of control over the highest position within their organization.

The importance of the Nisei within the BCA was underscored in May 1968 with the selection of the Reverend Kenryu T. Tsuji, a Canadian-born Nisei, to succeed Bishop Shinsho Hanayama after his retirement. Not only was the new bishop a Nisei, but for the first time, the inaugural ceremony was conducted in the United States. Heretofore all inaugurals had taken place in Kyoto at the Nishi Hongwanji headquarters. These changes concerning the bishop's position, the selection method, and the inauguration in America reflect a large transfer of authority from Japan to the United States. At this time, there is no reason to believe that the BCA will not abide by these new procedures when the need again arises for the selection and investiture of a bishop.

As to the training of ministers, not until the late 1950s did the BCA make any systematic attempt to change the traditional system. Previously, all Japanese ministers and prospective Nisei and Sansei ministers underwent training in Japan. The American Buddhist Academy was started in the early 1950s in New York, and the Institute of Buddhist Studies (IBS) was initiated in 1966 at Berkeley.

The American Buddhist Academy, led by the founder and president Reverend Hozen Seki, was established as a center for Buddhist studies. The academy consists of a series of rooms with a library and dormitory adjacent to the New York Buddhist Church where Reverend Seki is also the resident minister. Donations were solicited throughout the BCA for books and supplies through the late 1950s until the inception of the IBS. The academy's activities include regular seminars and lecture series, and an ongoing Buddhist publication project. Reverend Seki has also given ordination rites to two lay persons.[11] The rites of ordination are apparently not officially sanctioned by the Hompa Hongwanji in Kyoto, and the two ministers are not registered within the BCA as is Reverend Seki.[12] The BCA continues its monetary support, about $1,000 per year, which is used to help defray costs in publications, lectures, additions to the library, and scholarships.

The academy's location on the East Coast made access difficult for the majority of the Jodo Shinshu followers. Thus, in 1966, the BCA initiated actions to establish the IBS, a ministerial training center, with instruction in English, on the West Coast. The site selected was Berkeley. In October 1966, the institute became fully functional and a building was purchased at 2717 Haste Street. The curriculum offered was accepted by the California State Board of Education, and the IBS, as an independent nonprofit corporation, qualified as a graduate school with the right to confer the Master of Arts degree in Buddhist studies.

> Other programs of the Institute in the Institute's curriculum are designed to orient the ministers newly arriving from abroad, to assist the practicing minister to keep abreast of the changing times, to help Sunday Dharma school teachers and the temple lay-readers to prepare better and to fulfill their duties in the religious world.[13]

The original endowment in 1966 consisted of $300,000 from the BCA Special Scholarship Fund. However, with no organized, continual fund-raising campaign, and an annual budget of $80,000 to $90,000 in 1972 and 1973,[14] the ever-increasing costs became a tremendous drain on the member churches. For this investment, IBS has offered Buddhist summer courses, prepared translations of Buddhist texts, and presented workshops in addition to training Nikei and Occidental students for the ministry.

By 1972, seven full-time students were enrolled and nine others were completing their studies in Japan. The Master of Arts degree was first conferred in 1972 upon June A. King, now a minister at the Fresno Betsuin, and Kenneth C. O'Neill, now a minister at the San Jose Betsuin.[15] They left for Japan for further studies and received the ordination rites and *kyoshi* certificate in Kyoto. The second commencement in 1973 featured three Sansei: Kanya Okamoto, Robert Oshita, and Ken Tanaka.[16] They are at present undergoing further training in Japan. A Sansei, Ronald K. Kobata, was the sole graduate at the third commencement in December 1973.[17]

The success of the IBS is an important development for the BCA and all Japanese Americans. It is the first accredited institution of higher learning established by the Japanese Americans. Moreover, the BCA has recognized the need to open its churches to other than just the Japanese and Japanese Americans. As one official BCA publication states in regard to the first commencement, "That the first two recipients of degrees were not Japanese Americans [i.e., Caucasians] is indicative of the Institute's hope to serve the community at large."[18] In 1973, there were four full-time continuing students, with two applications still pending.[19] Most important, the IBS has received official accreditation from the Hompa Hongwanji for its ministerial training courses. The privilege of sanctioning the clergy is crucial in any religion. To insure the capabilities, motives, religious spirit, and knowledge of any ministerial candidate is a right closely guarded by the major religious denominations of the world. The Nishi Hongwanji sect of Buddhism is no exception.

In the past, ministerial candidates trained at the IBS had to travel to Japan for further study and examination before being ordained. They were given certificates as *kyoshi*, but because they were not part of the Japanese clergy system and were unable to fully master the Japanese language, various requirements concerning residence time and training were relaxed for them.[20] Except for a few Nisei ministerial candidates before World War II, most students from America encountered language difficulties. Since the Jodo Shinshu texts were in Japanese, and more and more candidates were unfamiliar with the language, special provisions were necessarily made. For instance, though nearly all the candidates who came from America attended Ryukoku University in Kyoto, they were merely asked to translate an important work of a saint or patriarch to fulfill their thesis requirement for the Master of Arts degree. The academic quality of these American students has never been a problem, but their limited linguistic ability to learn and apply abstruse or complex Buddhist concepts has not been adequately resolved even to this day.[21]

The presence of American ministerial candidates also created difficulties for the Japanese university, which had to develop new methods of communication and examination. The professors were not fluent in the English language, and it became apparent that the language barrier precluded treatment of the Americans as if they were Japanese. Also, how could the professors adequately review the translations? At an *ad hoc* meeting between the BCA and the Hongwanji personnel, held in June 1972, Bishop Tsuji stated:

> I indicated that BCA now has a policy of sending only those students who have received their M.A. in Buddhist Studies from [the]

IBS to Japan. Both [Ryukoku University] and the [Hongwanji] are deeply concerned with the overseas students who speak little or no Japanese. It is impossible for them to take lectures or converse with their professors and fellow students. At the same time [Ryukoku University] is placing more emphasis on Japanese and is encouraging students to complete their thesis in Japanese, not just a translation of text.[22]

To clarify the requirements for *tokudo* (ordination), *kyoshi* (teaching certificate), and *kaikyoshi* (missionary work), guidelines were established for the American ministerial students.[23] First, all U.S. citizens applying for *tokudo* rites had to have a home temple. For the BCA-sponsored students, the designated temple would be the Buddhist Church of San Francisco. Second, the *tokudo* training and ceremony would last for one week. Third, the courses taken during the week would consist of rituals (e.g., sutra chanting), "missionary" activity (e.g., preaching), religion (origins and history), Buddhism (doctrine and history), Jodo Shinshu (doctrine and creed), present condition of Nishi Hongwanji, and an "awareness of the Buddhist ministry." Fourth, the *kyoshi* courses beyond those required for the *tokudo* would include preaching, Buddhist education, Hongwanji activities, intensive Shinshu doctrines, "Religion and Modern Man" and a personal understanding and faith. The *kyoshi* training would last for ten days, including examinations. The Hongwanji also agreed that all U.S. *tokudo* candidates had to have prior approval from the BCA before obtaining initiation rites.[24]

Because the IBS is an accredited educational institution chaired by a professor, Buddhist scholar,[25] and a former faculty member at Ryukoku University, the IBS representative requested a waiver of the required examination for their Master's candidates. This request was approved in 1973, and the IBS became a Hongwanji-accredited ministerial training school. Even in Japan, only three or four institutions are accredited by the Hompa Hongwanji.[26] The students still have to journey to Japan for the training and ceremonies, but all examinations are conducted in America.[27]

The IBS is a clear departure from past tradition. BCA ministers can now be educated and trained in their native language without losing contact with their homeland. The level and content of instruction are monitored not only by the Hompa Hongwanji, but also by the State

Board of Education, and ministerial training instruction is reviewed by both the Hongwanji and BCA ministerial personnel. Provided that a high quality of education and training is maintained, an institutional means to continue the replacement of Issei with English-speaking ministers has become a reality. Although the Issei ministers recognized the problem in the training of new ministers with the creation of the NABM *Zaidan* (Endowment Fund) in 1929, the BCA in 1966 appears to have the first positive and workable solution.

Even so, the IBS has problems of its own, the greatest of which involves finances. In 1973, an additional total contribution of $76,707.30 was asked of the member temples through a complex formula based upon their respective BCA dues. Ninety-five percent of the assessment has been received, and unspecified plans have apparently been initiated to obtain other funds in the coming years.[28] Additional special assessments from the BCA member churches will probably also be necessary.

Because of the specialized subject matter at IBS, the student body is small. IBS is perceived as a graduate training institution, and the general Buddhist population has not been enticed by its course offerings, which have included Tutorial in Asian Philosophy, Kegon Buddhism, Sanskrit Grammar, Shinran's Letters, *Ojoraisan* (hymns of Zendo), and the like. IBS must maintain its high academic standings; however, there are summer session courses that have slightly broader appeal, but not to the average Buddhist member. Given the choice between a broader student base or quality education for future ministers, the latter appears to be the preferred path for now.

The Temple or Church

There are problems in the very designation of the individual constituent bodies collectively known as the BCA, as well as in the district organization of these bodies and in the financial relationship between them and the BCA. Let us start with the problem of definition.

The predominant official designation, used by fifty-six of the present fifty-nine dues-paying or independent suborganizations, is the "Buddhist Church of *(location)*" or the "*(location)* Buddhist Church." This title was first instituted in 1905 by the San Francisco YMBA and approved by the fourth director *(kantoku)*[29] of the NABM as the official English equivalent for the more proper Japanese term *bukkyokai* (literally,

Buddhist Association). Seven suborganizations use the title temple rather than church, while one calls itself an association and another a *Sangha* (Buddhist Brotherhood).[30]

The problem concerning the title of each member organization within the BCA has recently become an official issue.[31] The Issei members still refer to their place of worship in Japanese, and there is little concern about the translation of the word *bukkyokai* to the Buddhist Church. A church, for the Issei, signifies a place of worship and reverence, and the term does no injustice to the many activities housed by their Buddhist structures. Since the Issei are not generally fluent in English, their everyday designation is the proper Japanese title.

The change from the NABM to the BCA in 1944, as previously stated, was a reaction to the catastrophic event of World War II and the recognition of the Nisei within the Jodo Shinshu organization.

Some ministers and members within the BCA are now evaluating the appropriateness of the designation "church" to their organization. Some BCA ministers, as part of the Ministerial Research Committee,[32] aware of the symbolic significance of titles, investigated the words "church," "temple," and *"Sangha"* to determine if any corrections or additions should be made.

The term *church*, as applied to a Buddhist place of worship, has been recognized by at least one Issei Buddhist as less than adequate:

INT: Do you think "church" is a good name for or description of the places to which you have been a *Sensei* (priest)?

Rev. S: The name of our organization is the Church [Santa Barbara Buddhist Church]. I don't like it, but it's there. It's better expressed as a temple.

INT: What is the idea of a temple, then, in Japan, and how would you see it in America?

Rev. S: Well, of course, a temple in Shinshu doctrine, is understood as another place where the Shinshu doctrine is propagated. And of course there are other religious activities connected with Jodo Shinshu doctrine.

INT: If they were temples, rather than churches, how different would they be?

Rev. S: I think that before we can learn about that matter, we need to know, what is a church? What is meant by Christianity? Then that way the difference will be found.[33]

The problem of nomenclature is not easily solved, since the particular English translations utilized are already imbued with Christian overtones. The term *church*, the Ministerial Research Committee found, derives from Old and New Testament Greek,[34] and could therefore be regarded as inappropriate for use by English-speaking Buddhists. The term *temple* is somewhat less problematical, although it derives from Latin and is also used in the Old and New Testament. However, as the committee states, *temple* denotes merely a sanctuary or sacred area, and "due to its pre-Christian usage . . . is religiously neutral."[35]

The term *Sangha* has been used by the Washington, D.C., association in its title. *Sangha*, in Sanskrit, indicates a Buddhist crowd, company, gathering, or community. Utilized by the Buddhists from their beginnings, the word has come to mean simply a gathering of Buddhists.

After examining the three terms *church, temple,* and *Sangha,* Reverend Fujitani concluded that

> the first is exclusively Christian, while the latter two are neutral or of very thin dogmatic flavor. [The] idea of a Buddhist Church puts us in mind of *Hanamatsuri* translated as "Buddhist Christmas," etc. In order not to have Buddhist Sunday schools [appear as] a preparatory school to make good Christians, we are obliged to confront the semantic problem more seriously.[36]

The final suggestions of the Ministerial Research Committee were to change the words "Buddhist Church of (*location*)" to "Buddhist Temple of (*location*)," to refer to adherents of Buddhism as the Buddhist *Sangha*, and to call the BCA the Buddhist Sangha of America.

Among the Buddhists as a whole, the implications of using the word "church" have not been generally recognized. To most members, "church" is still an everyday term. Whether an alteration of the term will actually occur cannot be ascertained. Any change will hinge on the

Buddhist members' recognition of the significance, necessity, and desirability of making such an alteration. So far, the differences between "church" and "temple" are slight to the members; however, the BCA has not made a large-scale effort to educate them as to the need for redefinition.

Is "church" an appropriate designation for the BCA activities? One can argue that if "church" is defined as a body of religious adherents or as a religious society, then it is apt. The Buddhist churches, through their ministers, do hold religious ceremonies, conduct services, solemnize weddings and funerals, and host other activities similar to those of other religious denominations. Yet, as one Sansei minister has stated, this is not as it should be:

> Another name for a temple in Buddhism is the term "Dojo." Historically, "Dojo" means a "place where the Way is cultivated." The Way referred to here is the Way of Buddha, the Way of Enlightenment, the Way of Awakening. . . . The temple or Dojo then is a place where one attempts to cultivate an understanding of Buddhism.[37]

The problem of definition—whether a religious assembly should be called a church, temple, *Sangha*, or *Dojo*—is very serious for the BCA. The minister's main concern is with the religion and the propagation of the Teachings of Buddha; yet, the members' conception of their temples is somewhat different. To the extent that they utilize their house of reverence for other than strictly religious purposes, their indifference to such matters as title becomes clear. As many ministers have pointed out, the problem of teaching the Buddhist religion has been a major obstacle to successful propagation of Buddhism. Reverend Sakow, an Issei minister, has summarized the issue:

INT: Do most Buddhists in America have a strong understanding of Buddhism?

Rev. S: I don't think so. I guess almost 80% of the so-called American Buddhists just don't know. They just don't know. Of course they know a little bit about Buddhism, but it's rather merely common sense about Buddhism.

INT: They why do they continue to go to the Buddhist Church?

Rev. S: What do you mean?

INT: If . . . knowledge about Buddhism is very minimal . . . then why have we had a Buddhist church since 1899? What purpose do you think the Buddhist church has served?

Rev. S: I guess for a long time the Buddhist Church in the United States has served as the Japanese Community Center. This should be stressed more than the missionary work.[38]

When a Nisei minister was asked to explain the Nisei's continual involvement in their church, he stated:

Perhaps it could be guilt or family pressure. What my parents [Issei] have done for the temple, and therefore . . . I must carry on. And the other one would say I must do it for my children. These may be some of the reasons why they do it. But not so much from the religious standpoint, but I do it for myself. . . . [One Nisei] said, "I don't know anything about Buddhism, I'll come not to the service but to other things. To carnivals, but not to study class or the *Hondo* [temple hall]."[39]

And a Sansei minister observed:

"For my children" is a very common reason given, almost always. And this is why like one guy told me honestly that he didn't think he could understand Buddhism. He was too old to change, but as for his children he could do it. He was quite honest about it.[40]

Although many ministers agree that the Nikkei Buddhists in America are not as conversant with their religion as they would like them to be,[41] there have always been devout followers. The Nikkei Buddhists' difficulty in understanding their religion has previously been traced to the lack of adequate English religious texts and to the ministers' inability to translate Buddhist teachings from Japanese to English. The problem of understanding lies not with the Issei but with the Nisei. The Sansei are becoming involved in religious-centered activities such as meditation and the Kinnara group, and apparently are more likely to read and discuss with their ministers the few available books on Jodo Shinshu Buddhism.

The other difficulty for Buddhists is their lack of a unified body of religious thought such as the Old or New Testament, which the Christians possess. The Teachings of the Buddha are spread throughout many volumes, and if a dedicated Buddhist desires to become knowledgeable, he must adopt not only a scholarly and intellectual approach but also a deeply personal and subjective concern. Thus, as Reverend Sakow has estimated, 80 percent of the American Buddhists do not know about their religion.

The percentages given by Reverend Sakow are not easily verified. But his beliefs concerning the inherent irreligiousness of many American Buddhists are quite verifiable, and as such the BCA, member temples, and ministers are faced with a serious problem. Sakow's conclusions are certainly compatible with the apparent insensitivity of Buddhist followers to the semantic problem of speaking of Buddhist "churches" rather than temples, *Sanghas*, or *Dojos*. It is impossible to predict the outcome of this terminology problem. For the present, the word "church" remains the predominant designation given by the Nisei and most Sansei to their Buddhist place of reverence. The Issei, of course, continue to use the Japanese title *bukkyokai*.

Temples and Districts

Between the individual BCA temples and the headquarters in San Francisco lies another collective level. With the wide geographic dispersion of churches throughout the United States, eight divisions, called districts, were created after World War II to facilitate communication between the member churches and headquarters. Figure 8 presents the breakdown by districts, and also lists branch, nonindependent Buddhist groups, under the jurisdiction of certain churches. Thus, there are fifty-nine churches with thirty-nine branches, for a total of ninety-eight localities where Buddhist services and activities can be found.

Figure 8
BCA District Breakdown

DISTRICT I
(Bay District, California)

   Alameda
   Berkeley
   Enmanji (Sebastopol)
   Marin
   Oakland
     Ashland
     Concord
   Palo Alto
   San Francisco
   San Mateo
   South Alameda County

DISTRICT II
(Central California)

   Bakersfield
   Delano
   Dinuba
   Fowler
   Fresno
     Bowles
     Clovis
     Del Rey
     Fresno City
     Kingsburg
     Lone Star
     Madera
     North Fresno
     Sanger
     Selmer
     West Fresno
   Hanford
   Parlier
   Reedley
   Visalia

DISTRICT III
(California Coast)

   Monterey Peninsula
   Mountain View
   Salinas
   San Jose
     Gilroy
     Morgan Hill
   Watsonville
     Hollister
     San Juan Bautista

DISTRICT IV
(Eastern United States)

   Cleveland
   Detroit
   Midwest (Chicago)
   New York
   Seabrook
   Twin Cities
   Washington, D.C., Sangha

DISTRICT V
(Mountain United States)

   Honeyville
   Salt Lake City
   Tri-State
     Alamosa-LaJara, Colo.
     Brighton, Colo.
     Denver, Colo.
     Fort Lupton, Colo.
     Greeley, Colo.
     Longmont, Colo.
     Rocky Ford-Swink, Colo.
     Scottsbluff, Neb.
     Sedgwick, Colo.

Figure 8
(continued)

DISTRICT V (continued)

Utah-Idaho
Ogden, Utah
Corinne
Syracuse

DISTRICT VI
(Northern California)

Florin
Lodi
Marysville
Placer
Sacramento
Vacaville
Stockton
Cortez
French Camp
Walnut Grove

DISTRICT VII
(Northwest United States)

Idaho-Oregon (Ontario, Oreg.)
Oregon
Seattle
Spokane
Tacoma
White River
Yakima
Moses Lake

DISTRICT VIII
(Southern California and Arizona)

Arizona
Gardena
Guadalupe
Los Angeles
Hollywood
Long Beach
San Fernando Valley
Sun Valley
Orange County
Oxnard
Pasadena
San Diego
Brawley
Coachella
El Centro
San Luis Obispo
Santa Barbara
Senshin
Venice
West Los Angeles

The districts are divisions created for convenience. Each district may sponsor yearly conferences for the YBA, Junior YBA, Sunday School teachers, and other like groups for fellowship, discussions of mutual problems, or dissemination of information that might be helpful to the individual temples. This geographical breakdown is especially beneficial to churches outside California, since most of the Buddhist activities center in that state. The district conferences held, for example, in the Eastern District help prevent Nikkei church members from feeling isolated. When there are national conferences for the YBA, WABL (Western Adult Buddhist League), or the Federation of Buddhist Women, participants unable to attend can be represented by their district delegates, and thus retain a voice and interest in the actions taken at the national level.

Finances

Financing within the Buddhist Church has always been a long-term problem. The economic basis of the NABM and BCA has been fulfilled by a variety of programs and fund drives. The earliest large-scale collection of monies was the NABM *Zaidan* fund, later retitled the BCA Endowment Foundation, started in 1929. Since then, programs such as the Sustaining Membership Program, Special Projects Fund, and the Ministerial Appreciation and Pension Fund have been incorporated into the economic situation of the BCA. At the member temple level, membership dues, contributions, pledges, and profit from food and carnival bazaars have constituted the main sources of monetary supply.[42]

Only one economic pattern has arisen at the headquarters or member temples: in cases of a perceived financial problem, fund-raising programs and different methods of collection have been instituted. Every temple has a continual problem concerning income. The minister's salary, along with charges for sundry items such as utility bills, must be met on a monthly basis. In the early 1900s, the major request for funds went to the construction of temple structures; presently, construction plans at many temples include new additions for Sunday School buildings, parking lots, or reconstruction of older temple buildings. Major expenses such as new buildings are paid for by pledges or income generated by food or carnival bazaars or special project funds. Membership dues are generally utilized for the salary of the ministers, upkeep of present structures and, in most churches, defraying the dues paid by the temple to the San Francisco headquarters.

The pledge system has been most effective when there is a need for large donations over a span of years. This system originated in Japan; priests would go to each household within their territory to solicit the necessary funds according to the economic capability of each family. In America, especially the Issei priests would use the pledge method not only to solicit funds, but also to maintain personal and religious contact with Buddhist families unable regularly to attend church services or functions. The San Diego Buddhist Church minister, for instance, would travel to Westmoreland, Brawley, and El Centro in Imperial County in the east and Oceanside, Fallbrook, and Vista in the north. The arrival of the San Diego minister often gave the Japanese agricultural farmers a respite from their daily tasks. He would bring news from the city, enjoy their company, and often be asked to conduct religious services in their homes. In return, the minister would receive a truckload of produce for distribution to the Japanese in the city.

The generation of church revenue by food or carnival bazaars is a Buddhist innovation in America. As discussed earlier, bazaars are not only an effective money-raising endeavor, but they also aid in maintaining ethnic community solidarity. Most temples have building expansion programs, the desire to purchase a new automobile for their minister, and the continual need to support projects, such as the Institute for Buddhist Studies, instituted by headquarters. Both the churches and headquarters have been seeking an adequate solution to the financial problem; meanwhile, the present programs will continue to be used.

Notes

1. Interview with Reverend M. Fujitani, Oxnard, Calif., October 26, 1974.
2. Nishu Utsuki, "The History of Hongwanji," pamphlet, San Francisco, Buddhist Churches of America, n.d., p. 10.
3. Interviews with Reverends S. Sakow, December 3, 1973, and M. Fujitani, October 26, 1974.
4. In 1932, Kosei Ogura stated that the *kantoku* received a salary of $1,500 from the NABM plus 3,000 yen from Japan (approximately $1,500); op. cit., p. 6. The salary augmentation from Japan was followed

until at least 1938, with the 3,000 not directly sent to the BCA *kantoku*, but handcarried by the newly assigned ministers. See Shigetsu Akahosi, "The Bishop Masuyama Period: Part II," San Francisco *Wheel of Dharma* 1, no. 2 (October 16, 1973): 2.

5. Interview on October 26, 1974.

6. A comparison of Figures 1 and 4 (ecclesiastical) shows some slight changes: the *shugyo* has been renamed the *sokyoku* and has been expanded by one priest; and most of the previous departments have been upgraded to bureau status. By comparing Figures 2 and 3 (legislative), it appears that another group (*Honzan, Chokuzokujiin,* and *Ippanjiin*) came under the legislative headquarters after World War II. Actually, some temples have always been directly under the administrative and financial control of the main temple in Kyoto (*Honzan*). N. Utsuki (the source for Figures 1 and 2) did not indicate the *Honzan* (headquarters temple) nor the *Chokuzokujiin* nor the *Ippanjiin* since they are the responsibility of the main temple and not the *Shu-e* or the *Shukai.*

7. Interview with Dr. Ryo Munekata, Los Angeles, November 22, 1973.

8. Utsuki, "History of Hongwanji," p. 42.

9. Interview with Reverend S. Sakow, Santa Barbara, December 3, 1973.

10. Ogura, op. cit., p. 2.

11. The two persons are Kyojo Vergara and Alan Kyojun Klaw. See the "American Buddhist Academy," BCA, *Annual Report, 1971,* p. 69, and *1973,* p. 74.

12. Interview with BCA ministers.

13. "The Institute of Buddhist Studies," pamphlet, n.d.

14. BCA, *Annual Report, 1972, 1973.* See section on the IBS.

15. *BCA Newsletter* 10, no. 7 (July 1972): 1.

16. *BCA Newsletter* 11, no. 4, (June 1973): 1.

17. San Francisco *Hokubei Mainichi,* no. 8196, December 13, 1973, p. 1.

18. *BCA Newsletter* (July 1972).

19. BCA, *Annual Report, 1973,* p. 47.

20. Interview with Reverend S. Sakow, December 4, 1973.

21. Personal interviews with Reverends Sakow and A. Takemoto, as previously cited.

22. BCA, *Annual Report, 1972,* p. 10.

23. Ibid., pp. 10–11.

24. Ibid.

25. Dr. Ryotetsu Fujiwara was the resident professor; he has since returned to Japan; the selection of his replacement is now under way.

26. BCA, *Annual Report, 1973*, p. 46.

27. One notable exception to the IBS-Hongwanji relationship is Ken Yamaguchi, a past president of the BCA. At fifty-two years of age, after twenty years of successful practice as an optometrist in Pasadena, California, he decided to become a Buddhist minister. In March 1973, Dr. Yamaguchi, with his family soon to follow, enrolled at Ryukoku University for a period of two years in preparation for his ordination to the priesthood. See San Francisco *Hokubei Mainichi*, no. 7941, February 12, 1973, and no. 7961, March 8, 1973.

28. BCA, *Annual Report, 1973*, p. 48.

29. Munekata, "Introductory," op. cit., p. 49.

30. The seven temples are the Los Angeles Hompa Hongwanji Buddhist Temple, Buddhist Temple of Alameda, Buddhist Temple of Utah-Idaho, Midwest Buddhist Temple (Chicago), Mountain View Buddhist Temple, Buddhist Temple of Marin, and Venice (California) Hongwanji Buddhist Temple. The remaining two are the Twin Cities Buddhist Association and the Washington, D.C., Sangha.

31. See Fujitani, "BCA and Buddhist Sangha of America"; Reverend Mas Kodani, "Dojo," San Francisco *Hokubei Mainichi*, no. 8130, September 24, 1973, Part I, and no. 8136, October 1, 1973, Part II.

32. Ibid., and personal interviews 1972 to 1974.

33. Interview with Reverend S. Sakow, Santa Barbara, January 17, 1973.

34. "The English term CHURCH is a translation from EKKLESIA in Greek, which literally stands for a 'called-out assembly.' . . . English CHURCH is not directly associated with EKKLESIA at least phonetically. The term church as CIRICE appeared even before the official entrance of Christianity in 597 A.D. into the Old English language. CIRICE is the product of metamorphosis through Teutonic transliteration of Christian Greek KYRIAKON which means 'of the Lord.' . . . The etymological genealogy of the church as the house of Lord Jesus Christ is endorsed by Peter's concept of CHURCH: 'people of God.' " Fujitani, "BCA and the Buddhist Sangha of America."

"Temple, from the Latin, templum, is 'derived from a Greek verb to cut,' points to a sacred enclosure. The Ancient Roman soothsayer would stretch out his hands and mark off a section of the sky and name it sacred. This he called a templum. . . . He would often mark off a piece of ground in the same manner. . . . Eventually, that name was applied to the building or temple called there." Fujitani, "BCA and the Buddhist Sangha of America," p. 2.

35. Ibid., p. 2.

36. Ibid.

37. Kodani, op. cit., p. 1.

38. Interview with Reverend S. Sakow, January 17, 1973.

39. Interview with Reverend A. Takemoto, Los Angeles, February 26, 1972.

40. Interview with Reverend M. Kodani, Los Angeles, February 26, 1972.

41. For the ministers' response to the questionnaire, especially concerning the problems facing them, see Chapter 6.

42. A future paper will discuss each of the economic programs and the fund-raising procedure.

CHAPTER 8 | *The American Buddhist Church and the Japanese Ethnic Minority Face the Future*

Both the BCA headquarters and member temples have changed now that the Issei are passing on and the Nisei are in firm control of the various boards of directors and many other leadership positions within the religious institution. But already the Sansei are viewed as the promise of the future, and they are asking for more changes in the organizational structure. The differences among the three generations are highlighted by the Reverend Koshin Ogui:

> As history shows, the Issei had to work to support their families, nothing but work. The Nisei were educated by the Issei to build up their lives the same as the *hakujin* [Caucasian] people. So you see the majority of Nisei people out to buy cars and homes. They don't think about spiritual matters. They are more satisfied with fancy cars and homes. The Sansei are raised in such a background and are getting tired of it. Of course, they respect their families. But they're looking for more importance in life—to go forward to fight for human rights, against racial discrimination and to help the community instead of building up their abundance.[1]

Reverend Ogui also points to the changes that are occurring within the Buddhist churches: "Ten years ago there were more Buddhist Conventions and conferences, but the young people were more interested in the dances. Today more young people come and talk to me about Buddhism. They're struggling [for] meaning. . . . They are seeking after the truth, the Buddha Dharma."[2] We have already discussed the various changes within the BCA instigated by and for the Sansei, particularly the Kinnara and Relevant American Buddhists groups. But what of the future? Is it possible to make any meaningful generalizations about the BCA as its churches enter their seventy-eighth year? Today, Jodo Shinshu Buddhism is almost entirely a Japanese American ethnic religious organization; but even though the temples were built by and for the Japanese, "Buddhism is not for one race, but for all races."[3]

The present BCA bishop predicts an interethnic base for Jodo Shinshu in future years:

> Bishop Kenryu Tsuji of BCA told the group [Nisei Buddhist Society], San Jose, California, that the forthcoming 75th anniversary celebration of the founding of BCA is drawing mostly Japanese delegates from the Asian countries, Hawaii, Canada and United States, but when the 100th anniversary of BCA is celebrated in 1999, there should be a strong delegation of non-Japanese Shin-Buddhists, black, brown, white and red, from the Southern states as well as from [the] general community.[4]

Is this idealistic, interethnic mixture within the BCA a real possibility, or is it merely wishful thinking? What will the future hold for the BCA and its member temples?

All prognostications must, of course, be tentative, for crisis and catastrophe, so typical of BCA history, are inherently unpredictable. However, past experience is sufficiently broad to allow for reasonable inference. We shall therefore review the various problems and solutions discussed in previous chapters, and consider their implications for the future.

The Current and Future Status of the Japanese Americans

The 1970s are a time of turmoil and uncertainty for the Japanese Americans. On the one hand, official statistics concerning social, economic, occupational, and political indicators show that the members of this group have achieved far in excess of what their early history might have allowed them to expect. As one scholar writes, ". . . the Japanese case [in America] constitutes the outstanding exception to the generalization that past oppression blocks present progress."[5] On the other hand, many Japanese Americans maintain that they are part of an underprivileged minority group. This contention rests upon continual evidence of discrimination and prejudice and the lack of total acceptance by American society. There are numerous examples of underemployment, lack of social support services, insensitivity in the educational field as well as in literature, arts, and communication media.

The turmoil is best indicated by the lack of consensus among members of the group as to their present status in America. A few Japanese American writers concentrate on the "success-story" image—that is, that the Japanese Americans have made a success of their stay in America. One salient image frequently placed upon this group is that of America's "Model Minority." A minority, however, model or not, is inherently separate from the mainstream society. Also, an ideological problem inherent in this label makes it objectionable to some Japanese Americans. That is, some argue that the rise from the status of an oppressed minority to that of a successful American group gives evidence to many that the American ideal of equality, liberty, and justice works for all. Those groups still in the "minority" category, the evidence suggests, can make it, can succeed if they desire, since diverse groups have assimilated in the past, the Japanese American group being but one in a long list of examples.

Let us then examine briefly the current and future status of the Japanese Americans. This short section will provide a backdrop for a discussion of the future of the Buddhist Churches. Since lack of space precludes an in-depth treatment of the entire realm of social characteristics, the focus will be upon economy, employment, and education.

As a whole, Japanese Americans no longer qualify as an economically depressed group. The median income, using 1970 figures, is reported to be $12,515, a figure quite high when one considers that the total U.S. median income is $9,590. Also, male Japanese Americans are found more frequently in professional, technical, managerial, and administrative fields; 33 percent of their work force is in these fields, compared with 25 percent of the total U.S. male work force. The percentage working in sales and clerical jobs is the same (15 percent) for both groups. The largest disparity between the two groups is in the percentage of craftsmen, foremen, and operatives; 30 percent of the Japanese American work force is in this category, compared with 41 percent of the total male work force. In service work, farm managing, farm laboring, and other laboring fields, the percentage of the Japanese American male work force is 22 percent, and that of the total U.S. male work force is 19 percent. The occupation statistics on the females, both Japanese American and total U.S., are quite similar.

What is indicated above is a twofold picture. Although many Japanese Americans are becoming economically and professionally successful, a large proportion still works in manual, menial, and service trades. This latter group is often composed of the elderly, the unschooled, and the untrained. The move upward occupationally is especially difficult for this group. For example, the following assertion has been made about the lack of equal employment opportunities for blue-collar workers and those at other levels of employment:

> By comparison with other minorities, it may be true that Japanese Americans have gained a degree of parity at the entry level of employment. However, this does not mean that we have had an equal employment opportunity in all areas of employment, especially blue collar jobs, management and executive positions, union and skilled crafts, political appointments, and public media.[6]

The less prestigious occupations have received less attention than the professional, managerial, or administrative fields. Thus with prior research accenting the positive or those who are "successful," it is precisely these people to whom the community's and the general public's eyes are turned and who make the model minority image a seemingly accurate stereotype.

As in many stereotypes, however, there appears to be a grain of truth. One pillar of the image is the high educational attainment of the Japanese Americans. There is usually a positive relationship between income, occupation, and educational level in America, leading one to expect that the most highly educated persons will have occupational positions with high annual incomes. Perhaps many of the early Issei saw the importance of this relationship. Comments such as "You can lose everything but a good education" or "Obey your teacher, she is always right" are still prevalent in the Japanese community. They might have aided the Nisei in their high achievement. A complete explanation of this process is beyond the scope of this section; however, since as early as the 1930 census the proportion of Japanese Americans in school, from primary schools to institutions of higher education, has been higher than all other groups in America, including native whites.[7] This disparity, in completion of one or more years of high school and one or more years of college, has continued almost without exception to recent times. The 1970 census reports that of all Japanese males sixteen years and older, 70 percent have finished high school and 19 percent have finished college; for the females the figures are 67 percent and 11 percent. In comparison, of the total U.S. males sixteen years and older, 54 percent have finished high school and 13 percent college, and of the woment, 55 percent and 8 percent. The high level of educational attainment does not mean an absence of educational problems. Some Japanese community representatives talk about a steady rise in the school-drop-out rate; others show at various institutions lack of Japanese American faculty and secondary school administrators with respect to the students' Nikkei population.[8]

By combining the statistics on education, employment, and occupation, we can explicate a tentative finding: there appears to be an over-achievement in educational attainment and an underachievement in occupational level and income. We have already talked about males being overrepresented in the service and manual employment areas. However, even with the high educational level, the Japanese American males are in fact underachieving with respect to income.

> An analysis of income levels of men in the total U.S. population and in the Japanese population relative to the proportions with a college education . . . reveals that the income levels of Japanese in the United States are lagging behind those of the total population . . .[9]

Within the total U.S. white population, there are, to every person with a college degree, 1.5 men and 0.1 females, ages twenty-five to thirty-four, earning $10,000 or more. For the Japanese American males in the same category, there is less than one person, 0.9, and for the females, 0.1. If the age range is expanded to include twenty-five to sixty-four years, the U.S. white population figure for males is 2.33, for females, 0.3; for the Nikkei males 1.99, for females 0.4. Within the work force, then, especially in light of their higher educational attainment, Japanese American males are receiving proportionately less money. The females are about equal with the U.S. total females.

These three important areas—employment, education, and income—were highlighted in this section because they are important cornerstones to the image of the Japanese as a successful minority. However, even a cursory view of these areas reveals an ambiguous picture of success. Other areas of social concern show that Japanese Americans are facing many of the particular social ills confronting the rest of society. For instance, where once the official statistics could show a low incidence of crime, juvenile delinquency, and mental illness, such indicators are now undergoing closer examination. Such problems were prevalent in the past, but they were rarely made known to the wider public. One reason for the biased statistics is that the Japanese community was socially closed to outside investigators. Individual social pathologies were kept within the confines of the families or within the communities if at all possible. Within the past decade, however, the Japanese Americans appear to have become less hesitant about discussing personal and community problems.

Although the major problems still center around discrimination and prejudice, there are other problems in areas of social support services, rising delinquency rates, the elderly, rising mental illness rates, redevelopment or urban planning, drug offenders, adjustment of new immigrants, etc. The degree or extent of such problems differs from one community to another.

Thus the current status of the Japanese Americans is in a state of turmoil and uncertainty. The change in economic and social status since the mid-1940s cannot be denied. But the group still has less than total acceptance, and internal dissension is now open for public examination; internal problems cry out for solutions.

Furthermore, there is another unpredictable factor: Japan's relationship to and image in America. So long as Japan is seen as a friend, an ally to America, the Japanese Americans may look forward to tolerance and more acceptance by the American populace. But as the events after December 1941 point out, factors beyond the control of this American minority may have a bearing on its future status. Thus, not only is the present status still in flux and turmoil, the uncertainty is heightened when we speak of the future.

Uncertainty of Futures

All the problems and crises documented in this work demonstrate that the outcomes or solutions could not have been predicted. Where there was a crisis, either at the individual temples or at BCA headquarters, leaders or members banded together to effect a solution, which in turn sometimes created the background for a future crisis. It is always difficult to foresee results; even in a laboratory, where all factors can be controlled, one would do well to maintain a probability statement concerning the outcome of any experiment. The problem is so much the greater in a large social setting, where the experimenter/observer is all but powerless to control events. The vagaries of individual conduct, multiplied by the number of individuals, gives in most instances only the slightest hint as to the eventual outcome of any set of occurrences.

We have previously detailed the problems and crises of the BCA and its temples to demonstrate that the present situation is the outcome of a unique history. This history has been rooted in habit and disrupted by crises and continuing problems whose solutions or outcomes in their aggregate have shaped the institution as it now exists. Only through analysis of this complex process can the BCA be clearly understood.

At any particular point, individuals have the option of choosing among a multiplicity of realities.[10] We can literally choose the reality that we desire to perceive and interact with the surrounding social world at any particular moment. Individuals have all chosen the particular reality from which their consequent actions arose, and the history of the BCA appears to be a single continuous stream of events emanating from prior events. Yet, at any particular juncture the members of the BCA had a choice of paths, and those they elected not to follow must also be considered. For example, if the members at large had rejected the decision of the Issei ministers and NABM in 1929 to start the Endowment Fund (*Zaidan*) and to encourage the initiation of Nisei ministerial training, today there might have been few or no English-speaking ministers and no Institute for Buddhist Studies.

Such "what if" speculations are not conducive to defensible analysis: what might have been is past. However, it is important to bear in mind that what did occur was not the only possible occurrence. Where realities are subjective, and their numbers infinite, the same analysis can be made for the future.

The future of the BCA is shrouded in uncertainties because the members can choose from many present realities, all of which would produce different future conditions.

Although the idea of the future is itself flexible, to the minds of the actors themselves it may *seem* inflexible. At any time the members and ministers may feel and act as if their decision is the right and only problem-solving course possible. In the days just prior to the evacuation, the NABM leaders prepared for the eventual dislocation into assembly centers and internment camps; hardly a voice was raised in opposition by the Buddhists or by the Japanese American population as a whole.[11] However, when viewed from the present perspective, the calm and accepting entrance into the evacuation camps can be perceived as only one possible course of action. The inmates might have protested; they could have objected en masse; the Issei might have all decided to return to Japan. Yet, most saw the situation as an inevitable byproduct of the war with Japan and Germany, and peacefully prepared for the dislocation into an unknowable situation. Men may believe that their chosen reality is inflexible and thus unwittingly practice "bad faith."[12]

From the beginning of the NABM in 1899, a multitude of futures has been possible. The present, as it is known today, is not the only possible one. There has been a continual reassignment of priorities, and old choices have sometimes reappeared with new images (or old ones resuscitated). The previous chapters have discussed in detail the impact of Japanese immigration (and the immigration laws) on the NABM-BCA institution. The traditional Buddhist swastika was habitually utilized until 1941, then largely abandoned until it was readopted by a Sansei group, the Kinnara. The traditional method of financing churches, by pledges and donations, has now been made obsolete by the large financial programs initiated by the headquarters. The importance of the Issei generation has declined, and the problem of keeping the Nisei and Sansei within the membership has grown more serious. The traditional method of training ministers—sending them to Japan for their Buddhist education—has now been modified to a large degree by the institutionalization of an American Buddhist training center called the Institute of Buddhist Studies. Buddhist practices and ceremonies have in the main withstood the changes in the Japanese American generations, but the encroachment of the Judeo-Christian-based English language has created problems in the proper translation of key Buddhist concepts. Now, at least one group, the Kinnara, is attempting to return to the purely Japanese, or traditional, methods of religious worship, emphasizing meditation and the use of Japanese musical instruments (instead of the piano), and again stressing sutra chantings.

Looking ahead, we may easily conceive of many futures for the BCA, which is really just another way of saying that the future is uncertain. The distinguished historian H. A. L. Fisher has, in another context, made some highly applicable remarks:

> One intellectual excitement has . . . been denied me. Men wiser and more learned than I have discovered in history a plot, a rhythm, a predetermined pattern. These harmonies are concealed from me. I can see only one emergency following another, as wave follows upon wave, only one great fact with respect to which, since it is unique, there can be no generalization . . . the play of the contingent and the unforeseen.[13]

All this does not, of course, preclude our seeking patterns in the life of individuals or groups. It does, however, throw into question theoretical assumptions on the directions of change, especially the prevailing Aristotelean and neo-Aristotelean theories concerning the evolutionary changes in race relations so well exemplified by Robert E. Park.[14]

Trends, patterns, and cycles exist only in the mind of the observer; the data of individual or group lives do not inherently support such constructs. By themselves, data are simply events or occurrences made salient by the actor or observer and then "made sense of."[15] The data of the social world, as Herbert Blumer points out, are merely the actors' actions and reactions to events in which they discern social meaning, themselves always open to some new interpretation. Events can, and often do, occur outside the involved groups; however, for the events to be perceived as a crisis, they must be recognized by the members themselves. World War II and the subsequent internment of the Japanese and Japanese Americans are obvious examples of events unforeseen by the affected group. Once the evacuation process was started, meanings were given by the group and actions were taken on the basis of those meanings. When one talks about the predictability of the future and/or a theory of the directionality of an inherent change in groups, one must keep in mind that "the proper picture of empirical science . . . is that of a collective quest for answers to questions directed to the resistant character of the given empirical world under study. One has to respect the obdurate character of *that* empirical world under study."[16] The object of our empirical study is the Buddhist church, and its past and present actions must be respected if we hope to predict a future.

Another fact that should be emphasized is that predictions become steadily more difficult as they extend further into the future. Given the nature of crisis, unforeseen and in most cases unimaginable, differing meanings may be attached by an individual or individuals within a group, and different meanings arising *between* groups make the assumption of a unilinear change and predictable future very tenuous indeed. The possibility also exists that multidimensional changes will take place at the same time. At any one moment, a multitude of forces may impinge upon the total institution, necessitating an immediate decision, while at other times the continuity of social life will flow onward, only periodically punctuated by particular events or decisions affecting a single church or sector of the BCA. An example of the former circumstance was the evacuation during World War II, when the entire lifeworld of the Japanese Americans was involved, as they prepared for the eventual encampment to the relocation centers. But clearly in the latter category is the method by which each church attempts to meet its peculiar financial encumbrances, through donations, bazaars, membership dues, and so forth; here, each church has its own yearly method, depending upon such variable factors as the financial base of the membership and the participation of the surrounding community.

Possible Futures

Although any discussion of the future is inherently fraught with peril, certain problems presently facing the BCA, and recognized by the ministers and laymen, deserve our attention here. It is difficult to ascertain which problem or problems will continue and will later become more pressing. Historically (except in rare instances such as the creation of the *Zaidan*) the BCA has not taken much action to forestall future problems. But they have attempted to solve them as they occurred, treating them as immediate rather than continuing needs. Richard Beardsley, in explaining Buddhism, suggests one reason for this lack of planning by contrasting the Christian and Buddhist traditions in Japan:

In simple terms, Christianity is activist where traditional Buddhism and Shinto take a position of passivity or retreat; the Christian position accords with the expectation that man can mold and improve the external world rather than with the premise that he must accommodate himself to immutable, external realities.[17]

While Buddhism implicitly teaches acceptance, it places no stricture against forthright confrontation of clear and present threats. The recent membership- and BCA-sponsored arguments concerning the book *Japanese Americans: The Untold Story*, as well as the inclusion of the Divine Creation Theory in California school textbooks, attest to the involvement of Buddhists in the wider political sphere.

Yet, patterns of action rooted in historical tradition are difficult to eradicate. One possible future is the continuation of the past, with the BCA and member temples reacting to problems only as they become insistent. One year would be like the next, with each temple occupied with its own services, bazaars, and Japanese movies, and with the members attending or sponsoring district conferences, annually passing the BCA budget, and so on.

But there are other possible futures, which will be determined by how a number of present problems are resolved: (1) decreasing and changing membership; (2) the ethnic character of the membership; (3) economic problems at many churches, especially at headquarters; (4) the proper techniques for teaching Buddhism; and (5) interrelated problems with the ministry concerning number, composition, and finances. Each of these issues will be discussed in turn, to show the multiplicity of futures that may arise. All of the problems are ultimately interconnected, and the solution to any one of them may affect all the rest.

The first problem is that of the decreasing number and changing composition of the members. The strong and continual support of the Issei generation will soon disappear, as their numbers dwindle. Already in 1972, the BCA census reported that 49 percent of the persons tallied came from the zero to thirty-nine-year-old age bracket; 33 percent from the forty to fifty-nine group; and 18 percent from the over sixty group. Obviously, the Sansei generation has been gaining in numerical importance; even so, little direct attention has been devoted to this phenomenon. RAB, Kinnara, Scout awards, and Sunday Schools have been established for this generation, but whether programs are sufficient to retain the young as Buddhists in the future is an important question. Within the next ten years, over 35 percent (or 10,914) of the present membership, as tallied by actual BCA statistics, will be sixty years of age or older. This group cannot realistically be expected to be active participants in the financial support of the member temples and BCA.

A few communities, such as Los Angeles, San Francisco, and Salinas, have received a sizable influx of new Buddhist immigrants from Japan, but only in Salinas has this migration produced a significant increase in church membership. At other temples, newly arrived individual families may greatly aid the Buddhists, but the Nisei generation continues to dominate the present BCA.

If present trends continue, the BCA will dwindle in size, although in ten to fifteen years the Sansei will become the most active members of the church. One solution that has been offered to the BCA involves actively encouraging more Japanese Americans to become Buddhists. If a Buddhist study retreat center, or center for Buddhist learning, were created, ministers freed from the administrative duties encountered at individual temples could give prospective members intensive instruction in the rudiments of the religion.[18]

The problem of membership is closely tied to the ethnic character of the BCA. Not a few ministers believe that Jodo Shinshu Buddhism and the Buddhist temples must be open to persons of all nationalities. Bishop Tsuji has strongly advocated this stance, and he has stated his desire that in twenty-five years the general membership should include Buddhists from all ethnic and minority groups in the United States.[19]

Although this is the bishop's official position, and many ministers do agree with it, a few ministers have voiced their doubts as to whether this policy can in fact be implemented:

> This temple [San Francisco] was built by the Japanese pioneers, in the Japanese community, and most of its members are Japanese. So it has to work for the Japanese. . . . [However], Buddhism is not for one race but for all races. . . . I find it very difficult to think of Buddhism as flowing from the Issei, Nisei and Sansei to the rest of society.[20]

Another minister in opposition to the present situation stated, "The door is open, but they are not made welcome."[21]

One option available to an ethnic church desiring to attract other
groups is to create new temples free from the historical ethnic makeup.
As Bishop Tsuji has remarked:

> We now have eighty ministers. By 1990 we should double that
> number to 160 and make them self supporting (we should get
> people to make their own congregations, for example even in
> Vermont or Maine). I don't care what they do, be it dishwasher
> or high school teacher—but they should go out and start their
> own temples.[22]

The crucial element in this equation, according to the bishop, is the ministers. Creating new temples with non-Japanese membership would be a
radical departure from the present condition. Moreover, it would alleviate problems only if there are excess numbers of Buddhist priests available to minister to a dwindling membership. In some temples today, the
non-Japanese play a vital role in the services and activities, but nowhere
is there a temple where the Japanese Americans do not comprise the
majority of members. The creation of new temples is not a problem.
BCA has the IBS to train new ministers, and, given some monetary support, any minister could attempt to start a new *Sangha.* At present, this
solution is in the discussion stage.

The third problem that will continue is one of economics. The increasing needs of most churches and the BCA for monetary support
necessitate an ongoing financial program. One solution is the Fraternal
Benefit Program. This program asks members to pledge $500 in install-
ments prorated according to their age. The full sum reverts to a designated beneficiary upon the death of the member. The capital is invested.
Some of the profits are used to reduce individual temple assessments by
as much as 10 percent, and the rest of the profits go to the BCA general
fund. If the program reaches the 10,000 membership goal, it will "represent an annual income sufficient or adequate to initiate needed programs and to sustain existing programs much in need of financial assistance."[23] Whether the goal will be reached is an empirical question; if it
is, then the member churches may devote most of their membership
dues to their own particular needs. With the present need for monies,
much time and energy are expended on fund-raising activities, both at
the local level and at headquarters. The future may be one of an organi-

zation again placing its primary emphasis on Buddhism, and on member social services and activities. At present, the financial situation is a serious area of concern.

The "future" of an adequate and proper method for propagating Buddhism is difficult to foresee. The BCA has been publishing an increasing number of English Buddhist texts and writings, and further books, translations, and manuscripts are anticipated.[24] However, the body of English works on Jodo Shinshu is still limited. For the youth, the Sunday Schools remain the backbone and main vehicle of their Buddhist education. Once a child reaches the late teen years, his opportunity for a formal religious education trails off. In most instances he must attain it on his own. Most ministers have instituted Buddhist study classes at their churches, but some of these classes are poorly attended, and such programs are an additional burden for their already overloaded schedules. Many ministers have voiced concern over the ineffectiveness of religious education and have indicated that their members lack even the most rudimentary facts and knowledge of Buddhism. Two proposals not yet implemented have been offered to deal with this situation. The first is the aforementioned retreat center or center for Buddhist learning; although the center would be primarily for prospective members, it could be utilized to instruct the present membership. A real problem here may be the member's lack of desire to learn about his own religion. This disinterest may be a function of the inadequate training they receive during their earlier years. Another proposal is the Pilot Program in Formal Buddhist Education, presented by Reverend Arthur Takemoto in 1972. The program would utilize a traditional educational format, with courses and lectures; it would "provide opportunities for Dharma School teachers, and others, to receive the Dharma on a planned, accredited and continued basis."[25] Thus far, the project has not been implemented.

The final future consideration here concerns the ministry. A minister at a local temple is deeply concerned with religious matters; he also serves as the temple administrator, financial advisor, and social director, and in some instances as a Japanese language teacher; and he might even hold a part-time job outside the temple to supplement his income. But his main concern ought to be religious matters. As one Nisei minister said, "What is the main role of the minister? *Oshieru*—to teach and to cultivate Buddhism among the people."[26] The teaching of Buddhism goes hand in hand with social, financial, and administrative duties. Some churches cannot financially support more than one minister; because this man is their most visible representative, most members of the congregation expect him to carry out all the additional duties beyond those identified with services or religious activities. It is a most demanding task, calling for a very dedicated person. So far, over 300 men and women have served in the NABM or BCA, maintaining a close relationship between the *kaikyoshi* and the membership. Why do they continue to take on such a difficult task? Whatever any one minister does, there will always be someone within the congregation who will question his decision or action. The financial remuneration is small, the hours long, the private areas of his life limited, and his family is subject to the same questions concerning his decisions. One minister responded to this question by stating, "If I have at least one friend who can share the joy of Buddhism, then I have succeeded. It's not a matter of how many attend church if even one person attends. Then I can share my joy with him."

The ministerial problem is not with the individual priest; it is with the ministry itself. For example, at the present time, certain temples can afford to pay their ministers a larger salary (offering), while others, especially those with a smaller population, cannot. Regardless of the size of the minister's family, he must accept the local financial conditions. One solution would be to standardize all salaries by having the headquarters be the disburser, but then, as mentioned earlier, the local temples might lose control over their ministers. The local temples presently, in effect, hire and pay their ministers; in shifting their monies to the headquarters, some members might feel that they would lose their influence. The economic inequality of the present situation is difficult to resolve and will continue to trouble the BCA.

A relevant side-issue is that in the near future there may be more ministers available than can be accommodated within the local churches. One minister estimated that, given present conditions, by 1985 there will be only twenty-three independent churches with from fifteen to nineteen branches.[27] The number of active ministers by that time would number sixty-nine, with only forty-eight actually necessary. By 1990, the minister estimated, only twenty independent and thirty branches will be in existence, with nine other temples possibly surviving. Moreover, the active ministers would number around fifty-eight, with only thirty-five actually necessary. This minister's pessimism concerning the survival of the temples is probably realistic: decreasing membership, financial inability to sustain existing temples, and the migration and dispersion of Japanese Americans from agricultural to urban settings, all suggest that some temples will suffer. It is in any case true that such temples as those at Bakersfield and Vallejo, California, are no longer as active as before, and others are finding it increasingly difficult to maintain independent church status. One solution for the excess supply of ministers is the early retirement, with compensation from the BCA Ministerial Pension Fund, of older ministers, and the establishment of new temples in new locales as previously advocated by the bishop. The present physical temple structures will remain, and so will a number of Buddhist members in any casualty area. Any decision here will be difficult to make.

The training of new ministers in America is now the responsibility of IBS. With a decreasing membership, the pool of financial donors will also decrease, thus making the continuation of IBS problematical. Outside funding from other than Buddhist sources is one possible answer; another may be to make IBS a nonsectarian Buddhist center, drawing support from all Buddhists in America. The outcome remains to be seen.

This brief enumeration of present difficulties that will undoubtedly continue into the future is hardly exhaustive. In discussing membership, the ethnic character of the BCA, economics, propagation techniques, and the ministry, only the most obvious problems have been highlighted. Whether additional crises and catastrophes will occur is a matter for conjecture—although past experience suggests that they will. But it is the nature of such crises that is most important and most difficult to predict. The BCA will certainly have to continue to change and adapt to meet new emergencies and problems. What the institution will be like in ten, fifteen, or twenty-five years is an interesting question. But present problems are already large, and these will have to be dealt with: they will not simply fade away.

"Protestantism," Interreligiosity, and Pluralism

The year 1974 marked an important anniversary for the BCA and its members: their seventy-fifth year of existence. The commemoration ceremony, held in San Francisco, drew recognition statements from, among others, the president of the United States and the governor of California.[28] The mayor of San Francisco designated the week of August 24 through September 1 as "Shin Buddhist Week" in his city.[29] While an anniversary celebration is an occasion for festivities, it should not cloud the very real and important decisions that must be made. The future of the institution will depend to a large degree on the solutions it finds for its problems and on the ever-present possibility of crisis or catastrophe.

Three possible trends might characterize future changes within the Buddhist institution: "Protestantism," interreligiosity, or continual borrowing from other religious denominations and sects, and religious pluralism. Of these three, the latter two are most probable under present circumstances, and the first the least likely.

Some scholars presume the eventual assimilation of Buddhism into the American mainstream. Furthermore, they see this assimilation process to be moving toward a particular religious denomination in America, the Protestant.[30] This perspective assumes that the Buddhist church has no alternative but to accept Protestantization—that not to do so would be to jeopardize its own survival.[31]

This immense and overpowering influence by one American denomination is one possibility for the future of the BCA. However, given the pluralistic nature of the United States, both in religious and secular organizations, the path along the narrow walkway toward only Protestantization is very limiting.

A second alternative concerns the continued borrowing from other religious denominations and sects, i.e., interreligiosity. The BCA ministers and leaders are not isolated from other religious traditions in the United States. Since the 1950s, the members and clergy have shown increasing interest in entering into dialogues with other denominations. Although these dialogues have in some instances been less than satisfactory to the Buddhist ministers,[32] there have been many opportunities for ideational exchange, intra-Buddhist and extra-Buddhist. These contacts and exchanges have been twofold: non-Jodo Shinshu Buddhists and non-Buddhists coming to the individual temples or conferences, and Buddhists attending non-Buddhist religious and secular activities.

Let us start with the first category. Since the mid-1920s, Buddhist seminars have been sponsored by the NABM for the Nisei to encourage their knowledge of their religion.[33] Those who attended the seminars during these early years were Sunday School teachers, and the instructors were most often NABM priests. The seminars were suspended during World War II and were not reintroduced until 1952. Since then, they have been held on an annual basis in California and at other locales where they are sponsored by the various BCA district councils. Since 1952, the seminar speakers have not been exclusively Jodo Shinshu ministers; there have been Zen monks, Protestant ministers, Catholic fathers, Indian philosophers, authors such as Alan Watts, and many professors of religion and instructors from the universities.[34]

Within the individual temples there have been instances of non-Jodo Shinshu participation. At the Buddhist Church of San Francisco, for example, the head priest of the San Francisco Zen Center, Roshi Richard Baker, and Dr. Ajari Warwick of the San Francisco Buddhist Kailas Shugendo Temple spoke at the 1972 Nirvana Day Service.[35]

There have also been instances of combined services between sects and denominations. For example, in 1972, a combined Buddhist service was held at the Los Angeles Higashi Hongwanji Buddhist Church between Nishi and Higashi priests to commemorate the birth of Shinran Shonin and the birth of the Buddha.[36] Combined Christian and Buddhist services have also been held. Since at least 1972, the Memorial Day Service held in San Diego has featured a joint interreligious service at the local Mt. Hope cemetery with the Jodo Shinshu priest and ministers from the San Diego Japanese Holiness Church and Church of Christ Congregational.[37] The spirit of interdenominational cooperation is relatively new in San Diego. Until 1970, the three Japanese-dominated churches had little to do with each other; each church held separate services on Memorial Day at the place in the cemetery where the deceased Japanese were buried. The three church ministers decided to pool their efforts and hold a joint service: each would include, in the ceremony, important elements of his own religion for his own adherents, and each would give a brief talk or sermon to the congregants. There are about a hundred participants at Mt. Hope, and another ceremony follows at Fort Rosecrans Military Cemetery for interred Japanese American soldiers. At the latter site, about fifty people gather for a joint service. Whether this interdenominational practice will continue is up to the ministers; the congregants all know each other, and there seems to be no objection to the combined service.

Buddhist ministers have also been asked to other denominational services. For example, in 1962, at Manhattan's Community Church, a Unitarian minister, Donald Harrington, invited Buddhist priests and scholars to conduct a service in his church. This was probably the first Buddhist service in a Christian church in America.[38]

A few joint Christian-Buddhist wedding ceremonies have been held. When the couples have two different religions, instead of forcing a choice some ministers have entered into a cooperative ceremony:

> Buddhism and Christianity merged recently in a unique marriage ceremony between Cynthia Jeannie Seid and Richard K. Ishizaki. The bride, a Presbyterian, and the groom, a Buddhist, were united in wedlock on August 15 at the Buddhist Church of San Francisco in a special ceremony written and officiated by Rev. Koshin Ogui and Rev. Dennis Loo of the United Presbyterian Church.
>
> The marriage vows combined aspects of Buddhism and Christianity. It avoided mention of "God" or "Buddha," employing instead the concepts of "the Awakened One," "Universal Truth," the "Blessed Teacher" and "the All Compassionate One."[39]

The ceremony included an interesting syncretic synthesis. The usual Buddhist English service always includes the three homages "I put my faith in Buddha; I put my faith in Dharma (teachings); I put my faith in Sangha (brotherhood)." In the Christian-Buddhist wedding ceremony, the couple recited the following: "I take refuge in the Awakened One; I take refuge in the Universal Truth; and I take refuge in the Universal Brotherhood."[40] The roots of the new vow are Buddhist; however, its acceptance by all parties is an example of interdenominational cooperation. The acceptance of this type of ceremony indicates that the BCA and the ministers can adapt to particular situations while retaining their emphasis on a Buddhist heritage.

Interdenominational participation has occurred in areas other than religion. As mentioned earlier, the BCA has participated in a Boy Scout program since 1955, with Buddhist chaplains attending National Scout Jamborees since 1957. Boy Scout chaplains represent all religious faiths; moreover, the Jamborees present many opportunities for the Buddhist priests to cooperate with rabbis, fathers, and Protestant ministers to discuss topics of mutual interest and concern.[41]

The Japanese American Religious Federation of San Francisco is another example of interfaith cooperation. Here, as previously mentioned, eleven different Japanese American churches or missions joined together to sponsor a $6.1 million housing project for low-income families and the elderly. The 272-unit apartment, dedicated in September 1975, is probably the largest cooperative interfaith project entered into by Japanese Americans. The Buddhist Church of San Francisco and the BCA are participants, along with other Buddhist, Catholic, Protestant, and other independent churches.

In southern California, there are two large interfaith organizations in which the Jodo Shinshu Buddhist churches participate: the Buddhist-Christian Clergy Fellowship of Southern California (BCCF) and the Interreligious Council of Southern California (ICSC). The BCCF, formed in December 1969, seeks to create an atmosphere wherein the ministers may "understand each other's religions and work together on common community problems."[42] They have, for example, aided the Little Tokyo Redevelopment Agency by sending out questionnaires concerning a proposed home for the elderly, and they have cooperated in sending a letter of disapproval to the California State Board of Education concerning the book *Japanese Americans—The Untold Story.*[43]

The BCCF spirit is to work together. As one minister states, "Not that we compromise our religious convictions, but we cooperate with each other in regard to some of the social issues that are confronting many people."[44] This organization was an outgrowth of two previous organizations: the Los Angeles Buddhist Church Federation, of which the many Jodo Shinshu Buddhist churches in the area were participants, and the Japanese American Church Federation of Southern California. The composition of the BCCF does not reflect the religious background of the surrounding populace. It includes forty Buddhist priests and thirty Christian clergymen; the Japanese American population is estimated to be 60 percent Buddhist, 20 percent Christian, and 20 percent Shinto or no religion.[45] However, the fact that religious leaders are now able to work together on matters of mutual concern for their membership portends a hopeful future for the many Japanese Americans in southern California.

The largest interfaith group in which Jodo Shinshu Buddhists participate is the ICSC. Created in 1970, ICSC now includes participation by Christians (both Protestant and Catholic), Jews, Muslims, Buddhists, and Hindus.[46] The purpose of the council, according to the council president Rabbi Wolf, "is to provide the opportunity at the inter-faith level of dealing with issues that affect the total religious community and sharing our common concern for our community, nation and world."[47] Thus, through various groups in northern and southern California, the BCA and its member temples are now participating in cooperative religious organizations where dialogues can be conducted, ideas exchanged, and mutual problems discussed. There will undoubtedly be a continual exchange between the religious denominations, occasionally with direct input to temples from guest ministers or invited experts. Any borrowing will probably have little to do with the *content* of Buddhism, but there will almost certainly be discussion of the various problems facing not only the Buddhist churches, but all churches, temples, and synagogues in the United States.

Besides "Protestantism" and borrowing from other institutionalized religions, the BCA has a third alternative: religious pluralism. Given the democratic tradition in the United States, which has created a climate of acceptability of major religious beliefs, the Buddhists in America are free to practice their religion. Furthermore, the relatively short history of the BCA reveals an ethnic religious institution whose members are aware of, and have maintained, a particular identity. There is little inherent reason for the change, but at some point in its history, the Buddhist churches did become an "Americanized" religion. With the coming of the Nisei generation, the change from a Japanese- to English-language orientation was begun: services were held on Sundays, pianos or organs playing the *gathas* became prevalent, and the BCA-sponsored Camp Fire and Boy Scout troops and wedding ceremonies became as important as funeral services. These changes may be currently labeled as evidences of an Americanization process. Except for the scouting program and the use of English, however, the Sunday Schools, hymns, and wedding ceremonies are found in Jodo Shinshu Japanese Buddhism.

Americanization is not Protestantism; to label it as such is to severely delimit the change process of one particular denomination. Americanization is, if anything, the process whereby an institution or individual adapts, by making additions and deletions, to the American culture. There has been, in the past, contact between the NABM-BCA, non-Buddhist religions, and other Buddhist sects in America, and these contacts have become more numerous since the 1950s. Thus, a two-way exchange has been suggested, with all religious institutions benefiting from their interactions.

The influence of past priests, such as Reverend Ernest Hunt in Hawaii (from an Anglican religious background) and Reverend Julius Goldwater (from a Jewish religious background), has been noted. They were influential in the Buddhist institution from the 1920s to the early 1940s. For instance, many of the early English *gathas* for Buddhists were written by Reverend Hunt and his wife, and the *gathas* were apparently influenced by Christian melodies. With more priests and members becoming aware of the problem of translations, the older "hymns" have been replaced by new *gathas* written by Japanese Americans. For example, in 1950, BCA headquarters created a Music Department. Since then, a number of new *gathas* have been written by Japanese Americans and incorporated in the Buddhist service book and Sunday School *gatha* book.

The music used by the Buddhist churches comes from a variety of sources (and, as we will soon see, even from the present soft rock). However, the use of Buddhist music found in the BCA has its origins in the *gathas* and "hymnals" instituted in Japan *prior* to the Japanese immigrants' arrival in America. Buddhist music, with accompanying musical instruments, has had a long tradition in Japan:

> Buddhist music has long been sung to praise Buddha in the form of *Shomyo.* As *Shomyo* is sung in Oriental melody with Oriental instruments, it may sound heathen and strange to American ears that are used to Western Music. That is why the Buddhist chorus [Ryukoku University Male Chorus] is striving to find new Buddhist music in the Western style. The new style is only 100 years old.[48]

Thus, since at least 1874, Buddhist music in the Western tradition has been available at Ryukoku University, which is the main "seminary" for all priests within the Nishi Hongwanji Jodo Shinshu sect. It is not unreasonable to suppose that all missionary priests studying at Ryukoku came in contact with Buddhist music; therefore, the incorporation of such music into the Buddhist churches in America is not surprising.

Since the 1960s there have been increasing changes in the format of service presentation. With leadership coming from the Nisei and Sansei ministers, many churches have instituted experimental services without piano music, relying instead on sutra chanting and group recitation of Buddhist texts.[49] Differing seating arrangements have also been used, with participants sitting on cushions rather than on the chairs that are traditionally utilized. These changes are not to be found at all temples, and where they have been tried, they have constituted superficial changes in form: the contents of the services remain Buddhist. Furthermore, the changes have been made at the explicit behest of the Sansei. Many Sansei, and now an increasing number of Nisei, feel that the religious service pattern has become a ritual. The usual service format, instituted before World War II, is considered only a habit and not a sacred rite. Thus, in order to renovate the *Sangha* gatherings, the temples are experimenting with new formats.

A dramatic example of this change occurred at a San Francisco Bay area Junior YBA conference.[50] The main service opened with the Buddhists entering a dark seating area, each carrying a candle. The music played over the entrance was soft rock; the seats were placed in a U-shape configuration rather than in the usual straightline arrangement. The usual altar was modified; in front was placed a sacred Buddhist scroll, flanked merely with two candles instead of the ornate candle holders and vases of flowers. First, there was an informal introduction, and then adherents were asked to meditate. In place of a sermon by a minister, a talk was presented by a Sansei ministerial candidate. More meditation was followed by a candle-lighting ceremony, closing words, and a recessional out of the hall. As a result of this format change, the participants at the conference actually discussed a religious service instead of social activities, which is the usual topic of discussion. Whether this type of service will be instituted at the member temples is not the point: the fact that a few churches had initiated changes before the conference, and that others have since, indicates that the usual services are not held sancrosanct and may be altered.

Inherent in religious pluralism is a recognition and sanctioning of the various religious institutions in America. The acknowledgment of the BCA as an official organization, representing the many Buddhists in America, has been late in arriving. Probably the first time that a BCA priest was asked to participate in a secular activity, in his religious capacity, occurred during the University of California at Berkeley commencement ceremony on June 11, 1959. The Reverend Shozen Naito served as the chaplain and recited the aspiration and benediction.[51]

The most recent recognition of the Buddhists in America, and the BCA, came in December 1974, when Reverend Shoko Matsunaga, *rimban* of the Sacramento Buddhist Betsuin, was selected to serve as the new chaplain for the California State Senate. While this one-year appointment is largely symbolic and ceremonial, the selection of Matsunaga did have a small dramatic moment. The pastor of Southern California Baptist Church protested the appointment, stating: "In a day when so few things remain sacred . . . we see still another of the eternal truths being trampled . . . the existence of one God." Because the Buddhists do not invoke the blessings of a personal Judeo-Christian God, he continued, "there is no justification for an idol worshipper serving as a Senate Chaplain."[52] Many letters of support from Buddhists, non-Buddhists, newspapers, and secular organizations were sent to the Senate in support of its nomination and selection. The specific nominator, Senator Albert S. Rodda (D-Sacramento), with the support of most senators, has remained firm in his decision: "I think they [the Senate] are proud of the fact that we alternate Chaplains. It reflects the diversity of religion in California.[53]

Thus, religious pluralism posits a heterogeneous religious situation. The religious institutions in America are identifiably different. This is even more true of the Buddhist churches, whose prevalent ethnic composition, coupled with their identification as an Asian religion, has made them a stark contrast to other denominations. The Buddhist churches will continue to change, as they attempt to solve their many problems. As Buddhism becomes more acceptable to Americans in general, as is presently occurring, the reaction to this acceptance is difficult to foretell. To date, Jodo Shinshu Buddhism has remained a vital institution for the Japanese Americans by meeting their religious and ethnic needs while reinforcing their Buddhist identity. There is little reason to suppose that this situation will change in the near future. For the distant future, the leaders and ministers of the BCA envision a wider representation of racial groups within their institution. If this occurs, Buddhism will indeed become fully Americanized.

Notes

1. Interview by Glenn Omatsu, "Church Future: Buddhist Church," San Francisco *Hokubei Mainichi*, January 10, 1973, p. 1.

2. Ibid.

3. Ibid.

4. "Bishop Tsuji Looking Forward to 100th Anniversary," San Francisco *Hokubei Mainichi*, February 6, 1974, p. 1.

5. William Petersen, *Japanese Americans* (New York: Random House, 1971), p. 4.

6. Edison Uno, quoted in "Asian Americans and Pacific Peoples: A Case of Mistaken Identity." Report of the California Advisory Committee to U.S. Commission on Civil Rights, February 1975, p. 37.

7. Robert W. O'Brien, *The College Nisei* (Palo Alto: Pacific Books, 1949), pp. 12, 126.

8. Edison Uno, op. cit., pp. 37–38.

9. 1970 Census, vol. 2, p. 104.

10. The term *multiple reality* is derived from Alfred Schutz, but I use it somewhat differently than he does. See Alfred Schutz, "Don Quixote and the Problem of Reality," in *Collected Papers: Studies in Social Theory*, Vol. 2 (The Hague: Martinus Nijhoff, 1964), p. 135.

11. There were three important exceptions: Gordon Hirabayshi, Minoru Yasui, and Fred T. Korematsu. See tenBroek, et al., op cit.

12. "To put it very simply, 'bad faith' is to pretend something is necessary that in fact is voluntary." See Peter L. Berger, *Invitation to Sociology* (New York: Doubleday and Co., 1963), pp. 143–145.

13. Quoted in Robert A. Nisbet, *Social Change and History: Aspects of the Western Theory of Development* (New York: Oxford University Press, 1969), p. 284. From Geoffrey Barraclough, *History in a Changing World* (Oxford: Basil Blackwell, 1956), pp. 222–223.

14. See Robert E. Park, "Our Racial Frontier on the Pacific," *Survey Graphics* 6 (May 1, 1926): 196, and discussion by Stanford M. Lyman, *The Black American in American Sociological Thought: A Failure of Perspective* (New York: G. P. Putnam's Sons, 1972), pp. 27–70.

15. For a statement of a sociology based on this concept of "actors making sense," see Lyman and Scott, op. cit., pp. 1–28.

16. Herbert Blumer, *Symbolic Interactionism* (Englewood Cliffs, N.J.: Prentice-Hall, 1969), p. 23.

17. Richard K. Beardsley, "Religion and Philosophy," in *Twelve Doors to Japan*, edited by John W. Hall and R. K. Beardsley (New York: McGraw-Hill, Inc., 1965), p. 338.

222 / BUDDHISM IN AMERICA

18. See Tetsuden Kashima, "Center for Buddhist Learning," Typescript, March 3, 1973.

19. "Bishop Tsuji Looking Forward."

20. Omatsu, op. cit.; and an interview with the Reverend Koshin Ogui, San Francisco *Hokubei Mainichi*, January 10, 1973, p. 1.

21. Reverend S. Oi, at the BCA Ministers' Conference, Oakland, Calif., August 28, 1973.

22. Bishop K. Tsuji at the BCA Ministers' Conference, Oakland, Calif., August 28, 1973.

23. "Fraternal Benefit Program," BCA, *Annual Report, 1973*, p. 138.

24. Two recent publications include *Shin Buddhist Handbook* (1972) and *Jodo Shinshu Book* (1973).

25. Reverend Arthur Takemoto, "A Proposal for a Pilot Program in Formal Buddhist Education," mimeographed, June 6, 1972.

26. Reverend Laverne Sasaki at the BCA Ministers' Conference, Oakland, Calif., August 28, 1973.

27. Interviewed minister desired to remain anonymous. February 12, 1972.

28. "President Ford Sends Greeting to BCA Event," San Francisco *Hokubei Mainichi*, August 26, 1974, p. 1.

29. "Buddhist Week Proclaimed," San Francisco *Hokubei Mainichi*, August 20, 1974, p. 1.

30. This is the position taken by Robert Spencer and Isao Horinouchi in their respective dissertations on the Buddhist church. Both of these studies are informed by the acculturation-assimilationist approach and tend to equate assimilation with Protestantism. Spencer, writing in 1946, focuses on acculturation and implicitly points toward Protestantization. Horinouchi, writing in 1973, discusses the Protestantism of the BCA. Note that Horinouchi and Spencer suggest that Protestantism is the *only* possibility for the future; what we must now see is that this is only one possible future. See Spencer, op. cit., and Horinouchi, op. cit.

31. Horinouchi has stated, "The Protestantization of Buddhism is not merely one of emulating the dominant culture because of economic gain or other utilities; but the process became necessary as part of survival in an indigenous religion in a new environment." Op. cit., p. 15.

32. One interviewed BCA minister stated: "I used to be on a panel of the National Conference for Christians and Jews; they used to almost tell me what to say rather than what I wanted to say. They said, 'you can't give answers like that, don't give answers like that.' But how else can I give an answer? They were really mad about it—especially the Catholic fathers—they used to get on my back." Los Angeles Betsuin Temple, February 26, 1972.

33. Munekata, op. cit., p. 96.

34. For example, at the most recent BCA Northwest District Seminar held at Seattle Betsuin, Washington, on September 21–22, 1974, the speakers were a religious editor for a Seattle newspaper, Earl Hansen; a Soto Zen priest, Reverend Soryugen Fisher; and a sociologist.

35. "Ecumenism Enhanced at Buddhist Temple Service," San Francisco *Hokubei Mainichi*, no. 7650, February 24, 1972, p. 1.; and "Another Ecumenical Rite at S. F. Buddhist Temple," San Francisco *Hokubei Mainichi*, no. 7702, April 25, 1972, p. 1.

36. "Joint Service to Mark Two Buddhist Holidays," Los Angeles *Times*, June 3, 1972, Part 1, p. 29.

37. Personal observation, May 30, 1972, 1973, and 1974.

38. "Buddhism in America," *Time* (October 26, 1962): 60.

39. "Christian, Buddhist Vows Said at Nuptial Ceremony," San Francisco *Hokubei Mainichi*, August 20, 1971.

40. Ibid.

41. "National Scout Jamboree East," *BCA Newsletter* 11, no. 10 (October 1973): 2–3.

42. John Dart, "Japanese-American Clergy Work Together," Los Angeles *Times*, May 22, 1971, Part 1, p. 25.

43. Ibid.

44. Ibid.

45. Ibid.

46. "Interreligious Council Supports United Way," Los Angeles *Times*, August 19, 1972, Part 1, p. 24; John Dart, "Southland Interreligious Council Perhaps Broadest Group in U.S.," Los Angeles *Times*, April 14, 1973, Part 1, p. 27.

47. John Dart, "Los Angeles Buddhist Group Joins Interreligious Council," *BCA Newsletter* 10, no. 8 (August 1972): 4.

48. "Brief History of the Ryukoku University Male Chorus," program notes for the BCA 75th Anniversary Celebration, San Francisco, August 29, 1974. (The booklet was printed in Japan; no author, date, or pagination was given.)

49. From interviews with Buddhist ministers at Reedley, Palo Alto, Oakland, Fresno, and Guadalupe Buddhist churches in California. They stated that they have sanctioned services with differing formats as discussed in the text.

50. July 29, 1972.

51. Munekata, op. cit., p. 73.

52. Los Angeles *Times*, January 26, 1975, Part 1, p. 3; Los Angeles *Times* editorial, February 12, 1975, Part 2, p. 6.

53. Ibid.

APPENDIX 1 | *List of BCA Churches and Temples*[1]

	Name	Date of Establishment
1.	Buddhist Church of San Francisco (Cal.)	July 1898
2.	Buddhist Church of Sacramento, Betsuin (Cal.)	Dec. 1899
3.	Fresno Buddhist Church, Betsuin (Cal.)	Jan. 1901
4.	Seattle Buddhist Church, Betsuin (Wash.)	Nov. 15, 1901
5.	San Jose Buddhist Church, Betsuin (Cal.)	Aug. 28, 1902
6.	Oregon Buddhist Church (Portland, Oreg.)	Nov. 29, 1903
7.	Oakland Buddhist Church (Cal.)	June 1904
8.	Placer Buddhist Church (Cal.)	Jan. 1905
9.	Los Angeles Hompa Hongwanji Buddhist Temple, Betsuin (Cal.)	1905
10.	Hanford Buddhist Church (Cal.)	1905
11.	Stockton Buddhist Church (Cal.)	1906
12.	Watsonville Buddhist Church (Cal.)	July 7, 1907
13.	Guadalupe Buddhist Church (Cal.)	Jan. 1909
14.	Bakersfield Buddhist Church[2] (Cal.)	Feb. 1909
15.	Vacaville Buddhist Church[3] (Cal.)	1909
16.	Berkeley Buddhist Church (Cal.)	May 10, 1911

1. From Dr. Ryo Munekata, Los Angeles, November 22, 1973.
2. Not dues-paying churches; independent status.
3. No longer independent churches: Vacaville is under the Sacramento Betsuin; El Centro is under San Diego; Brawley is under San Diego; Ft. Lupton is under Tri-State Buddhist Church.

Name	Date of Establishment
17. Salt Lake Buddhist Church (Utah)	1912
18. White River Buddhist Church (Auburn, Wash.)	Oct. 1912
19. Palo Alto Buddhist Church (Cal.)	June 7, 1914
20. Tacoma Buddhist Church (Wash.)	1915
21. Buddhist Temple of Alameda (Cal.)	Jan. 4, 1916
22. Tri-State Buddhist Church (Denver, Colo.)	Mar. 13, 1916
23. Florin Buddhist Church (Cal.)	Mar. 1918
24. Buddhist Church of Santa Barbara (Cal.)	Jan. 4, 1922
25. Buddhist Church of Salinas (Cal.)	Mar. 9, 1924
26. El Centro Buddhist Church[3] (Cal.)	Feb. 1925
27. Buddhist Church of San Diego (Cal.)	May 19, 1926
28. San Luis Obispo Buddhist Church (Cal.)	Feb. 3, 1927
29. Brawley Buddhist Church[3] (Cal.)	Oct. 1927
30. Buddhist Church of Lodi (Cal.)	Apr. 1929
31. Oxnard Buddhist Church (Cal.)	1929
32. Yakima Buddhist Church (Wash.)	1929
33. Delano Buddhist Church[2] (Cal.)	June 22, 1929
34. San Mateo Buddhist Church (Cal.)	1930
35. Buddhist Church of Marysville (Cal.)	Apr. 26, 1931
36. Gardena Buddhist Church (Cal.)	1931
37. Buddhist Church of Parlier (Cal.)	July 1931
38. Arizona Buddhist Church (Phoenix, Ariz.)	Sept. 3, 1933
39. Enmanji Buddhist Church (Sebastapol, Cal.)	Apr. 15, 1934
40. Visalia Buddhist Church (Cal.)	1935
41. Reedley Buddhist Church (Cal.)	1936
42. Dinuba Buddhist Church (Cal.)	May 1937
43. New York Buddhist Church (N.Y.)	1938
44. Ft. Lupton Buddhist Church[3] (Colo.)	1938
45. Buddhist Temple of Utah-Idaho (Ogden, Utah)	1943
46. Midwest Buddhist Temple (Chicago, Ill.)	July 10, 1944

2. Not dues-paying churches; independent status.

3. No longer independent churches: Vacaville is under the Sacramento Betsuin; El Centro is under San Diego; Brawley is under San Diego; Ft. Lupton is under Tri-State Buddhist Church.

Name	Date of Establishment
47. Cleveland Buddhist Church (Ohio)	Jan. 1945
48. Detroit Buddhist Church[2] (Mich.)	June 1945
49. Idaho-Oregon Buddhist Church (Ontario, Oreg.)	1945
50. Spokane Buddhist Church (Wash.)	Nov. 1945
51. Twin Cities Buddhist Association[2] (Minneapolis, Minn.)	Apr. 14, 1946
52. Monterey Peninsula Buddhist Church (Seaside, Cal.)	Dec. 15, 1946
53. West Los Angeles Buddhist Church (Cal.)	1950
54. Senshin Buddhist Church (Los Angeles, Cal.)	1951
55. Pasadena Buddhist Church (Cal.)	Sept. 1, 1958
56. Mountain View Buddhist Temple (Cal.)	1961
57. Southern Alameda County Buddhist Church (Union City, Cal.)	1965
58. Orange County Buddhist Church (Anaheim, Cal.)	Apr. 25, 1965
59. Seabrook Buddhist Church (N.J.)	1965
60. Buddhist Temple of Marin (Cal.)	1968
61. Buddhist Church of Fowler (Cal.)	Jan. 1, 1969
62. Honeyville Buddhist Church (Utah)	Apr. 1, 1971
63. Venice Hongwanji Temple (Cal.)	Mar. 1, 1976
64. Washington, D.C., Sangha[4]	
65. Buddhist Fellowship of Sunnyvale[4] (Cal.)	

4. A gathering of Buddhists; neither a church nor temple. It is not a dues-paying member of the BCA.

APPENDIX 2 | *Questionnaire*

UNIVERSITY OF CALIFORNIA, SANTA BARBARA

BERKELEY · DAVIS · IRVINE · LOS ANGELES · RIVERSIDE · SAN DIEGO · SAN FRANCISCO

SANTA BARBARA · SANTA CRUZ

DEPARTMENT OF SOCIOLOGY

SANTA BARBARA, CALIFORNIA   93106

10 November 1972

Dear Reverend :

I am writing to you to ask for a little of your time in completing the enclosed questionnaire. This questionnaire is part of a study on the Buddhist Churches in America, and the results of the study, and in particular this questionnaire, will aid in understanding the present status of the church, and the particular church you are at now.

The enclosed questionnaire will take a little time to fill out, so I hope you will spare the time, and then return it to me in the pre-addressed envelope. As you can see there are two questionnaires, one in English and the other in Japanese. Please complete only _one_ of them, whichever you desire, and then return the completed one to me.

I realize that this is asking you to take time out of a busy schedule. Yet, the research on the church and its ministers has been very sparse, and the topic is very important. Let me add that this is a study being conducted independently of the B.C.A., but that when completed the results will be made available to the church if they so desire.

In some churches there may be more than one minister. Even if that is the case I would like all ministers to fill out the questionnaire as if you were the sole minister. This is necessary because some of the questions deal with subjective areas and thus responses are needed by everyone. There are also some ministers who have no official affiliation with one temple or one church. If you are in this category, please fill in the non-appropriate questions with the mark "n/a" (not applicable) and complete the rest of the questionnaire.

Your time and effort is greatly appreciated. If there are any questions about the questionnaire or the study itself, please do not hesitate to contact me at the above mailing address or to call on the telephone: (805) 968-4625, (805) 961-3048.

Thank you. I remain yours,

In Gassho,

Tetsuden Kashima
Acting Assistant Professor
Department of Sociology and
Asian American Studies Program

UNIVERSITY OF CALIFORNIA, SANTA BARBARA

BERKELEY · DAVIS · IRVINE · LOS ANGELES · RIVERSIDE · SAN DIEGO · SAN FRANCISCO   SANTA BARBARA · SANTA CRUZ

DEPARTMENT OF SOCIOLOGY

SANTA BARBARA, CALIFORNIA   93106

前略

今度米國に於ける佛教會の研究を行う事になりまして、是非とも開教使諸先生方の御協力をお願いしたいと存じます。

ここに貴佛教會に関する質問表を同封いたします。これは米國佛教會研究の一部です。その研究の結果は、特にこの質問表の回答は現在先生が在職されている佛教會の現状を理解する為に貴重な資料となります。

同封の質問表を記入するには、少し手間がかかりますが、どうぞ時間をさかれて記入され、備え付の封筒で返送されるようお願いいたします。御覧の様に二種類の質問表があり、一部は英文で他は和文です。どちらか都合の良い片方のみを記入され、返送して下さいませ。

このお願いが先生のお手数を取る事は十分承知しております。しかし、佛教會及び開教使先生についての研究は、誠に少く、この課題は極めて重要であります。なおこの研究はBCA・（米國佛教団）とは関係なく行っておりますが、結果は御要望がありますればBCA・及び貴佛教會に御報告

致します。

佛教會によっては、一人以上の開教使がおられるかも知れませ
ん。もしその場合でも、全部の開教使の方々が、各人が、
その佛教會で唯一の開教使であるとの見解に立たれ、御
自分の意見を質問表に記入して頂きたく思います。そう
お願いします訳は、質問の幾つかは主観的なものであり、
皆の方からの御回答がいただきたいからです。

寺院又は佛教會を持たれない開教使先生がおられます。
その場合、該当しない質問に ✓印を引かれ、残りを記入
されるようお願い致します。

先生が時間をさかれて質問表に御回答なされる事をこころから
感謝っております。もし質問表又はこの研究自体に疑問、ある
いは不審な点がありましたら御遠慮なくお手紙下さるか、
次の番号にお電話下さいませ。自宅(八〇五)九六八一四六二五、
オフイス(八〇五)九六一一三〇四八。心から御協力感謝致します。

合掌

加州大學サンタバーバラ校 社会學部・次助教授

昭和四十七年十一月十日

開教使先生各位

鹿島哲典

QUESTIONNAIRE FOR MINISTERS

The questionnaire is composed of various types of questions dealing first with the particular church to which you minister, and then to a section dealing with the ministers themselves. Please fill in the blanks with responses to the best of your knowledge. It is important that you feel that you are expressing your true feelings as you answer the questions so feel free to write comments in the margin when you feel that a question is unclear, or doesn't allow you to express exactly how you feel.

I. To begin, this section deals with your church or temple:

1. What is the official name of the temple or church? _____

2. What is the address of the temple or church? _____ .

3. When was your church organized? _____ .

4. What was(were) the reason(s) for organizing a church in your particular area? _____
    _____
    _____
    _____

5. a. Is the church incorporated as a religious church under state law? Yes ____ No ____ .

    b. If the answer is yes, when was the church first incorporated? _____ .

    c. If the answer is no, how is the church organized? _____
        _____
        _____

6. If the church is incorporated please answer the following questions. If the church is not yet incorporated, or will not be, please skip this question.

    a. Did the church utilize the form, "By-Laws of the Buddhist Church of _____" sent by the Buddhist Church of America in 1967 as a model of incorporation?

        Yes _____ No _____ .

    b. If the answer is "No", how is the church organized? _____
        _____
        _____
        (use other paper if necessary)

7. Most Buddhist Churches in America have a Board of Directors as having the powers of the corporation. Is this true of your church?

    Yes _____ No _____

    a. If the answer is "Yes" how many persons constitute the board? _____

    b. How are the Board members selected? _____
        _____

    c. Does the minister have a voting position on the Board? Yes ____ No ____

    d. If the answer to 7c is "yes" is the right to vote permanent? Yes ____ No ____

2

8. If the answer to question 7 is "No", who has the power of the church and how are important decisions made? _____

    _____

    _____

9. What percentage of the Board of Directors, or persons in Question 8:

    Issei? _____ Kibei? _____ Nisei? _____ Sansei? _____ Others (please specify)? ____
    (Please use approximations if the real figures are unknown.)

10. What other areas besides the city in which your church is located does the church have jurisdiction? _____ .

11. This section deals with the membership in the church or temple. (Please use approximations where necessary.)

    a. How many families are members of your church? _____

    b. What is the total number of individuals? _____

    c. Approximately how many individuals in the church jurisdiction are Buddhists regardless of actual membership or not in the church? _____

    d. Approximately how many Japanese or Japanese Americans (totally) are there in the area regardless of church affiliation? _____

    e. Is there a local Japanese Christian Church?   Yes _____   No _____ .

    f. If the above question is answered "Yes" is there a full-time minister?   Yes _____   No _____

    g. Approximately how many families are members of the J. Christian Church? _____

12. What percentage of your church membership is: Issei? _____   Nisei? _____   Sansei? _____

    Others? (please specify) _____

13. What is the number of individuals (approximately) that the church aid outside of the main temple? (For example, the San Diego Church also conducts services in Vista, Calif.) Please give the location and the number of individuals.

    _____

    _____

14. The following section deals with the economic aspects of the church. Confidentiality will be observed.

    a. What is the annual expenditure of the church?   1971 _____   1972 (est) _____

    b. What is the annual income of the church?   1971 _____   1972 (est) _____

15. From what sources does the church derive its income?

(indicate the degree of importance)

	LOW	(CIRCLE ONE)			HIGH
Membership dues	1	2	3	4	5
Contributions	1	2	3	4	5
Pledges (what kind?)	1	2	3	4	5
Movies	1	2	3	4	5
Bazaars (Food)	1	2	3	4	5
Bazaars (Carnival)	1	2	3	4	5
Others (Please list)	1	2	3	4	5
_____	1	2	3	4	5

16. What organizations are in the church and what is their approximate number?

Fujinkai	Yes _____	No _____	Number _____
YABA	Yes _____	No _____	Number _____
YBA	Yes _____	No _____	Number _____
JR. YBA	Yes _____	No _____	Number _____
Sunday School	Yes _____	No _____	Number _____
Study Group	Yes _____	No _____	Number _____
Jr. Fujinkai	Yes _____	No _____	Number _____

Others
(Please list with approx. numbers) _____ .

17. Please rate the following activities of the church according to the degree of importance that you think is important to your church.

(PLEASE CIRCLE THE DEGREE OF IMPORTANCE)
(CIRCLE ONE)

		Low				High
( ) a.	Social life and social activities	1	2	3	4	5
( ) b.	Participation in communities affairs	1	2	3	4	5
( ) c.	Concern over local economic questions	1	2	3	4	5
( ) d.	Concern over local political questions	1	2	3	4	5
( ) e.	Religious beliefs and activities	1	2	3	4	5
( ) f.	Helping members of the congregation (other than religious)	1	2	3	4	5
( ) g.	Helping others than those in the congregation	1	2	3	4	5
( ) h.	Sports or athletic activities	1	2	3	4	5
( ) i.	Fund raising activities for the church	1	2	3	4	5
( ) j.	Attempt to get more new Japanese or J. Amer. members	1	2	3	4	5
( ) k.	Attempt to get other than J. or J. Amer. members	1	2	3	4	5
( ) l.	Foster education other than religious (e.g. language)	1	2	3	4	5

Now please go back and rank order (from 1 to 12) the above activities according to the relative degree of importance for the church. Please use the parenthesis ( ) to the left of each item for this purpose. Place the number 1 next to the item that you think is most important, a "2" next to the second most important and so on. The number 12 should indicate the least important activity that you feel is for the church.

4

18. What other activity or activities is or are important for your church? _____

_____

19. This section deals with the church during the second world war:

   a. What happened to the church during the second world war? _____

   _____

   _____

   b. What happened to the members of the church during this time? _____

   _____

   c. How has the church or its membership changed since the end of relocation days? _____

   _____

   _____

20. This section deals with religious services:

   a. Do you have Sunday Schools? Yes _____ No _____ If "Yes" how often in a year _____

   b. Do you have regular services? Yes _____ No _____ If "Yes" how often in a year _____

   c. Do you have other Special Services? (e.g. Obon, Ohigan, etc.) Yes _____ No _____

   If "Yes" please list them _____

   _____

21. What do you see as some of the problems of the Buddhist Church today? _____

   _____

   _____

   _____

   _____

                                                        (use other paper if necessary)

22. What do you foresee as the problems of the church five or more years from now?

   _____

   _____

   _____

                                                        (use other paper if necessary)

23. What do you think your church should or could do about the problems? _____

   _____

   _____

24 What do you think the BCA Headquarters should or could do about the problems?

   _____

   _____

   _____

II. This section deals with the minister:

    25. a. What is your name?_____

        b. What is your age? (check one)   26-30 ____ , 31-35 ____ , 36-40 ____ , 41-45 ____ , 46-50 ___
           51-55 ____ , 56-60 ____ , 61-65 ____ , 66-70 ____ , over 70 ____ .

        c. Where were you born? _____

        d. Are you a(n) (please check one) Issei ____ , Kibei ____ , Nisei ____ , Sansei ____ ,
          Caucasian ____ , Other (please explain) _____

    26. Where were you ordained? _____

    27. When were you ordained? _____

    28. When did you start your ministry in America? _____

    29. What schools have you attended? (What Universities or colleges) _____
        _____

    30. Please list the churches that you have ministered to with the approximate years.
        _____
        _____

    31. How long have you been at the present church? _____

    32. Why did you become a minister? _____
        _____
        _____

    33. If your birthplace is from Japan, what reasons did you have to become a minister in America?
        _____
        _____
        _____

    34. What are the most difficult tasks of being a Buddhist minister in America? (Please use other
        paper if necessary) _____
        _____
        _____
        _____

6

35. What are the greatest rewards or joys of being a Buddhist minister in America?

(Please use other paper if necessary) _____

_____

_____

_____

_____

36. Please rate yourself on your ability to speak Japanese:

Fluent _____   Good _____   Passable _____   Poor _____   Unable _____

37. Please rate yourself on your ability to speak English?

Fluent _____   Good _____   Passable _____   Poor _____   Unable _____

38. How can ministers influence the decisions made within their church? _____

_____

_____

Please use the space below, and any additional sheets for any comments you would like to make with respect to the above questions or any part of this study.

開教使の方々への質問表

この質問表は各種の質問から構成され、第Ⅰ部は現在在職しておられる仏教会に関するもの、第Ⅱ部は開教使の方自身に関するものです。どうぞ知り得る範囲で空欄に記入して下さい。答えられる際に御自分の本当の感情を卒直に表明されることが重要でありますので、もし質問が明白でない時、又はその問い方では自分の気持が正確に表現出来ないと思われます時は、どうぞ余白に意見なり、批評なり自由にお書き下さい。

Ⅰ 貴仏教会又は寺院に関する事柄:

　1. 仏教会又は寺院の正式の名前は何ですか？
　　　＿＿＿＿＿＿＿＿＿＿＿＿＿＿＿＿＿＿＿＿

　2. 仏教会又は寺院の住所はどこですか？
　　　＿＿＿＿＿＿＿＿＿＿＿＿＿＿

　3. いつ仏教会は（以下寺院略）、組織されましたか？
　　　＿＿＿＿＿＿＿＿＿＿＿＿＿＿＿＿＿＿＿＿

　4. 仏教会が特にその地域に組織された理由は何ですか？
　　　＿＿＿＿＿＿＿＿＿＿＿＿＿＿＿＿＿＿＿＿＿＿＿＿＿
　　　＿＿＿＿＿＿＿＿＿＿＿＿＿＿＿＿＿＿＿＿＿＿＿＿＿
　　　＿＿＿＿＿＿＿＿＿＿＿＿＿＿＿＿＿＿＿＿
　　　＿＿＿＿＿＿＿＿＿＿＿＿＿＿＿＿＿＿＿＿＿＿＿

2

5. a. 仏教会は州法の基に宗教教会として法人とみなされていますか？（どちらかの答に×印をして下さい）
はい＿＿＿ , いいえ＿＿＿.

b. 答が"はい"なら、仏教会はいつ最初に法人となりましたか？

_____

c. 答が"いいえ"なら、いかにして仏教会は組織されましたか？

_____
_____
_____

6. もし仏教会が法人となっているならば、以下の問に答えて下さい。しかし、まだ法人となっていないか、あるいは将来も法人となりそうにないならば、この問は、とばして下さい。

a. 仏教会は1967年に米国仏教団（B.C.A.）から法人化のモデルとして送られた "By-Laws of Buddhist Church of ＿＿＿＿＿＿＿＿＿" の形式を取っていますか？
はい＿＿＿ , いいえ＿＿＿.

b. もし答えが"いいえ"なら、いかにして仏教会は組織されましたか？

_____
_____
_____
_____
_____

（もし足るらこのページの裏も使って下さい）

3

7.a. ほとんどの米国の仏教会はその法人の権限を持つものとして、理事会（ボード・オブ・ディレクター）を有しております。これは貴仏教会にあてはまりますか？
はい＿＿，いいえ＿＿．

b. もし答えが"はい"なら理事会（ボード）は何人で構成されていますか？
_____

c. いかにして理事会（ボード）の会員（メンバー）は選ばれますか？
_____
_____

d. 開教使は理事会（ボード）で投票権を持たされていますか？
はい＿＿，いいえ＿＿．

e. もし上の答え（7.d.）が"はい"なら、その投票権は恒久的なものですか？
はい＿＿，いいえ＿＿．

8. もし問7.a.の答えが"いいえ"なら、誰が仏教会の権力を持っていますか、又、重要な決定はいかにして下されますか？
_____
_____
_____

9. 理事会（ボード）の又は問8に該当する人の何パーセントが次の世代ですか？
一世＿＿，将来＿＿，二世＿＿，三世＿＿，

その他（明記して下さい）＿＿＿＿＿＿．（もし実数が不明なら概数を記入して下さい。）

4

10. 貴仏教会の所在する市以外に、どこの地域が
    管轄下にありますか？
    _____

11. 仏教会又は寺院の会員に関する事柄、(必要なる概数を
    記入のこと)
    a. 仏教会の会員は何家族ですか？ _____

    b. のべ会員数は いくらですか？ _____
       (家族単位でなく個人を単位として総数を記入のこと)

    c. 仏教会の会員であるか否かにかかわらず、貴仏教会
       の管轄地域に約何人の仏教徒がいますか？
       _____

    d. 仏教会に加入しているか否かにかかわらず、貴仏教会
       の管轄地域に全体で何人の日本人又は日系人が
       いますか？ _____

    e. 地元に日本人の(日系人の)キリスト教会があり
       ますか？ はい___, いいえ___

    f. もし上の問が "はい" ならその教会に常住の牧師
       がいますか？ はい___, いいえ___

    g. その日本人キリスト教会の会員は約何家族ですか？
       _____

12. 貴仏教会の会員の何パーセントが次の世代ですか？

    一世 ___, 二世 ___, 三世 ___, その他(明記
    すること) ___,

5

13. 貴仏教会は教会の外で約何人の人に恩恵を与えていますか？（たとえばサンデー：仏教会は加州パビスタに出張しています）その出張先の場所及び対象となる人数を明記して下さい。

_____

_____

14. 仏教会の財政に関する事柄、秘密は守られます。

　a、仏教会の年間支払は幾らですか？1971年_____ 、1972年(見積り)_____

　b、仏教会の年間収入は幾らですか？1971年_____ 、1972年(見積り)_____

15. 仏教会の収入はどこからきますか？（その比重の度合を数字の一つに丸をつけることによって示して下さい）

	(比重) 低				高
会費	1	2	3	4	5
寄付	1	2	3	4	5
予約劵(どんな種類ですか?)	1	2	3	4	5
映画	1	2	3	4	5
バザー(食事)	1	2	3	4	5
バザー(カーニバル)	1	2	3	4	5
その他(列記する事)	1	2	3	4	5
_____	1	2	3	4	5

16. どんな組織が仏教会にありその会員は約何人ですか

婦人会	有___,	無___,	会員数 ___
YABA	有___,	無___,	会員数 ___
YBA	有___,	無___,	会員数 ___
ジュニア YBA	有___,	無___,	会員数 ___
サンデースクール	有___,	無___,	会員数 ___
スタディーグループ	有___,	無___,	会員数 ___
ジュニア婦人会	有___,	無___,	会員数 ___
その他			

　　(概数で列記して下さい)_____

6

17. 次の仏教会の活動が貴仏教会にとってどの程度重要である度合を
　　評価して下さい。（その重要度合を数字の一つに丸をつけることによって
　　示して下さい。）

( ) a. 社交的活動　　　　　　　　　　　　　　1 2 3 4 5
( ) b. コミュニティーの行事参加　　　　　　　1 2 3 4 5
( ) c. 地元の経済問題への関心　　　　　　　　1 2 3 4 5
( ) d. 地元の政治問題への関心　　　　　　　　1 2 3 4 5
( ) e. 宗教的信仰及び宗教活動　　　　　　　　1 2 3 4 5
( ) f. 仏教会の会員を宗教以外の面で助ける　　1 2 3 4 5
( ) g. 仏教会会員以外の人を助ける　　　　　　1 2 3 4 5
( ) h. スポーツ又は運動　　　　　　　　　　　1 2 3 4 5
( ) i. 仏教会の基金集め　　　　　　　　　　　1 2 3 4 5
( ) j. 新しく日本人又は日系人を会員に入れる　1 2 3 4 5
( ) K. 日本人又は日系人以外の人を会員に入れる　1 2 3 4 5
( ) l. 宗教以外の教育活動の促進(例.日本語教育)　1 2 3 4 5

さて始めに戻って貴仏教会にとって上の諸活動が重要である度合を項目別に
1から12まで順位づけして下さい。各項目の左側にあるかっこ( )の中に
一番重要と思われるものに 1 を、二番目に重要と思われるものに2を、以下、
最も重要でないものに 12 をつけるよう、順に重要性を数字で示して下さい。

18. 以上の他に、どのような活動が貴仏教会にとって重要ですか？
_____

19. 第二次世界大戦中における仏教会について
　　a) 第二次大戦中仏教会に何が起りましたか？_____
_____
_____

　　b) この時期に仏教会会員に何が起りましたか？_____
_____

　　c) リロケーション(転住的)以後仏教会又は会員にどんな変化がありましたか？
_____
_____

7

20. 宗教 について

a. サンデースクールがありますか？　　はい___、いいえ___、はいなら年に何回ありますか？___回
b. 定例礼拝がありますか？　　　　　　はい___、いいえ___、はいなら年に何回ありますか？___回
c. 他の特別礼拝がありますか？（例、お盆、お彼岸等）は い___、いいえ___、
　　"はい"ならそれらを列記して下さい。_____

_____
_____

21. 今日の仏教会の問題として何を考えますか？_____

_____
_____
_____
_____

（と答える5紙の裏側を使って下さい）

22. これから5年後及びそれ以降の仏教会の問題として何を
　　予測しますか？_____

_____
_____
_____

23. そのような問題に対し、貴仏教会は何をすべきであり、何が
　　出きうると思われますか？_____

_____
_____

24. そのような問題に対し、米国仏教団（B.C.A）本部は何をすべき
　　であり、何が出きうると思われますか？_____

_____
_____
_____
_____

8

II. 開教使自身について

25. a. お名前は何ですか? _____

　　b. 年令は幾つですか? 26-30___, 31-35___, 36-40___, 41-45___,
　　　(チェックして下さい.) 46-50___, 51-55___, 56-60___, 61-65___,
　　　　　　　　　　　66-70___, 70以上___.

　　c. どこで生れましたか? _____

　　d. 次のどれにあてはまりますか?(チェックして下さい.)
　　　一世___, 帰米___, 二世___, 三世___, 白人___,
　　　その他(明記して下さい)_____

26. どこで正式の開教使になりましたか? _____

27. いつ正式の開教使になりましたか? _____

28. いつ米国で布教を始めましたか? _____

29. どの学校に行きましたか?(大学教育) _____
　　_____

30. 駐在された仏教会を列記して下さい. 又 各在職年も概算
　　で答えて下さい.

31. 現在の仏教会に何年在職していますか? _____

32. なぜ開教使になりましたか? _____
_____
_____

33. もし出生地が日本ならば、どんな理由で米国の開教使になり
　　ましたか? _____
_____
_____
_____

34. 米国の仏教開教使として何が最も困難な仕事ですか？
(必要なら紙の裏側も使って下さい)＿＿＿＿＿＿
＿＿＿＿＿＿＿＿＿＿＿＿＿＿＿＿＿＿＿＿＿
＿＿＿＿＿＿＿＿＿＿＿＿＿＿＿＿＿＿＿＿＿
＿＿＿＿＿＿＿＿＿＿＿＿＿＿＿＿＿＿＿＿＿

85. 米国の仏教開教使として何が最大の恩恵及び喜びですか？
(必要なら紙の裏側を使って下さい)＿＿＿＿＿＿
＿＿＿＿＿＿＿＿＿＿＿＿＿＿＿＿＿＿＿＿＿
＿＿＿＿＿＿＿＿＿＿＿＿＿＿＿＿＿＿＿＿＿
＿＿＿＿＿＿＿＿＿＿＿＿＿＿＿＿＿＿＿＿＿
＿＿＿＿＿＿＿＿＿＿＿＿＿＿＿＿＿＿＿＿＿

86. 日本語を話す力を自分で判定して下さい。
流暢 ＿＿, 良 ＿＿, まあまあ ＿＿, 下手 ＿＿, しゃべれない ＿＿,

37. 英語を話す力を自分で判定して下さい。
流暢 ＿＿, 良 ＿＿, まあまあ ＿＿, 下手 ＿＿, しゃべれない ＿＿,

38. どうやって開教使は仏教会で決定された事項に影響を及ぼすことが出来ますか？＿＿＿＿＿＿
＿＿＿＿＿＿＿＿＿＿＿＿＿＿＿＿＿＿＿＿＿
＿＿＿＿＿＿＿＿＿＿＿＿＿＿＿＿＿＿＿＿＿

以下の余白及び他の紙を使って以上の問又はこの研院に
関することは何でも意見なり批評なりのべて下さい。

Glossary

J. = Japanese, P. = Pali, Skt. = Sanskrit.

ABA. Adult Buddhist Association, an organization within the BCA.

Amida (Buddhism). A division of Buddhism founded in Japan. Amida is a transliteration of the Sanskrit word *a-mita*, a shortened form for *a-mitabha* (infinite light) or *a-mitayus* (infinite life).

Baishakunin (J.). Marriage match maker or go-between.

Bankoku Bukkyo Taikai. Literally: World Buddhist Conference.

BBA. Buddhist Brotherhood of America.

BBE. Bureau of Buddhist Education.

BCA. Buddhist Churches of America. See *Hokubei Bukkyo Dan.*

BCCF. Buddhist-Christian Clergy Fellowship.

Beikoku Bukkyo Dan (J.). Japanese translation of Buddhist Churches of America.

Betsuin (J.). Literally: Special temple. In America, this is an honorific designation given by the Hongwanji in Japan for an American Buddhist temple with a large congregation and administrative responsibilities for a cluster of dependent branch temples. The chief minister is called a *rimban.*

Bhikshu (Bhikkhu) (Skt.) (P.). An Indian word for a male Buddhist monk.

Bhikshuni (Bhikkhuni) (Skt.) (P.). An Indian word for a female Buddhist monk.

Bodhisattva (Skt.). A Buddha to be. One striving for enlightenment not only for oneself but for the aid of others.

Bonsan (J.). Literally: Mr. Temple. A colloquial Japanese term for a priest. Phonetic corruption from *Bo* (temple) and *San* (Mr., Mrs., etc.). Same as *Obosan.*

Buddhadharma (Skt.). Buddhism

Buddhist Mission of North America. See *Hokubei Bukkyo Dan.*

Bukkyo (J.). Literally: Teachings of Buddha. A formal term for Buddhism.

Bukkyokai (J.). A Buddhist temple or sangha (assembly). A term used by the Issei to designate a Buddhist temple or church.

Bukkyo Kyudo Kai (J.). Literally: Buddhist-searching-for-the-way association. A Buddhist study group.

Bukkyo Seinen Kai (J.). Young Men's Buddhist Association or YMBA.

Bussei (J.). An abbreviation of *Bukkyo Seinen Kai* or YMBA.

Chokuzokujiin (J.). Literally: Belonging-directly (mother) temple.

Dana (Skt.). Literally: Charity or offering.

Dharma (Skt.). The teaching, doctrines, or ultimate law of the Buddha. May apply to any religion, for example, *Khrishtiyadharma* (Christianity).

Dojo (J.). Literally: The place where the Way is cultivated. The term may refer to a religious or secular institution.

Enryo (J.). Undue restraint or reticence.

Fuho (J.). The simplest black robe worn by Jodo Shinshu priests while officiating in religious ceremonies. In Japan, *fuho* is often the usual daily attire for a priest.

Fujinkai (J.). Literally: Women's association.

Fuku-rimban (J.). Literally: Vice-rimban. See *Rimban.*

Fukyoshi (J.). Literally: Gospel messenger. A Jodo Shinshu title given to a person passing the *kyoshi* rites and having two to five years of experience

Gagaku (J.). Literally: Graceful music. Ancient Japanese court music derived from Chinese and Korean music and dance.

Gassho (J.). Literally: Join the palms. A Buddhist bow of respect.

Gathas (Skt.). Buddhist hymns.

Goingesan (J.). Literally: Resident priest at a temple.

Goinjusan (J.). Literally: Resident priest at a temple. Synonymous with *goingesan* but more frequently used in Japan.

Gomonshu (J.). Literally: School or denomination chief. It is usually translated as the lord or chief abbot in the BCA.

Gotan-E (J.). A religious service to honor the birth of Shinran Shonin, founder of Jodo Shinshu Buddhism. May 21.

Guntai Fukyoshi (J.). Naval or army chaplain. See *Fukyoshi.*

Hanamatsuri (J.). A religious service to honor the birth of the Buddha. April 8 is the accepted date among Japanese Mahayana Buddhists.

Higan-E (J.). A Buddhist religious service held on the spring and autumn equinox. March 21 and September 23.

Higashi Hongwanji (J.). Literally: The East School of the Original Vow of Amida Buddha. One sect of the Japanese Jodo Shinshu Buddhism. See also *Nishi Hongwanji.*

Hoji (J.). Memorial service or services.

Hokubei Bukkyo Dan (J.). North American Buddhist Mission. Original Japanese immigrants' term to designate their Japanese Jodo Shinshu Buddhist Institution in America. The name was changed to the Buddhist Churches of America (BCA), *Beikoku Bukkyo Dan*, in 1944.

Hompa Hongwanji (J.). See *Hongwanji-ha Hongwanji.*

Homyo Juyo (J.). Literally: Giving of a posthumous Buddhist name.

Hondo (J.). Literally: Main hall. The main worship hall of a temple or church.

Hongwanji (J.). Literally: Temple of the Original Vow. Applies to two subdivisions of Jodo Shinshu Buddhism. See *Hongwanji-ha Hongwanji.*

Hongwanji-ha Hongwanji (J.). Literally: School of the Temple of the Original Vow of Amida Buddha. One of the subdivisions of Jodo Shinshu Buddhism. The BCA is identified with this division. Often abbreviated as *Hompa Hongwanji* or *Nishi Hongwanji.*

Honzan (J.). Literally: Principal mountain. Translated as the headquarters of the *Hongwanji* found in Kyoto, Japan.

Ho-onko (J.). A religious ceremony to express gratitude; the memorial service for Shinran Shonin, founder of Jodo Shinshu Buddhism. January 16.

Howakai (J.). Literally: Sermon meeting. A Buddhist gathering to hear Buddhist sermons, often in homes rather than in a temple.

IBS. Institute of Buddhist Studies, Berkeley, California.

ICSC. Interreligious Council of Southern California.

Ippan-ji-in (J.). Literally: General temple. Part of the organizational structure of the *Hompa Hongwanji* and different from *Honzan* and *Betsuin.*

Issei (J.). Literally: First generation. Term for original immigrants from Japan to America. See also Nisei and Sansei.

JARF. Japanese American Religious Federation, San Francisco, California.

Jiin (J.). Literally: Temple.

Jodo (Buddhism) (J.). Literally: Pure Land. A sect of Japanese Amida Buddhism founded by Honen Shonin (1133–1212), teacher of Shinran Shonin.

Jodo-E (J.). Bodhi day. A religious service to commemorate the day that Shakamuni Buddha became enlightened. December 8 according to Mahayana Buddhists.

Jodo Shinshu (Buddhism) (J.). Literally: True Pure Land Sect. A sect of Japanese Amida Buddhism founded by Shinran Shonin (1173–1262). There are ten subsects in Japan; however, in America, the main division is between *Nishi* and *Higashi Hongwanji.* The *Nishi Hongwanji* is represented by the BCA.

Joya-E (J.). New Year's eve service. A religious service to close the present year. December 31.

Jugunso (J.). Literally: Engaging in a military Buddhist mission. A Jodo Shinshu term for a missionary traveling with the armed forces.

Junirai (J.). The Twelve Adorations. An important Jodo Shinshu gatha.

Jushoku (J.). Literally: Resident office. Chief resident priest at a Jodo Shinshu Japanese temple.

Kaikyoshi (J.). Literally: Open-teaching messenger. A Jodo Shinshu term for a priest completing the *kyoshi* course and qualified to work as an overseas missionary.

Kaki Koshukai (J.). Literally: Summer seminar. An NABM summer workshop to train Dharma school teachers.

Kantoku (J.). Literally: Supervisor or director. A title used by the NABM to designate its leader until 1918, when the title was changed to *socho*, or bishop.

Karuna Award. A recognized Campfire Girls religious award for Buddhist youths. Karuna is translated as "kindness" or "compassion."

Kenjinkai (J.). Literally: Prefectural associations.

Kibei (J.). A person born in and returning to America after spending part or much of his or her early life in Japan.

Kieshiki (J.). Literally: Taking-refuge ceremony. A Buddhist confirmation ceremony performed by the BCA bishop. Also called a Sarana Affirmation Ceremony.

Kikyoshiki (J.). Literally: Taking-refuge-in ceremony. A Buddhist confirmation ceremony performed by the chief abbot of the Jodo Shinshu Nishi Hongwanji Buddhist sect.

Kinnara. An incorporated nonprofit religious organization founded by BCA priests and followers but not formally within the BCA organization.

Koromo (J.). Literally: Robe or clothing. Buddhist robe worn by priests.

Koshukai (J.). Literally: Seminar. An NABM designation for a teacher's training program.

Kumi (J.). Literally: Class or division. Same as *So.*

Kyokai (J.). Literally: Teaching association. Also the place or temple.

Kyokaishi (J.). Appelation for prison chaplain.

Kyoku (J.). Literally: Parish. Similar to a diocese in the *Nishi Hongwanji* in Japan.

Kyoshi (J.). Literally: Teacher. The level of Jodo Shinshu ordination above the *tokudo.* Qualified to give sermons. Roughly equivalent to monsignor in the Roman Catholic Church.

Mahayana (Buddhism) (Skt. and P.). The Great Vehicle. One of the two major divisions of Buddhism, found in Northern Asia.

Makura-gyo (J.). Literally: Pillow sutra or chant. A religious service for the deceased performed just after death.

Mikado (J.). Emperor.

Monshu (J.). Literally: Gate master. Abbreviation of *gomonshu.*

NABM. North American Buddhist Mission or Buddhist Mission of North America. See *Hokubei Bukkyo Dan.*

Namu Amida Butsu (J.). Literally: Homage to the Amida Buddha.

Nehan-E (J.). Nirvana day. A religious service to memorialize the passing away of Shakamuni Buddha. February 15.

Nembutsu (J.). Literally: Thinking of Buddha. The recitation of the Amida Buddha. In Jodo Shinshu Buddhism, this is *Namu Amida Butsu*, or Homage to the Amida Buddha.

Nichiren (Buddhism) (J.). A denomination of Buddhism in Japan founded by Nichiren (1222–1283).

Nikkei (J.). Americans of Japanese ancestry. Synonymous with Japanese Americans.

Nirvana (Skt.). Enlightenment, salvation, or emancipation.

Nisei (J.).   Literally: Second generation. Term for the children of the original immigrants from Japan. See Issei and Sansei.

Nishi Hongwanji (J.).   Literally: The West School of the Original Vow. of Amida Buddha. One sect of Jodo Shinshu Buddhism in Japan. Represented in America by the BCA.

North American Buddhist Mission.   See *Hokubei Bukkyo Dan.*

NYBA.   National Young Buddhist Association.

Obasan (J.).   Aunt or if *obāsan*, then old woman.

Obon (J.).   A religious service and festival to memorialize those who have passed away. The formal term is *Ura-Bon-E.* July 15.

Obosan (J.).   A priest.

Ojoraisan (J.).   Literally: Praise for Rebirth. Hymns by Zendo.

Ojuzu (J.).   Religious rosary or beads.

Okusama (J.).   Literally: Madam. An informal honorific title used by Japanese or Japanese Americans to address the wife of a person with higher status, such as a minister or professor. Synonymous with *Okusan.*

Onaijin (J.).   Literally: Inside of the altar. The most sacred place within the temple.

Ondobo or *Ondogyo* (J.).   Literally: Fellow man or fellow traveler.

Oseibo (J.).   Literally: End of year. An informal term for a gift, "thank you" present, or recognition award.

Oshieru (J.).   To teach.

Oshoko or *Shoko* (J.).   Literally: Burning of incense. Offering of incense.

Otera (J.).   Literally: Temple.

Oterasan (J.).   Literally: A priest living at a temple.

Otsuya (J.).   Wake service.

Prefectures (J.).   A territorial division in Japan similar to a state in America.

RAB.   Revelant American Buddhist. One organization within the BCA.

Renraku (J.).   Literally: Liaison. Organization of NABM priests.

Renraku Bukkyo Dan (J.).   A term for an early NABM priest's association.

Rimban (J.).   Literally: Wheel-taking turn. Rotating temple keeper for the abbot in Japan. An honorific title bestowed by the BCA for a priest heading a *betsuin.*

Sake (J.).   Japanese rice wine.

San Butsu-ge (J.). "The Praises of the Buddha." An important Jodo Shinshu Buddhist gatha in the larger *Sukhavati-vyuha* sutra.

Sangha (Skt.). A Buddhist assembly or community or a brotherhood of Buddhists.

Sangha Award. A recognized American Boy Scouts religious award for Buddhist youths.

Sanji (J.). Literally: Counseling affairs office. Counselors of the NABM.

Sansankudo (J.). Part of the Japanese wedding ceremony in which the nuptial couple sip Japanese rice wine in a prescribed manner (three sips, three times).

Sansei (J.). Literally: Third generation. Term for the grandchildren of the original immigrants from Japan. See Issei and Nisei.

San Sei-ge (J.). "The Three Sacred Vows." An important Jodo Shinshu gatha in the larger *Sukhavati-byuha* sutra.

Sarana Affirmation Ceremony. See *Kieshiki.*

Senbei (J.). Japanese cookies.

Sensei (J.). Teacher.

Shashinkekkon (J.). Literally: Picture marriage. This term designates the picture-bride era from 1908 to about 1921.

Shikataganai (J.). Literally: Cannot be done; otherwise translated as "cannot be helped."

Shingon (Buddhism) (J.). A denomination of Japanese Buddhism founded by Kobo Daishi (744–835).

Shinjin (J.). Literally: Believing mind. Usually translated as "faith."

Shomyo (J.). Traditional Buddhist music or chanting.

Shotsuki hoyo (J.). Literally: Right monthly memorial. Monthly memorial service for the deceased.

Shu-e (J.). Legislative body of the *Nishi Hongwanji* in Japan. See *Shukai.*

Shugyo (J.). Literally: Take action. Directors of the *Nishi Hongwanji* in Japan within the ecclesiastical headquarters. Appointed by the chief abbot.

Shuji (J.). Literally: Take-office-affairs. Main secretary of the NABM.

Shukai (J.). The present term for the legislative body of the *Nishi Hongwanji* in Japan. The former term was *Shu-e.*

So (J.). Similar to a subparish or middle parish in the *Nishi Hongwanji* in Japan. Temples grouped under a particular administrative jurisdiction.

Soshiki (J.). Literally: Funeral. A formal funeral ceremony.

Shoshin-ge (J.). "The Hymn of Faith." An important Jodo Shinshu gatha.

Shusho-E (J.). A religious service dedicated to the start of a new year, January 1.

Socho (J.). Literally: Chancellor. Popularly translated as "bishop." A title used by the NABM to designate its leader after 1918.

Soryo (J.). A priest or qualified minister in Jodo Shinshu Buddhism.

Sushi (J.). Japanese rice flavored with various seasonings.

Sutra (Skt.). Holy words, sermon, or discourse of the Buddha.

Tanomoshi (J.). Rotating credit system.

Tendai (Buddhism) (J.). A Buddhist denomination founded by Chih-i (538–597) in China and introduced to Japan by Dengyo Daishi (767–822).

Theravada (Buddhism) (Skt.). The Doctrine of the Elders. One of the two major divisions of Buddhism. Found especially in Southern Asian countries and formerly called Hinayana Buddhism.

Tokudo (J.). Literally: Reaching the other shore. Shortened form of *Tokudocho*. The initial level of Jodo Shinshu ordination in the priestly ranks of this branch of Buddhism. The term means to "receive one's enrollment in the book of the laws [priest's sangha]."

Wagesa (J.). Literally: Ring Buddhist robe. A Jodo Shinshu religious lapel cloak which is placed around the neck. The term is a modified form of *kesa.*

YABL. Young Adult Buddhist League.

YBA. Young Buddhist Association.

YWBA. Young Women's Buddhist Association.

Zaidan (J.). Literally: Nonprofit treasury or finances group.

Zen (Buddhism) (J.). A Buddhist denomination established in Japan in the thirteenth century after importation from China.

Bibliography

Andrews, Paul. "A Brief Look at Young Buddhist Association History," Typescript, n.d.

Anesaki, Masaharu. *Religious Life of the Japanese People*. Tokyo: Kokusai Bunka Shinkokai, 1970.

Anon. "Bishop Tsuji Looking Forward to 199th Anniversary." San Francisco *Hokubei Mainichi*, February 6, 1974, p. 1.

Anon. "Brief History of the Tri-State Buddhist Church." Pamphlet, n.p., n.d.

Anon. "Buddhist Week Proclaimed." San Francisco *Hokubei Mainichi*, August 20, 1974, p. 1.

Anon. "Church Attendance Decline Continues." Santa Barbara *News-Press*, January 9, 1972, p. A-12.

Anon. "A Discussion on Early Missionary Work with Three Senior BCA Ministers." *Buddhist Churches of America Newsletter* 10, no. 3 (March 1973).

Anon. "The Evacuated People: A Quantitative Description." U.S. Department of the Interior, War Relocation Authority, p. 79. n.d.

Anon. "Hongwanji Hoki, Jodo Shinshu Hongwanji-ha Shu Sei" [Rules and regulations of the Jodo Shinshu religious sect]. Kyoto, Japan: n.p., n.d.

Anon. "JARF Gets Federal Approval for Apartment Construction: Building Work Will Start in Spring." San Francisco *Hokubei Mainichi*, December 2, 1972.

Anon. *The Jodo Shinshu Book* (Los Angeles: Nembutsu Press, 1973).

257

Anon. "Missionaries of the Buddhist Faith." San Francisco *Chronicle*, September 12, 1899, p. 1.

Anon. "New Era of American Buddhism with Youth in Focus Emphasized." San Francisco *Hokubei Mainichi*, February 29, 1972, p. 1.

Anon. "President Ford Sends Greetings to BCA Event." San Francisco *Hokubei Mainichi*, August 26, 1974, p. 1.

Anon. "Relocated Buddhists." *Newsweek* 23, no. 1 (January 3, 1944): 60-62.

Anon. "70th Anniversary Booklet: 1901-1971." Pamphlet. Oakland, Calif.: Oakland Buddhist Church, n.d.

Anon. "State Textbook Body Hears Buddhist Viewpoint Concerning 'Divine Creation.'" San Francisco *Hokubei Mainichi*, November 14, 1972, p. 1.

Anon. "U.S. Church Growth Comes to Standstill." Los Angeles *Times*, March 20, 1972, Part I, pp. 1, 9.

Anon. "Young Buddhists Pass Anti-War Resolution." Los Angeles *Kashu Mainichi*, May 25, 1971, p. 1.

Beardsley, Richard K. "Religion and Philosophy." In *Twelve Doors to Japan*, edited by John W. Hall and R. K. Beardsley, New York: McGraw-Hill, Inc., 1965.

Befu, Harumi. "Contrastive Acculturation of California Japanese: Comparative Approach to the Study of Immigrants." *Human Organization* 24 (Fall 1965): 209-216.

Benedict, Ruth. *Chrysanthemum and the Sword.* Boston: Houghton Mifflin Co., 1946.

Berger, Peter L. *Invitation to Sociology.* New York: Doubleday and Co., 1963.

Bloom, Leonard, and Reimer, Ruth. *Removal and Return.* Berkeley: University of California Press, 1949.

Blumer, Herbert. *Symbolic Interactionism.* Englewood Cliffs, N.J.: Prentice-Hall, 1969.

Boddy, E. Manchester. *Japanese in America.* Los Angeles: E. M. Boddy, 1921.

Bosworth, Allan R. *America's Concentration Camps.* New York: Bantam Books, 1967, 1968.

Buddhist Brotherhood of America. *Buddhist Gathas and Ceremonies.* Los Angeles: The Buddhist House, 1943.

Buddhist Churches of America. *Annual Report.* Mimeographed. San Francisco: 1970-1975.

———. *Buddhism and Jodo Shinshu.* San Francisco, 1955.

———. *Shin Buddhist Handbook.* San Francisco, 1972.

Bunce, William C. *Religions in Japan.* Rutland, Vt.: Charles E. Tuttle Co., 1955.

Chambers, John S. "The Japanese Invasion." *Annals of the American Academy of Political and Social Sciences* 93 (January 1921): 23-29.

Daniels, Roger. *Concentration Camps USA: Japanese Americans and World War II.* New York: Holt, Rinehart and Winston, Inc., 1971.

———. *The Politics of Prejudice.* Gloucester, Mass.: Peter Smith, 1966.

DeWitt, John L. *Final Report: Japanese Evacuation from the West Coast, 1942.* Washington, D.C.: U.S. Government Printing Office, 1943.

Drake, St. Clair, and Cayton, Horace. *Black Metropolis.* New York: Harper and Row, 1945.

Eidmann, Philipp K. (ed.). "The Lion's Roar." St. Paul, Minn., October 1957, January 1958.

———. *Young People's Introduction to Buddhism: A Sangha Award Study Book for Shin Buddhist Scouts.* San Francisco: Buddhist Churches of America, n.d.

Ethnic Studies Committee, Asian American Alliance, Stanford University. "Critical Reviews of *Japanese Americans: The Untold Story.*" Mimeographed. March 1971.

Feagan, Joe R., and Fujitaki, Nancy. "On the Assimilation of Japanese Americans." *Amerasia Journal* 1, no. 4 (February 1972): 13-31.

Fisher, Anne Reeploeg. *Exile of a Race.* Seattle, Wash.: F. and T. Publishers, 1965.

Freed, A., and Luomale, K. "Buddhism in the United States." Community Analysis Section: Community Analysis Report No. 9, Document Department. Washington, D.C.: War Relocation Authority, May 15, 1944.

Fujinaga, Kakumin. "A Brief History of the Buddhist Churches of America." San Francisco *Wheel of Dharma* (February 23, 1973): 2.

Fujitani, Masami. "BCA and the Buddhist Sangha of America." Typescript, February 25, 1971.

———. "English Nomenclature for *So-cho.*" Typescript, February 24, 1971.

Girdner, Audrie, and Loftis, Anne. *The Great Betrayal: The Evacuation of the Japanese Americans During World War II.* London: Collier Macmillan, Ltd., 1969.

Grodzins, Morton. *Americans Betrayed: Politics and the Japanese Evacuation.* Chicago: University of Chicago Press, 1949.

Gulick, Sidney L. *American-Japanese Relations 1916–1920: A Retrospect.* Quadrennial Report, Commission on Relations with the Orient of the Federal Council of the Churches of Christ in America, n.d.

Hanayama, Shoyu. *Buddhist Handbook for Shin-shu Followers.* Tokyo: Hokuseido Press, 1969.

Hansen, Marcus Lee. "The Third Generation in America." *Commentary* 14 (November 1952): 492–500.

Hompa Hongwanji Mission of Hawaii. *The Shinshu Seiten.* Honolulu: Hompa Hongwanji, 1955.

Horinouchi, Isao. "Americanized Buddhism: A Sociological Analysis of a Protestantized Japanese Religion." Ph.D. dissertation, University of California, Davis, 1973.

Hosokawa, William. *The Nisei: The Quiet Americans.* New York: William Morrow and Co., 1969.

Hunter, Louise H. *Buddhism in Hawaii: Its Impact on a Yankee Community.* Honolulu: University of Hawaii Press, 1971.

Ichihashi, Yamato. *The Japanese in the United States.* Stanford, Calif.: Stanford University Press, 1932.

Japanese American Curriculum Project. *Japanese Americans: The Untold Story.* New York: Holt, Rinehart and Winston, 1971.

Kanzaki, Kiichi. *California and the Japanese.* San Francisco: Japanese Association of America, 1921.

———. "Is the Japanese Menace in America a Reality?" *Annals of the American Academy of Political and Social Science* 93 (January 1921): 88–97.

Kashima, Tetsuden. "Center for Buddhist Learning." Typescript, March 3, 1973.

———. "Japanese American Patterns of Interaction: *Amaeru* and *Enryo.*" Typescript, n.d.

Kawai, Kazuo. "Three Roads and None Easy: An American Born Japanese Looks at Life." *Survey Graphics* (May 1, 1926): 164–166.

Kawakami, K. K. *The Real Japanese Question.* New York: Macmillan Co., 1921.

Kishimoto, Hideo. *Japanese Religion in the Meiji Era.* Translated and adapted by John F. Howes. Tokyo: Obusha, 1956.

Kitada, Ken. "Field Assignment: Placer Buddhist Church." San Francisco *Hokubei Mainichi*, March 19, 1973, p. 2.

Kitagawa, Daisuke. *Issei and Nisei: The Internment Years.* New York: Seabury Press, 1967.

Kitano, Harry. *Japanese Americans: Evolution of a Subculture.* Englewood Cliffs, N.J.: Prentice-Hall, 1969.

Kodani, Mas. "Dojo." San Francisco *Hokubei Mainichi*, no. 8130, September 24, 1973, Part 1, p. 1; and no. 8136, October 1, 1973, Part II, p. 1.

La Violette, Forrest E. *Americans of Japanese Ancestry: A Study of Assimilation in the American Community.* Toronto: Canadian Institute of International Affairs, 1945.

Leighton, Alexander. *The Governing of Men: General Principles and Recommendations Based on Experience at a Japanese Relocation Camp.* Princeton, N.J.: Princeton University Press, 1945.

Light, Ivan H. *Ethnic Enterprise in America: Business Among Chinese, Japanese and Blacks.* Berkeley: University of California Press, 1972.

Lyman, Stanford M. *The Black American in American Sociological Thought: A Failure of Perspective.* New York: G. P. Putnam's Sons, 1972.

——. "Generation and Character: The Case of the Japanese Americans," in *Asian in the West.* Reno, Nev.: Desert Research Institute, 1970.

——, and Scott, Marvin. *The Sociology of the Absurd.* New York: Appleton-Century-Crofts, 1970.

McClatchy, Valentine S. "Japanese in the Melting Pot." *Present Day Immigration with Special Reference to the Japanese. Annals of the American Academy of Political and Social Sciences* 93 (January 1921): 29-34.

McWilliams, Carey. *Prejudice/Japanese Americans: Symbol of Racial Intolerance.* Boston: Little, Brown and Co., 1945.

Madden, Maude W. *When the East Is in the West.* New York: Fleming H. Revell Co., 1923. Reprint. San Francisco: R and E Research Associates, 1971.

Matsumoto, Toru. *Beyond Prejudice: A Story of the Church and Japanese Americans.* New York: Friendship Press, 1946.

Mears, Eliot Grinnell. *Resident Orientals on the American Pacific Coast:*

Their Legal and Economic Status. New York: Institute of Pacific Relations, 1927.

Melendy, Brett H. *The Oriental Americans.* New York: Hippocrene Books, Inc., 1972.

Millis, H. A. *The Japanese Problem in the United States.* New York: Macmillan Co., 1920.

Modell, John (ed.). *Kikuchi Diary.* Urbana: University of Illinois Press, 1973.

Munekata, Ryo (ed.). *Buddhist Churches of America: Vol. 1, 75 Year History.* Chicago: Nobart, Inc., 1974.

National Young Buddhist Association. *Young Buddhist Handbook.* Mimeographed. San Francisco: Western Young Buddhist League Handbook Committee, 1958.

Nisbet, Robert A. *Social Change and History: Aspects of the Western Theory of Development.* New York: Oxford University Press, 1969.

Ogura, Kosei. "A Sociological Study of the Buddhist Churches in North America, With a Case Study of Gardena, California, Congregation." Master's Thesis, University of Southern California, Los Angeles, 1932.

Okano, Terukatsu (ed.). *A Guide to Buddhism.* Yokohama, Japan: International Buddhist Exchange Center Press, 1970.

Omatsu, Glenn. "Church Future: Buddhist Church." San Francisco *Hokubei Mainichi*, January 10, 1973, p. 1.

Pajus, Jean. *The Real Japanese California.* Berkeley: James J. Gillick Co., 1937. Reprint. San Francisco: R and E Research Associates, 1971.

Park, Robert E. "Our Racial Frontier on the Pacific." *Survey Graphics* 6 (May 1, 1926): 192-196.

——, and Miller, Herbert A. *Old World Traits Transplanted.* New York: Harper and Bros., 1921.

Petersen, William. *Japanese Americans.* New York: Random House, 1971.

Ratanamani, Manimai. "History of Shin Buddhism in the United States." Master's Thesis, College of the Pacific, Stockton, Calif., January 1960.

Reischauer, August K. *Studies in Japanese Buddhism.* New York: AMS Press, 1917, 1970.

Rust, William C. "The Shin Sect of Buddhism in America: Its Antecedents, Beliefs, and Present Conditions." Ph.D. dissertation, University of Southern California, Los Angeles, 1951.

Schrieke, B. *Alien Americans: A Study of Race Relations.* New York: Viking Press, 1936. Reprint. San Francisco: R and E Research Associates, 1971.

Schutz, Alfred. *Collected Papers: Studies in Social Theory.* Vol. 2. The Hague: Martinus Nijhoff, 1964.

Shibutani, Tamotsu. "The Buddhist Youth Movement in Chicago." Typescript, University of Chicago, 1944.

Smith, William Carlson. *Americans in Process: A Study of Our Citizens of Oriental Ancestry.* Ann Arbor, Mich.: Edward Brothers, Inc., 1937.

Sone, Monica. *Nisei Daughter.* Boston: Little, Brown and Co., 1953.

Spencer, Robert F. "Japanese Buddhism in the United States, 1940–1946: A Study in Acculturation." Ph.D. dissertation, University of California, Berkeley, September 1946.

——. "Social Structure of a Contemporary Japanese American Buddhist Church." *Social Forces* (March 1948): 281–287.

Spicer, Edward H.; Hansen, Asael T.; Luomala, Katherine; and Opler, Marvin K. *Impounded People: Japanese Americans in the Relocation Centers.* Tucson: University of Arizona Press, 1969.

Strong, Edward K. *The Second Generation Japanese Problem.* Stanford, Calif.: Stanford University Press, 1934.

Stroup, Dorothy A. "The Role of the Japanese American Press in Its Community." Master's Thesis, University of California, Los Angeles, 1960.

Tachiki, Amy, et al. *Roots: An Asian American Reader.* Los Angeles: UCLA Asian American Studies Center, 1971.

Tajima, Paul T. "Japanese Buddhism in Hawaii: Its Background, Origins and Adaptation to Local Conditions." Master's Thesis, University of Hawaii, Honolulu, 1935.

Takagi, Alpha H. "Mini Sermon: 95th Anniversary of Christian Churches." San Francisco *Hokubei Mainichi*, October 30, 1972.

Takahashi, Kyojiro. "A Social Study of the Japanese Shinto and Buddhism in Los Angeles." Master's Thesis, University of Southern California, Los Angeles, 1937.

tenBroek, Jacobus; Barnhart, Edward H.; and Matson, Floyd. *Prejudice, War and the Constitution.* Berkeley: University of California Press, 1954.

Terakawa, Chonen (ed.). *Hokubei Kaikyo Enkakushi* [History of the North American Buddhist Mission]. San Francisco: North American Buddhist Publication, 1936.

Thomas, Dorothy Swaine. *The Salvage*. Berkeley: University of California Press, 1952.

———, and Nishimoto, Richard S. *The Spoilage: Japanese-American Evacuation and Resettlement During World War II*. Berkeley: University of California Press, 1946.

Thomas, William Isaac (ed.). *Source Book for Social Origins*. Chicago: University of Chicago Press, 1909.

Tsuji, Takashi. *An Outline of Buddhism*. Toronto: Eastern Canada Publications, 1966.

Tsunemitsu, Kozen. *Nippon Bukkyo To-bei Shi* [History of Japanese Buddhism in America]. Tokyo: Bukkyo Shuppan Kyodo, 1964.

Tsunoda, Shodo; Masunaga, Shoko; and Kumata, Kenryo. *Buddhism and Jodo Shinshu*. San Francisco: Buddhist Churches of America, 1955.

U.S. Bureau of the Census. *Statistics of the Population*. Washington, D.C.: U.S. Government Printing Office.

U.S. Department of the Interior, War Agency Liquidation Unit. *People in Motion: The Postwar Adjustment of the Evacuated Japanese Americans*. Washington, D.C.: War Relocation Authority, 1947.

Utsuki, Nishu. *The Shin Sect: A School of Mahayana Buddhism*. Kyoto, Japan: Publication Bureau of Buddhist Books, Hompa Hongwanji, 1937.

War Relocation Authority. *The Evacuated People—A Quantitative Description*. Washington, D.C.: U.S. Department of the Interior, 1942.

Weglyn, Michi. *Years of Infamy: The Untold Story of America's Concentration Camps*. New York: William Morrow and Co., 1976.

Yamamoto, Giko, "Church History: Buddhist Church of San Diego." Typescript, April 1966.

Yanagita, Yuki. "Familial, Occupational, and Social Characteristics of Three Generations of Japanese Americans." Master's Thesis, University of Southern California, Los Angeles, June 1968.

Yoshida, Yasaburo. "Sources and Causes of Japanese Emigration." *Annals of the American Academy of Political Science* (September 1909): 157–167. Reprint. San Francisco: R and E Research Associates, 1970.

Index

About the Author

Tetsuden Kashima is the director of the Asian
American Studies program at the University
of Washington, Seattle, and a specialist in the
fields of social psychology, Asian American
Studies, and sociology.